SOCIOLOGY
AND SOCIETY
OF JAPAN

Japanese Studies
General Editor: Yoshio Sugimoto

Images of Japanese Society: *Ross E. Mouer and Yoshio Sugimoto*

An Intellectual History of Wartime Japan: *Shunsuke Tsurumi*

A Cultural History of Postwar Japan: *Shunsuke Tsurumi*

Beyond Computopia: *Tessa Morris-Suzuki*

Constructs for Understanding Japan: *Yoshio Sugimoto and Ross E. Mouer*

Japanese Models of Conflict Resoution: *S. N. Eisenstadt and Eyal Ben-Ari*

Changing Japanese Suburbia: *Eyal Ben-Ari*

The Rise of the Japanese Corporate System: *Koji Matsumoto*

Science, Technology and Society in Postwar Japan: *Shigeru Nakayama*

Group Psychology of the Japanese in Wartime: *Toshio Iritani*

Enterprise Unionism in Japan: *Hirosuke Kawanishi*

Social Psychology of Modern Japan: *Munesuke Mita*

The Origin of Ethnography in Japan: *Minoru Kawada*

Social Stratification in Contemporary Japan: *Kenji Kosaka*

Sociology and Society of Japan: *Nozomu Kawamura*

SOCIOLOGY
AND SOCIETY
OF JAPAN

Nozomu Kawamura

KEGAN PAUL INTERNATIONAL
London and New York

First published in 1994 by
Kegan Paul International Limited
UK: P.O. Box 256, London WC1B 3SW, England
USA: 562 West 113th Street, New York, NY 10025, USA

Distributed by

John Wiley & Sons Limited
Southern Cross Trading Estate
1 Oldlands Way, Bognor Regis
West Sussex PO22 9SA, England

Columbia University Press
563 West 113th Street
New York, NY 10025, USA

© Nozomu Kawamura 1994

Phototypeset in 10/12pt
by Intype, London

Printed in Great Britain by TJ Press, Padstow, Cornwall

ISBN 0 7103 0468 4

British Library Cataloguing in Publication Data
Kawamura, Nozomu
  Sociology and Society of Japan. –
  (Japanese Studies Series)
  I. Title II. Series
  301.0952

  ISBN 0–7103–0468–4

US Library of Congress Cataloging in Publication Data
Kawamura, Nozomu, 1931–
    Sociology and Society of Japan / Nozomu Kawamura.
      230pp.   21 cm. -- (Japanese studies)
    Includes bibliographical references and index.
    ISBN 0–7103–0468–4
    1. Sociology--Japan. 2. Japan--Social conditions--1945–
  I. Title. II. Series.
  HM22.J3K385 1994
  301'.0952--dc20
                                                              94–11715
                                                                 CIP

Contents

Preface   xi
PART I   1
1 Sociology in Japan   4
2 The Modernization of Japanese Society 1868–1945   14
3 Sociology and Socialism in the Interwar Period   40

PART II   75
4 A Critical Evaluation of the Sociological Thought of
   Tadashi Fukutake, Rural Sociologist of Postwar Japan   78
5 Tradition and Community Power Structure in Japan   97
6 The Citizens' Movement against Environmental
   Destruction in Japan   122

PART III   145
7 The *Tennōsei* Ideology and Japan's Wars of Aggression   147
8 Japanese Capitalism and the Extended Family System –
   Modernization and Tradition in a Local Community   170
9 The Japanese Images of the World   196

Bibliography   211
Index   221

Tables

2–1 Number of labour unions and union members by years, and number of labour disputes and labourers involved by year 25

2–2 Number of tenancy disputes by year, number of tenants and landlords involved by year, and number of litigation by year 26

2–3 Number of tenant union members by year 27

4–1 Numbers of farm households by full-time and part-time status 89

4–2 Farm households by scale of cultivated land 90

4–3 The class structure of Japan 92

5–1 Household members by industry 1954 in Shimoda city 107

5–2 Employed persons by industry in Shimoda city 108

5–3 Members of the city assembly by party in Shimoda city 109

5–4 The list of the leaders ranked within the top 30 by reputation scores in Shimoda city 112

5–5 The list of the leaders ranked within the top 20 by reputation scores in Yokoshiba town 116

5–6 Numbers of farm households in Yokoshiba town 117

5–7 Employed persons in Yokoshiba town 118

6–1 The bounty for enterprises of Kurashiki city 127

6–2 Public investment in the 1960s 129

6–3 Plans and past records of public investment 130

6–4 Damages awarded in pollution diseases litigation 135

6–5 Pollution disease victims 136

6–6 Results of development plan questionnaires 140

8–1 The silk industry in the Okaya area in 1875 175

8–2 Number of basins and silk produced by the workers in the Suwa areas 177

8–3 Main government enterprises transferred to merchants 180

8–4 The change of population and occupation by household in Hirano village 182

8–5   The mechanized silk factory in Hirano village   183
8–6   Number of mechanized silk factories by number of
       basins in the Suwa lake area in 1879   184
8–7   Number of mechanized silk factories by number of
       employees in the Suwa lake area in 1879   185
8–8   Number of mechanized silk factories listed by the
       amount of production in 1879   186
8–9   of mechanized silk factories by number of employees
       in the Suwa lake area from 1873 to 1879   187
8–10   The Katakura extended household and the share rate
       of common property of the members   193

Charts

2–1 Variations of *wakon-yōsai*   16
2–2 Family types   21
2–3 The idea of the *Dōzoku* relationship   23
5–1 Relationship among governing class, power elite and
    mass   104
5–2 Relationship between political and civic societies   105
8–1 Distribution of factories (more than 10 workers) in
    the Suwa lake area   176
8–2 The genealogical map of the Katakuras   189
9–1 Genealogy of the Emperor's household   203

Preface

I was completing this book in May 1992, at the time of the Los Angeles riots in the U.S. The Japanese press regarded these riots as legitimate anger at the verdict of an all-white jury which had exonerated four white policemen of guilt in their violent assault on a black man. However, there would be no justice or order if the legitimate rule of law were denied. A contradiction of modern society is clearly shown in this case. Is it truly possible to establish the universal rule of law in a multi-ethnic state? Is not the concept of a 'single' state itself contradicted?

The state or political society is an abstract whole – an abstract person (as it were), i.e. a sovereign. The concept of state is quite different from that of nation, folk, race or ethnic group. The decisions of political society are made by majority. Therefore it is imperative for political society to have an apparatus to enforce the will of the majority. In contrast, the autonomy of a community is to be achieved through consensus or cultural integration. In this context the existence of household and local community in Japan and the communal tradition itself affords a useful perspective for Japanese on the evaluation of post-modern society.

In the field of economics, the act of exchange in a market can reduce various concrete forms of useful labour to abstract human labour of a certain quality. Exchange values of commodities are objective measures of average labour time. Thus modern social sciences, of which economics is the king, may defend capitalist society. Reducing concrete societies to a capitalist society, and different individuals to commodity owners (the commodity of the labourer being his power of labour), are both useful methods for examining modern Western societies, which have the common cultural traits of the Judaeo-Christian tradition.

But other methods were needed for comparative studies of Western societies and Japanese society. In Japan communal relationships do not break down, but co-exist with individualistic relationships. For example, a man who buys wholesale and sells at retail calculates rationally to make a profit. But while he can be a green-grocer or fishmonger, he is also the head of a house-hold. His business is a family business. The economic unit is not the individual but the household. Economics does not apply within the family.

Likewise, for example, the ownership of premises in a suburb of Tokyo by a man of the new middle class, is not solely his individual concern. He cannot sell them on his own initiative. Rather that decision is one for the household to make, because the premises (like a grave)[1] are inseparable from the household, and the property should be inherited by one of his sons, usually the eldest. This principle operates in the same way in an enterprise. For the Japanese, an enterprise is a perpetuated whole with which the individuals involved in it – both capitalists and workers – must identify. A Japanese manager of a Japanese company abroad would be surprised when his secretary stops typing at five o'clock leaving a letter unfinished, when she could have completed it by typing only two more lines.

The Japanese have different spatiotemporal conceptions from Western people. This is shown clearly in drama. In the Japanese puppet play, *bunraku*, puppet operators, usually three, appear on-stage to operate the puppets. In a Western puppet play, the puppeteer never appears on-stage. In the West the stage is an inviolate space created and controlled (as it were) by God. So it should appear that no one but God has dominion over the puppet-people on-stage. Thus, at the cost of unnatural move-ments of the puppet, the unnatural presence of the puppeteers on-stage is avoided. In Japan all three operators used to wear black costumes and black veils. But now the main operator wears a formal stage costume and takes a role on-stage of one who inspires spirit into a puppet. In the world of Christianity this is absolutely impossible.

In Western drama the space and time of the stage are no different from those of ordinary life. Both are absolute space and time created by God. One step for the actor is no different from one step for the ordinary man in everyday life. So we can understand the meanings of actions on-stage. But in the Japanese *nō* play, the world on the stage is quite different from, for example, the scientific world with which sociologists are expected to deal. In *nō*, one step on the stage may symbolize thousands

[1] In Japan a grave is the family grave, and people who live together in this world are thought to live together in the other world.

of miles. A main player, *site*, plays various roles. He plays at one moment the role of the wife, and at the next the role of the husband; or he plays the man who died two hundred years ago, and next moment his ghost in the present.

So there arises the problem of how spectators understand the significance of the gestures of a *site*. *Nō* itself is a reification of the communal spirit by performers. The phenomena on the stage are aspects of the communal spirit. Thus each spectator can understand the significance of the performers on the stage by reference to the mind of his own community.

Many Japanese sociologists tend to regard the existence of local communal relationships in Japan as pre-modern, traditional and irrational. But the present author thinks of these as the primary charge of the move to post-modern societies in Japan. In Japan many disciplines, including sociology, have developed through imitation of Western scholarship. Within the Japanese academic world second-hand knowledge from the West has been regarded as learning. But seeking to offer Japanese knowledge to the original Western sources would be as foolish as trying to make ice by boiling.

It goes without saying that I am indebted to many people in publishing this book in English. It is almost impossible to present sociological studies of my own nation in English. Though this is my first English book, it will also be my last. Intellectually, two scholars played a decisive role in the studies presented in this book: Yanagida Kunio taught me the value of Japanese indigenous culture; Kizaemon Aruga informed me of the national character of Japanese capitalism. Also at this opportunity I would like to thank my two former teachers, sadly departed from this world: Takashi Koyama, late professor of Tokyo Metropolitan University; Tadashi Fukutake, late professor of the University of Tokyo.

Finally I would like to thank the people in the local communities in which I did field researches, i.e. Shimoda city in Shizuoka prefecture, Yokoshiba town in Chiba prefecture, Okaya city, Suwa city and Shimosuwa town in Nagano prefecture. Yokoshiba town is my wife's home town and therefore for me its people are also significant others. The people in the Suwa lake area instructed me on the process of reality reconstruction of community through the *onbashira* festivals which are held once in seven years. *Onbashira* means wooden poles, and in this festival four poles for each shrine are hauled from the mountains to the town and are established at the four corners of the shrine to deify local earthly deities. Through such communal activities the sense of common belonging revives, and people identify themselves with the spirit of community reified in the wooden poles.

Nozomu Kawamura
Tokyo, Japan

PART I

The three essays of Part I deal with the development of sociology in Japan. The first chapter presents a bird's-eye view of Japanese sociology from the end of the Tokugawa period to the present. The second chapter deals with the modernization of Japanese society from the Meiji Restoration to the end of World War II. The third chapter focuses on the interwar period and concentrates on the relationships between sociology, socialism and society.

Sociology in the West has developed as a discipline concerned with civil society, which is an historical product of Western bourgeois revolutions. In Japan, however, the idea of modern individualism did not take root. To the extent that modern Japanese society is based on communal relationships, it may not be fruitful to use Western sociological theories to analyse Japanese society; an indigenous approach to sociological issues would be more viable to successfully explicate the characters of Japanese society. Thus, as a Japanese sociologist, the present author has endeavoured to establish a sociological framework which does not imitate Western sociology.

Another problem of Japanese sociology concerns its relationship with Marxism or historical materialism in Japan. Marxism and communism had great influence among Japanese intellectuals, especially after the Russian revolution of 1917. Consequently, Lenin's scientific materialism rather than Marx's practical materialism influenced the development of historical materialism in Japan. Instead of being practical like American pragmatism, Japanese Marxism aspired to be scientific, attempting to emulate the modern sciences.

In the early 1930s Japanese Marxists criticized sociology as bourgeois. Scientific socialism was held to be the only legitimate doctrine and the only truly scientific sociology. Young revolutionary theorists who went abroad to Moscow[1] to study Marxist-Leninist literature and theories of scientific socialism, applied the formulae of historical materialism to concrete social conditions of Japan. These theorists held the belief that they knew the future direction Japan must take better than the ordinary Japanese people.

The breakdown of the Soviet socialist system in the 1990s

[1] Also to the Soviet Marx-Lenin University and German Universities.

1

evidenced the error of scientific so-called socialism. But in pre-war Japan both sociology and socialism were introduced as the ideas of a new enlightenment. Bolshevik-style communism was widely accepted in the Imperial universities by students. As a result of the competitive examination system many students felt they had already been chosen as the future leaders of Japan, even though they had committed themselves to the illegal revolutionary movement.

After the second world war communists were apprehensive because under the severe oppression of police violence they alone had opposed the war of aggression. In contrast, the defeat of Japanese imperialism and the occupation by American forces brought about circumstances different from war time. The new Japanese constitution was formed by GHQ and originally written in English. It proclaimed that the emperor system should co-exist with democracy. Thus a traditional sociologist of the time stated the emperor's charter oath in the Meiji Restoration (which declared that everything should be decided by open discussion) proved the existence of democracy in pre-war Japan.

Conditions surrounding sociology also changed. Sociology and anthropology were re-imported as American sciences. Ruth Benedict's *The Chrysanthemum and the Sword*, for example, stipulated that those seriously seeking freedom and democracy had to supplant their national tradition with that of the West (particularly the U.S.). The traditionalists in reaction to this approach sought to preserve Japan's orthodoxy by adopting the anti-democratic ideology of the militaristic period. This culminated in intellectuals being advised not to 'trust those who speak English well!' It was generally believed that English-speaking Japanese were unreliable.

The basic problem of Japanese scholarship, including sociology, is that scholars often neglect the experience of ordinary people while trying to grasp an underlying scientific essence. Importance is attached to analytical methods developed in the West, while methods for understanding the unique characteristics of Japanese society and culture are dismissed. In Japanese academic circles the ideological stance of enlightenment has become convention. In such a context the scholarship of Kunio Yanagida's work, with its emphasis on folkloric studies and culture specific approach must be appreciated as a truly original form of Japanese sociology. Japanese sociologists must also learn from pragmatic

American sociologists and social psychologists such as George
Herbert Mead and John Dewey, placing emphasis on social life,
including the aspect of individual life.

1 Sociology in Japan

Importation of Western Sociology

Japan is the only major industrial society yet to emerge outside the West. Differences between Japanese and Western societies are found not so much in organizational and industrial structures as in the Japanese conceptions of the individual and society, and the relationship they share.

Along with other social sciences, sociology was introduced from the West soon after the Meiji Restoration of 1868. Though their understanding of modern Western society was very limited by the end of the Tokugawa feudal era, several Japanese scholars had begun to explore Western ideas of civil society, civil rights, and freedom. For example, Keiu Nakamura, the translator of John Stuart Mill's *On Liberty*, wrote in the 1871 introduction to the text that:

> the liberty with which this book deals has, of course, nothing
> to do with our emperor's policy. However it is a very
> important and necessary matter for the people of Western
> countries. Therefore it might be convenient for those who
> are inquiring into Western polity to have this book translated
> into Japanese. This is the reason why I have been so bold
> as to do this translation.

The tragedy which modern Japan suffered was expressed by Mill in this book as: 'A state which dwarfs its men in order that they may be more docile instruments in its hands even for beneficial purposes, will find that with small man no great things can really be accomplished' (Mill, 1912, p. 141).

Similarly the first Japanese scholar to introduce sociology to Japan, Amane Nishi, in 1870 wrote 'Sociology . . . came from the term "society", which means the cooperative way of life of human beings', and added that 'birds and beasts can live alone but human beings cannot. Therefore, the way of life of human

4

beings is communal, within which people are interdependent on each other'. For Nishi, as for other Japanese scholars, the societal type of *Gesellschaft* (or association) was foreign. He could only understand the type of *Gemeinschaft* (or community) in which individuals were interdependent.

The conditions under which Comte's sociology was used to justify Japan's pre-modern social hierarchy were somewhat similar to those which existed when sociology was introduced to the Southern United States in the 1850s. This sociology was based not on individualism but on the paternalistic relations between master and slave. As is widely known, Comte's theory of social organicism served to justify slavery, and provided an ideological foundation for critiques of the 'free society' of the North.

In contrast the leading liberal theorists in the 1880's movement for people's rights and freedoms, relied on Herbert Spencer's sociology. In *Social Statics*, Spencer insisted on the individual's right to ignore the state or government. Those who opposed the Meiji government wishing to replace it with an elected assembly and representative government were much influenced by the liberal theories of Bentham, Mill, and Spencer. But conservatives also used Spencer's sociological theories for suppression. For example, Hiroyuki Katō, the first president of Tokyo Imperial University, attacked the doctrine of the natural rights of man with the weapon of Spencer's social Darwinism. Katō insisted that there were no equal rights in the jungle. He said that in human society too, the law of the right of the strong – that 'the stronger prey upon the weaker' – is the only law that can be proved empirically and scientifically. However, Katō's social Darwinism was less optimistic and more inconsistent than that of William Graham Sumner. Sumner, who brought social Darwinism from England in the form of Spencer's sociology, was convinced that the 'survival of the fittest' was a law of civilization, and that the socialist view – that it would be possible to nourish the weak whilst advancing civilisation – was unrealistic.

Katō, on the other hand, was concerned that the weaker might prey upon the stronger. He distinguished between 'good' and 'bad' forms of survival of the fittest. According to Katō, the law of the 'survival of the fittest' might undermine the basis for and justification of relations between the emperor and his subjects, and could also destroy the harmonious hierarchical ordering of social relationships. Katō later relinquished this theory because of

5

its focus on conflict between classes or groups. Katō's theoretical emphasis was on harmony within society and he abandoned his theory of 'might is right' in favour of an organicist model of society and the state, in order to justify the emperor's absolute power. He wrote in 1903:

> If the state is regarded as needing to pursue the greatest happiness of the greatest number, as in Bentham's theory, this proposition has to rest on the individualistic assumption that the state should be regarded as a mere aggregation of individuals like a small hill of gravel . . . In the first place, the state is an organic unity in which every institution and agent has organic and harmonious relations (Katō, 1903, p. 240).

Katō's theory of social organicism influenced many sociologists who began to compare the state with the family or household, stressing their close relationship. In the extreme nationalist formulations of social history, Japanese people are all thought to have descended from a common ancestor. The Imperial Family represents the line of direct descent; all other families in Japan are collateral branches founded by sons of earlier generations. The whole nation is therefore seen as one vast lineage group, which is hierarchical in structure. The hierarchy being rooted in the Imperial Family's superiority and legitimized by the kinship relations existing (or thought to exist) between families.

Relationship Between Sociology and Socialism in Japan

However, the development of capitalism did undermine the bases of the emperor system and the family system. Traditional values became irrelevant to the further development of capitalism: capitalist enterprise reorganized itself to the rational pursuit of profit. As to the traditional social order, it is instructive to consider the land-tenure system of the prewar period. The relationship between landlords and tenants was not on a contractual one, but was based upon traditional authority. Originally, landlords were called *oya* (parents) and tenants were *ko* (children). Tenants believed that they could make a living under the landlord's favour, although almost half of their rice crop was taken as rent. Tenants also were obliged to perform certain domestic services for their landlord as an expression of their personal subordination. However, the stable relationship between landlords and tenants was disturbed by the development of a commodity economy. The expansion of the rice market called for a uniform quality for rice; the landlords, who sold the rice they collected as rent, put pressure on their tenants to improve quality so that a higher price could be gained for the product. These requirements undermined the traditionally paternalistic relationship between landlord and tenant and aggravated tensions between them. The situation became more acute after the Russo-Japanese war of 1905, and developed further following World War I.

Meanwhile, the establishment of the modern labour movement occurred just after the Sino-Japanese war of 1895. In the labour movement (as in other socialist movements) the seeking of wider liberties, universal suffrage, and various rights (including women's rights) became a part of its charter. The labour and socialist movements regarded themselves as heirs of the movement for rights and freedom which occurred in the early Meiji period. A labour leader stated in 1908:

As for us commoners and workers, we did not enjoy freedom of assembly, printing or speech. The Meiji liberals have bequeathed to us, as unfinished business, the championing of these rights. Accordingly, the winning of these liberties is the responsibility which has fallen upon our shoulders.

In this context, the development of modern social theory in Japan was possible only in connection with the democracy movement. At the turn of the century, sociologists without governmental ties and who had studied in the United States, adopted a position very close to socialism. They became influential in the developing labour and socialist movements in Japan. The first sociological society in Japan (founded in 1896) laid stress on the close relationship between sociology, socialism and social reform, in its policy. Its most influential members were socialist (social reformist) sociologists, influenced by American liberal sociology and theology, and Christian socialism. Among them was Sen Katayama, a pioneer of the labour and socialist movements. In his youth Katayama travelled to the United States where he studied liberal theology and sociology, becoming a Christian socialist. On his return to Japan he engaged in settlement activities in Tokyo. He later organized the first labour unions in Japan. At this time A.W. Small and G.E. Vincent's *An Introduction to the Study of Society* (published in 1894) was widely read; in 1912, Arthur Lewis' *An Introduction to Sociology* gained popularity in its Japanese edition, *Socialist Sociology*. Small's article, 'Socialism in the Light of Social Science', which appeared in the *American Journal of Sociology* in May 1912, was also influential for those socialist sociologists interested in the relationships between sociology, social science and socialism.

It is interesting to note that early socialist leaders in Japan largely ignored German and Russian socialist theories. This occurred because many of them had been exposed to socialism in the United States (whilst studying sociology and liberal theology) and had become Christians. However, from the early twentieth century, a nationalist sociology which insisted on the unique national polity of Japan, became dominant in academia. Often sociologists who stressed the close relationship between sociology and socialism were subjected to severe restrictions by the government and lost influence. Professional sociologists began to criticize socialism as an enemy of Japanese national polity and denied there was any connection between sociology and socialism.

In 1912 Tatebe and other conservative sociologists established the Society of Japanese Sociology. Tatebe was the association's first president and chief editor of its yearbook. According to Tatebe, Japanese national polity was characterized by the notion that the prosperity of the Imperial Throne must be as eternal as heaven and earth. To maintain the prosperity of the Imperial Throne, Japan should be a first-class nation, and in order to be a strong nation, the Japanese population had to increase to more than one billion. Since the establishment of a strong nation was the purpose of the Society, it published an article entitled 'The Fundamental Policy of Education in Japan', which emphasised respect for the emperor and maintenance of the prosperity of the household. Individualism was seen as a deviant form of behaviour which undermined lineage. Individual desires were seen as being unrelated to, or at least as existing in a separate sphere from the nation's needs.

However, most young sociologists of the time maintained the liberal standpoint. The Japan Sociological Society was established in 1923 by young liberal sociologists including Teizo Toda, who was then an assistant professor of the Department of Sociology at the Tokyo Imperial University. In the 1920s (the era known as '*Taisho* democracy') empirically oriented sociology began to develop in Japan. The introduction of empirical social research mainly came from the United States, and some young sociologists participated in fieldwork focussing on families and communities in urban and rural areas. By the late 1930s the liberal sociologists had submitted to the nationalist sociologists and converted to criticizing liberalism and socialism as un-Japanese. 'Japanism' became the mainstream academic sociology and served as an ideological basis for the emperor system.

Within a similar time frame, new considerations which had a bearing on sociological theory, were being promoted. Drawing on history, and the realm of traditional Japanese belief and social practice, a number of influential thinkers, including sociologists, developed theories that grew out of what they understood as the bedrock of national experience.

Even in the fascist period, Japanese fascist sociologists emphasized the close connection between the emperor system and the family system. For example, Kōzō Tsuda, in his 1934 article 'The Present State of Japanese Fascism', wrote as follows:

In the family-system principle of Japan, the keynote of society is not the demand for individual rights, as in the modern countries of the West, but service to the family as a whole. Socially each family is an independent animate body, a complete cell. Our nationalism should be the extension and enlargement of this family-system principle. This is perhaps because our nationalism is nothing but the union of these families at the national level. The Emperor is the sovereign, family head, centre, and general representative of the state as a united body (Quoted by Maruyama, 1963, p. 37).

9

The Influence of American Sociology after World War II

After World War II nationalistic sociology lost its prestige. The Emperor renounced his divinity and the new Constitution proclaiming the people's sovereignty was announced. Land reform was carried out and the landlord system dissolved. A new civil code was promulgated and the legal basis of the family system was abolished. The legal rights of the household head were eliminated. Policies to dissolve the *zaibatsu* (giant family-controlled conglomerates) and to encourage the formation of labour unions were implemented. All of these changes came from the so-called 'democratization' policies of the American occupation forces. At that time high priority was given to the demilitarization and decentralization of the Japanese economy by General Headquarters (GHQ) and the Supreme Commander for the Allied Powers (SCAP). Giant enterprises such as Mitsui, Mitsubishi, and Sumitomo were considered by GHQ and SCAP as inherently anti-democratic, and a policy aimed at dissolving the *zaibatsu* was promoted. Indeed the occupation forces attempted to reorganize and in doing this reorient almost every facet of Japanese life, Japanese social psychology and national attitudes.

In this period of social change and restructuring the American disciplines of sociology, social psychology, and anthropology were introduced to Japan. In the postwar environment Japan adopted the American system of education. As a consequence many universities and colleges established departments of sociology and courses in sociology at both the undergraduate and graduate levels. Once introduced into the mainstream of academia the disciplines of sociology and anthropology became popular.

In the prewar period Japanese sociologists had been influenced by German sociology. During wartime, those sociologists opposing the war and Japan's extreme nationalism, had studied the sociology of Max Weber. At that time, the study of Marx and Marxist social theories was totally prohibited. Consequently, most leading Japanese sociologists were unfamiliar with the empirical research methodology and pragmatic ideas of American sociology. Immediately after World War II the focus on German sociology had been replaced by a focus on U.S. sociology.

Japanese sociologists in the postwar period became involved practically and theoretically in the democratization of Japanese society. They believed that the occupation's 'democratization' policies would endure. However, within a few years these policies were changed. In January 1948, the objective of the occupation had changed from anti-militarization to developing 'a deterrent against any other totalitarian war threats'. In 1948, also as part of the shift in occupation policy, the drafting of an economic rehabilitation plan encouraged industrialization. The cultural revolution in China forced the United States to promote Japan from (ex)enemy to partner.

From this period onwards the term 'democratization' was supplanted by 'modernization'. By the 1960s the ideological implications of 'modernization' had become clear. The basis of the modernization approach was succinctly characterized by Marius Jansen, one of the leading historians of modern Japan in the United States, in the spring of 1961:

> the important thing is that people read, not what they read, that they participate in the generalized functions of mass society, not whether they do so as free individuals, that machines operate, not for whose benefit, and that things are produced, not what is produced. It is quite as 'modern' to make guns as automobiles, and to organize concentration camps as to organize schools which teach freedom (Jansen, 1962, p. 10).

After the reversal in American policy, Parsonian structural-functional sociology, with its special vocabulary, enjoyed popularity among Japanese sociologists. With the influence of American sociology two quite different schools became evident. The more conservative sociologists were interested in system theories. In the empirical field these sociologists paid much attention to such subjects as human relations in industry, in the interest of higher production. The more radical Japanese sociologists paid attention to the work of C. Wright Mills, Barrington Moore Jr. and others who believed that the methodology of sociology needed to be grounded in historical understanding. In the 1950s conservatism was predominant, but in the 1960s the radicalization of sociology in the United States strongly influenced young Japanese sociologists. At this time, Gouldner's *Coming Crisis of Western Sociology* and Friedrichs' *A Sociology of Sociology* were widely read and highly appreciated among young sociologists.

11

The influence of Marxist sociology also increased, particularly following the war. In Japan the so-called orthodox Marxists (who were influenced by Russian Marxism) criticized sociology as a bourgeois science. Their aim was to destroy bourgeois sociology and to replace it with historical materialism, but following Stalin's death their position became ambivalent. In Japan, as elsewhere, Marxist sociology faced difficult theoretical problems, such as: how could the critique of sociology and critical sociology be distinguished? What of the liberation of sociology and liberation from sociology? In essence, just as a sociology of sociology was needed, so was a Marxism of Marxism. Aside from this, in Japan as has happened in the West, the young humanist Marx, rather than Marx the mature economic determinist, received higher esteem. In general, classical sociologists such as Marx, Weber and G.H. Mead are regarded as requiring Japanese reinterpretation.

Tasks Indigenous to Japanese Sociology

Finally, I will highlight some problems indigenous to Japanese sociology. The research undertaken by Japanese sociologists has primarily been based upon the family and the rural community. Both have a considerable history of study. Although Japan underwent substantial change and became the only non-Western nation with a highly developed capitalist system Japanese society still retained many traditional elements after the Meiji Restoration. Yet in sociological theory, the unitary development of society, or its universal historical development, has been emphasized. Maine's theory of passage from status to contract, Durkheim's theory of development from mechanical solidarity to organic solidarity, Tönnies' conception of the movement from community to association, and Parsons' pattern variables are all examples. With this theoretical background sociologists in Japan tend to regard the society's traditional elements as pre-modern or backward. In contrast anthropologists tend to emphasize the cultural features peculiar to Japanese society. The discipline of Japanese studies as undertaken in the West is a prime example of this. When Ruth Benedict wrote *The Chrysanthemum and the Sword* she was criticized by R.P. Dore in his book, *City Life in Japan*, for her main assumption that there was an entity as homogeneous 'Japanese culture' (or a 'Japanese culture pattern') which persisted through time and pervaded all regions and social classes. Dore may be correct in his criticism, but he himself had limited exposure to the diversity of Japanese society and culture. Dore dealt with one aspect of Japanese society: the movement from a closed and cooperative agricultural structure to an open and competitive industrial structure. He postulated that Japanese society might become 'a society which differs from none of the Western industrial societies more than they differ from each . other'. Dore believed that many of the features common to Western societies were the inevitable concomitants of industrialization. They were the functional prerequisites for any industrial society in the East.

When examining their own society most Japanese sociologists use universal societal models and identify Japan with the highly industrialized Western societies. In contrast to this there are some sociologists who are concerned with the minutiae of everyday life in Japan. This difference in focus leads those sociologists to argue that the traditionally cooperative way of life will remain in many aspects of Japanese culture despite increasing westernization. This concept of the traditional and cooperative way of life differs from the concept of 'Japanese spirit'. 'Japanese spirit' as emphasized during the war, was nothing but an ideology which served to suppress individual rights and freedom. At that time the concentration on hierarchical, rather than egalitarian relationships was an ideologically biased use of traditional values.

Traditional values placing emphasis on communal interests are preserved in the everyday lives of the Japanese. This cultural tradition originates from the reality of centuries of communal life in Japanese families and communities. In certain circumstances, movements to establish new communities or new communal ways of life could begin. However, it is unlikely that in Japan there would first emerge complete independence of each person, followed by the development of some kind of solidarity between independent persons. Such mechanical distinctions between two stages of development do not seem relevant to the Japanese experience. The search for the possibility of revitalizing traditional communal relationships or solidarity among ordinary people, can be seen as an important task for Japanese sociologists.

2 The Modernization of Japanese Society: 1868–1945

Introduction

Classical sociology consists of both social dynamics and statics. In social dynamics, sociological dichotomies that are based upon two-stage models of social development have gained currency. Herbert Spencer proposed such a dichotomy in his two-stage model of the development from militaristic to industrial society. Similarly, such dichotomies are discernible in Henry J.S. Maine's model of development from status to contract, in Ferdinand Tönnies' model of passage: *Gemeinschaft* to *Gesellschaft*, and in Emile Durkheim's model of development: mechanical to organic solidarity.

Furthermore, Max Weber, who interpreted the change towards *Gesellschaft* as a process of rationalization, thought the transformation from traditionalism to rationalism to be a major trend. In this sense, he too followed the dichotomous sociological model. Talcott Parsons' model of pattern variables is another case in point. To the extent that it was based on Tönnies' dichotomy, development – (1) from affectivity to affective neutrality, (2) from particularism to universalism, (3) from functional diffuseness to functional specificity, (4) from quality to performance, and (5) from collectivity orientation to individual orientation – is implied in the Parsonian model.

In *Japan's Emergence as a Modern State*, E. Herbert Norman observed that 'in Japan there has been a time-lag between the adoption of a new mode of life and the full maturity of its cultural and psychological expression.' He observed that, with the lag eliminated, 'it will scarcely leave any space for the patriarchal and often genial tradition of its medieval past.' Norman maintained:

> The ideal of feudal loyalty, the patriarchal system, the attitude toward women, exaltation of the martial virtues, these have acquired in Japan all the garish luster of a tropical sunset.

14

This metaphor is used to suggest that there is a waxing and a waning even in what often appears to be the inherent and inalienable spiritual or cultural tinting of a nation (Norman, 1940, p. 9).

If the sunset had displayed its last garish lustre in 1941, it must be the case that in 1991 the sun had fully set. But if the process of 'modernization' from the pre-modern phase is the only process of any significance, little need be added to the above-quoted passage. The crucial point is that the process of 'modernization' spans not only the transition from the pre-modern to the modern phase, but also that of the modern to post-modern.

In *British Factory and Japanese Factory* (1973), Dore changed his view about the direction of change in industrialized societies and suggested the possibility of the British industrial system moving 'in a Japanese direction'. Britain 'began grudgingly to accept a new collectivism', but remains differentiated from 'a society like Japan which jumped from feudal forms of corporatism without ever experiencing either the sturdy indifference to one's neighbour or a completely laissez-faire market economy' (Dore, 1973, p. 420).

Similarly, Robert Bellah criticizes his own *Tokugawa Religion* (1957) in the 1985 'Introduction to the Paperback Edition': 'The book's weaknesses . . . come from . . . unwillingness to count the costs that Japanese modernization would exact'. He maintains that:

> the great weakness of the book has nothing to do with Japan but with a weakness in the modernization theory I was using: I failed to see that the endless accumulation of wealth and power does not lead to the good society but undermines the conditions necessary for any viable society at all (Bellah, 1985, p. xviii).

In Japan there has been great doubt about equating modernization with Westernization. Modernization is no longer construed as catching up with the West. Thus, the return to tradition as a form of conquest against modernity has appeared, together with Japanism and right-wing nationalism. But, aside from right-wing interests there have been many attempts to re-evaluate Japanese cultural tradition.

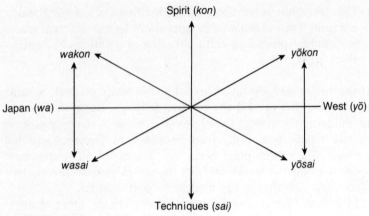

Chart 2–1 Variations of *wakon-yōsai*

The Meiji era slogan of '*wakon-yōsai*' (Japanese spirit, Western techniques) has again emerged. In *Japan as Number One* (1979), Ezra F. Vogel suggested that the American people take up the principle of '*yōkon-wasai*'. Vogel emphasised *wasai* because, while he initially attributed the so-called Japanese success to a Japanese virtue, in the process of his research he realized that 'Japanese success has less to do with traditional character traits than with specific organizational structures, policy programs, and conscious planning' (Vogel, 1979, p. ix). However, there are other possible constructions of this concept: '*yōkon-yōsai*' (Western spirit, Western techniques), '*wakon-wasai*' (Japanese spirit, Japanese techniques) and '*yōkon-wasai*' (Western spirit, Japanese techniques). The situation underlying these four concepts requires explanation: obviously '*wakon-wasai*' is the normal state of Japan and '*yōkon-yōsai*' is that in the West. '*Wakon-yōsai*' and '*yōkon-wasai*' are valid only in a period of transition. Yet in such cases, we cannot imagine a society being modernized in the spheres of science and technology whilst remaining premodern in its social relationships. Modernization as a universal process takes place both on the material and spiritual levels. Living by traditional values while trying to accept modern technology would create a contradiction in social life.

Bellah, who delivered a public lecture entitled 'Cultural Identity and Asian Modernization' in Japan in 1983, supported the slogan '*wakon-yōsa*' to provide a harmonious solution to the contradictory requirements of modernization and tradition

(Bellah, 1983, p. 20). In Bellah's analysis, *wakon* is the sole agent for the determination of national purpose, and modernization is simply a means to achieve this. He maintained:

Perhaps we are approaching the day when the tradition can set the end and modernization can be reduced to providing the means, and, where it undermines the ends, modernization itself might have to be brought under control (Bellah, 1983, p. 27).

However, it is difficult to comprehend modernization solely as a means to an end. As long as *yōkon* represents the universally modern and rational spirit, the process in which *yōkon* is firmly established can only be modernization. We have seen two forms of modernization Western and Japanese, both would be involved in their own process to overcome the alienation and reification which, as ever, accompany modernization.

Characteristics of Modernization in Japan

The modernization process as experienced by Japan has revealed idiosyncratic elements. Japan experienced a major transformation following the Meiji Restoration in 1868. Becoming in less than fifty years the only non-Western nation with a highly developed capitalist system. The Japanese process of modernization, however, differed from what occurred in Western societies.

Most importantly, Japanese society retained many of its traditional elements. In overthrowing the Tokugawa feudal regime the Meiji government established a new order. But in Japan (as contrasted with England and France especially) there existed no third estate that could promote a thoroughgoing civil revolution. The successful overthrow of the *bakufu* was achieved with the leadership of *samurai* (albeit of lower rank) and with the financial backing of merchant-landlords. Japan's transition from feudal to modern took place not from below, through mass-revolutionary or democratic processes, but autocratically from above.

At that time, Japan faced a crisis of national independence. To maintain Japanese independence the newly-established government needed to adopt capitalist modes of production. However, the internal conditions necessary for the development of capitalism did not yet exist. Because of highly populated rural areas modernization of Japanese society could not take the same course it had in the West. The people living in these areas were strongly bound by the traditional ties of the household and village community.

After the Restoration, the discontented former *samurai* and small landlords joined forces with peasants to promote the *jiūmin-ken* ('liberty and people's rights') movement. It demanded an open national assembly of elected representatives. This movement was suppressed by the government and the *Jiyūtō* (the Liberal Party) which had provided its leadership, was dissolved in 1882. The Constitution proclaimed in 1889 established the Japanese empire was to be governed by the emperor, whose line was unbroken for ages eternal, as absolute sovereign (Article I); that the throne was dynastic, and descended through the male side of the imperial line (Article II); and that the emperor was sacred and inviolable (Article III).

From its inception the Meiji government promoted policies designed to encourage industrialization and greater production. To realize the goals of enriching the nation and strengthening the military, the Meiji leaders introduced modern institutions and techniques from the West. They borrowed heavily from Western industrial, military, educational, legal and communication systems. Yet these leaders were also keenly aware of the advantages of keeping Japanese traditional values specifically for the maintenance of autocratic control. Therefore their catchcry was *wakon yōsai* – 'Western techniques, Japanese spirit'.

In the feudal era, the village was an administrative unit which gathered land taxes; for that purpose, the village was organized into groups of five households, each group was collectively responsible for its taxes. If one group failed to pay, the entire village was held responsible. In 1868 the new government's official policy was that 'all the land of the village should belong to the peasants'. Three years later saw the recognition of the freedom for peasants to cultivate paddy and upland crops. People were free to buy and sell land. The peasant was no longer bound to the land in the traditional feudal ways.

With the new land reforms came the obligation for owners to pay land tax (in cash). The five-household organization was formally abolished, along with the feudal rice tax, and the village was no longer the administrative unit for tax collection. In the process of this administrative reform, numbers of small, older villages were merged into new towns and villages. The former villages continued to function as communal units for mutual assistance in farming and other day-to-day activities. The matter of rights to the use of common land and irrigation was left for the village community to deal with. The head of the village was no longer an official, but continued to exercise power in the settlement of disputes centred around collective work, irrigation, common pasture and forest, roads and rights of way, and so on.

The household played an important role within the village. Legally, for example, the ownership of land was vested in individuals, but in actual practice land belonged to the household; the individual 'owned' it solely in his capacity as head of the household, and could only pass it down to the next generation.

The Development of Capitalism

In the early Meiji period no indigenous manufacturing industry existed. In order to promote the growth of a modern mechanized industry in line with its policies, the Meiji government purchased plant and equipment and established factories owned and operated by the state. However, the government enterprises were soon transferred to the control of privileged merchants. Under state management they had not fared well, because neither the managers (former *samurai* now in official posts) nor the workers (who in many cases had come straight from farming) were accustomed to the rational discipline of a modern factory system. Japan did not got through a 'pre-capitalist' phase; nor did it have a Protestant 'work' ethic for providing inner drive.

With the transfer of the government enterprises to private hands conditions did not considerably change. However the merchants, (who acquired the factories at bargain prices) managed their new properties more like household businesses. Ownership did not fall to individuals but to the 'house'; workers recruited from the peasantry were treated like members of the household, and were expected to work hard for its development and prosperity.

The concept of the enterprise as one large household concealed the actual exploitative relationships existing between the owners and workers. The Japanese spirit of communality could be used quite effectively to veil antagonism. The privileged merchants were protected by the government; they were therefore loyal and obedient supporters of national policy. Ultimately these merchants formed giant family trusts called *zaibatsu*, in which the main families. (such as Mitsubishi and Mitsui) and the heads of those families in turn, controlled branch families. The enterprise was organized and run as a household (*ie*); the combination of enterprises was a *dōzoku* – a unification of the various parts of a single family. Managers were regarded as equivalent to head clerks in the older household businesses; workers were at the bottom of the hierarchy of status.

The ideology of paternalism's function was to create docile workers. If the enterprise was like a household, the state itself was envisioned in the same terms: a 'family' with the emperor at the head. The worker who sacrificed himself for the state also sacrificed himself for the company. These traditional values were of course, irrelevant to the further development of capitalism. Profitmaking is the end to which a capitalist enterprise must rationally organize itself. Yet even today the managers of large business concerns insist their companies are 'one big family', and that managers and workers are much like parents and children.

Family System and the Emperor System

Originally the Japanese term *ie* referred to the extended compound family. However, the institution essentially dissolved at the beginning of the Tokugawa period, and *ie* came to mean a small stem family. The perpetuation of the household as small stem family is illustrated below: the *ie* embraces and takes precedence over the individuals in it, so that a new bride, for example, completely and unconditionally becomes a member of the family she enters. The eldest son succeeds as head of the family; younger sons establish branch families; and when daugh-

(1) The Extended Compound Family   (2) The Stem Family

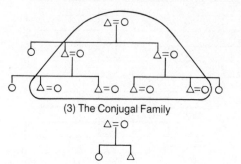
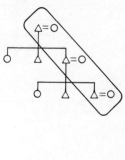

(3) The Conjugal Family

Chart 2–2 Family types

ters marry they enter other households. This system is also illustrated in the custom of the family grave. In Japan, a grave is not
for an individual but for the *ie*; only members of the stem family
(the head of the family and his wife, his successors and their
wives) can be buried in the family grave.

Each family constitutes a lineage group (*dōzoku*). If the head
of a family has two sons, for example, the elder succeeds his
father and the younger establishes a branch of his own; the lines
on the Chart 2–3 indicate the process whereby branches and sub-
branches are created in subsequent generations. The original
family remains at the top of the genealogical hierarchy, and the
other families can be traced back to it. Relationships within the
dōzoku are analogous to those within the nation as a whole,
under the rule of the emperor.

Before World War II, the *ie* was also a legal institution. The
prewar civil code defined the legal rights of the householder,
specifying that the head of the family had to be male and over
the age of twenty. It also specified that the *ie* itself consisted of
the householder, all relatives who lived in his house, and their
wives. Children belonged to their father's household; the head
of the family controlled and managed the family's property; and
the property in turn devolved to the eldest son. The head of the
household was a link in the line of continuity from the ancestral
past to the future. As such he commanded the obedience of
everyone in the *ie*, for the continuity of the household itself was
considered of primary importance.

The head of the household was called *oya* or *oyakata* (parent);
other members were *ko* or *kokata* (children). However, these

21

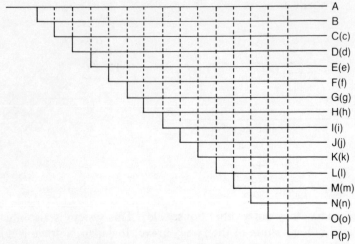

Chart 2–3 The idea of the *dozoku* relationship

terms originally had nothing to do with blood relations: the *oya* was the leader of a cooperative work organization in an extended family or lineage group, and the *ko* were his followers. In the state-as-family, the emperor was *oya* and his subjects were *ko*; the present constitution defines the emperor as 'the symbol of the Japanese nation and national unity'. Even now, as in the past, national integration cannot be maintained without the emperor – who also must be succeeded by his eldest male child.

The Landlord System

Under the prewar land tenure system, the landlord demanded absolute obedience and loyalty from his tenants; the relationship between landlord and tenant did not in the modern sense have a contractual basis but was based on traditional authority. Originally, landlords were *oya* and tenants were *ko*. Tenants believed that they could make a living with the landlord's favour, even though almost half of their rice crop was taken as rent. Tenants were also obliged to perform certain services for the landlord, in order to express their personal subordination. On the first day of each New Year and on All Souls Day (*Bon*) they would go to the landlord's house with small presents, and offer their services for domestic work. At funerals and marriages in the landlord's family, they willingly provided much of the help.

Such relationships were maintained and strengthened by the structure of the village community. In order to understand the landlord's power, one should note the different aspects of his role: the landlord was both owner and lender. As a leaser of land his basic relationship was with his tenants; as landowner, he was tied to the village community as a whole. Only landowners were members of this community; landlords and peasants who farmed their own land had the right to attend village meetings to decide upon community affairs; tenants had no such rights.

Each household's status was determined by the amount of land it owned; the domination of the village community by landlords depended on the extent of their holdings not on the number of tenants they had. As household heads (the primary units of the village community) with the highest status, the landlords effectively governed village life. Eventually the emergence of large-scale absentee landlords, who had little relation to the land and its people, undermined the stability of the community. In turn, because almost all of the people in a village became tenants, they gained the opportunity to unite against domination.

The stable relationship between landlords and tenants was disturbed by the development of a commodity economy. The expansion of the rice market called for uniform rice quality and a uniform sack measure; to gain a higher price for the rice they collected as rent and then had to sell, the landlords put pressure on their tenants to improve quality. The landlords established inspection systems and rice that fell short of the standard could not be accepted as rent. These requirements undermined the traditionally paternalistic relationship between landlord and tenant and aggravated tensions between them, becoming most acute after World War I.

Changes in the 1920s

After the War, labour disputes became frequent in the cities and strikes broke out in many large factories and mines. In 1915 as many as 64 such disputes were recorded, with some 8,000 workers taking part. Two years later there were 398 labour disputes involving 57,000 workers; and in 1919 the number of disputes increased to 497, with 63,000 workers involved. The general labour unrest in the cities also helped to bring about an agrarian movement, but it was not until after the Rice Riot of 1918 that many large-scale actions were attempted by tenants. The number of actions rose from 85 in 1917 to 256 in 1918. In 1919 there were 326 such disputes, 1,680 in 1921, and 2,751 in 1926. The later disputes lasted longer, and more involved litigation. (See Table 2–1.)

In response, the government passed oppressive legislation to control both labour and tenant disputes. These measures were strengthened as disputes became more frequent and widespread. In 1925 the Law for the Maintenance of Public Peace was enacted; this was followed in 1926 by the Violence Control Law.

Along with the labour and tenant disputes came attempts by intellectuals to secure democratic rights and freedom; and the protest of workers, peasants and intellectuals was called the Taisho Democracy Movement. While this took the form of a demand for universal suffrage, it did not extend to a demand for the sovereignty of the people; all three elements of the movement acknowledged the inviolability of the emperor as defined by the Meiji Constitution. Radical elements sought to give the movement a proletarian character, and in 1922 formed the Japanese Communist Party, but this was soon outlawed.

Universal suffrage was enacted in 1925, the same year as the passage of the Law for the Maintenance of Public Peace. The suffrage law was in effect for the local assembly election of 1926 and the national election of 1928. In the 1928 election for members of the House of Representatives, eight proletarian candidates were elected. The initiative created by universal suffrage, however, was taken over by liberal groups (composed of bureaucrats and big business managers) who sought to modernize the *zaibatsu* and to resolve conflicts between landlords and the large business concerns. They also tried to raise the status of parliamentary politics under the basic system of imperial rule, through the creation of political parties. In 1918, before the Universal Suffrage Law was enacted, Prime Minister Hara, leader of the Seiyūkai Party, organized the first party cabinet. From then until 1932, cabinets were in turn formed by two parties.

Table 2–1 Number of labour unions and union members by years, and number of labour disputes and labourers involved by year

Year	No. of unions	No. of union members(A)	No. of total employee(B)	A/B (%)	No. of disputes	No. of persons involved
1914					50	7,904
1915					64	7,852
1916					108	8,413
1917					398	57,309
1918	107				417	66,457
1919	187				497	63,137
1920	273				282	36,371
1921	300	103,442			246	58,225
1922	389	137,381			250	41,503
1923	432	125,551	3,958,877	3.2	270	36,225
1924	469	228,278	4,245,619	5.4	933	94,047
1925	457	254,262	4,485,810	5.6	816	89,387
1926	488	284,729	4,641,681	6.1	1,260	127,262
1927	505	309,493	4,703,757	6.5	1,202	103,350
1928	501	308,900	4,824,780	6.3	1,021	101,893
1929	630	330,985	4,873,081	6.8	1,420	172,144
1930	712	354,312	4,713,002	7.5	2,289	191,805
1931	818	368,975	4,670,275	7.9	2,456	154,528
1932	932	377,625	4,860,276	7.8	2,217	123,213
1933	942	384,613	5,126,719	7.5	1,897	116,733
1934	965	387,964	5,764,277	6.7	1,915	120,307
1935	993	408,662	5,906,589	6.9	1,872	103,692
1936	973	420,589	6,090,116	6.9	1,975	92,724
1937	837	395,290	6,422,333	6.2	2,126	213,622
1938	731	375,191	6,765,399	5.5	1,050	55,565
1939	517	365,804	6,961,457	5.3	1,120	128,294
1940	49	9,455	7,317,092	0.1	732	55,003
1941	11	895	7,771,960	0.0	443	17,258
1942	3	111	8,470,745	0.0	268	14,373
1943	3	155	8,739,915	0.0	443	16,694
1944	0	0	8,739,915	0.0	296	10,026

Cited from Shōbei Shiota, *Nihon Rodōundōshi*, Tokyo: Iwanami Shoten, 1982, p. 62.

Table 2–2 Number of tenancy disputes by year, number of tenants and landlords involved by year, and number of litigation by year

Year	No. of incidents	No. of tenants involved	No. of landlords involved	No. of litigation (cases)
1917	85			0
1918	256			0
1919	326			0
1920	408	34,605	5,236	0
1921	1,680	145,898	33,985	0
1922	1,578	125,750	29,077	0
1923	1,917	134,503	32,712	0
1924	1,532	110,920	27,223	27
1925	2,206	134,646	33,001	654
1926	2,751	151,061	39,705	954
1927	2,052	91,336	24,136	1,522
1928	1,866	75,136	19,474	1,686
1929	2,434	81,998	23,505	1,583
1930	2,478	58,565	14,159	1,638
1931	3,419	81,135	23,768	1,703
1932	3,414	61,499	16,706	2,020
1933	4,000	48,073	14,312	2,853
1934	5,828	121,031	34,035	3,323
1935	6,824	113,164	28,574	4,274
1936	6,804	77,187	23,293	4,249
1937	6,170	63,246	20,236	3,750
1938	4,615	52,817	15,422	2,777
1939	3,578	25,904	9,065	2,592
1940	3,165	38,614	11,082	2,500
1941	3,308	32,289	11,037	2,482
1942	2,756	33,185	11,139	1,876
1943	2,424	17,738	6,968	1,629
1944	2,160	8,213	3,778	1,391
1945	5,171			

Cited from Shiota, *ibid.*, p. 66.

Table 2–3 Number of tenant union members by year

Year	No. of unions	No. of union members
1921	681	
1922	1,114	
1923	1,530	163,931
1924	2,337	232,125
1925	3,496	307,106
1926	3,926	346,693
1927	4,582	365,332
1928	4,353	330,406
1929	4,156	315,771
1930	4,208	301,436
1931	4,414	306,301
1932	4,650	296,839
1933	4,810	302,736
1934	4,390	276,246
1935	4,011	242,422
1936	3,915	229,209
1937	3,879	226,919
1938	3,643	217,883
1939	3,509	210,208
1940	1,029	75,930
1941	294	23,595

Cited from *ibid*.

Japan-ism in the 1930s

In this period, the *zaibatsu* were reluctant to protect the interests of landlords. This was despite the fact that the two groups had formed a bloc, and the *zaibatsu* conditionally supported the landlords because the unrest caused by tenants threatened to undermine the *status quo*. The radical movement (led by communists and socialists) was a common enemy of the two groups. Liberal elements of the ruling class, in order to adjust to the new situation, adopted more flexible policies on the agricultural unrest. The liberals abolished the county office and class election system in the towns and villages, and finally brought about universal suffrage in the 1920s. The government also enacted special measures for the establishment of peasant-owners on the land to resolve the tenancy disputes. Had the Great Depression not followed, these efforts at liberal reform might well have succeeded. However, after 1930 with the advent of the 'Showa Depression', the situation dramatically changed. The economic crisis took the form of an agricultural depression, and the effects of the collapse of the market (which included the market for rice) were especially severe for tenants and peasants with small holdings. These people were particularly vulnerable to the influence of both militarism and fascism, particularly after the Manchurian Incident of 1931.

In this period, young right-wing radicals and young military officers demanded an effective solution to the problems of rural Japan; they saw farmers as the moral backbone of the nation. The *zaibatsu* with their modernization policies, the value of urbanizing and industrializing Japan, were all increasingly attacked as selfish and calculating. The 'Showa Restoration' would be seen as an attempt to offer the ideals of 'Japanism' as a solution for the crisis.

The fascist movements of Germany and Italy were supported by the majority of the urban middle class. In contrast Japanese fascism drew its support from and claimed to represent peasants and small landowners. Thus, in the early 1930s there appeared to be a basic conflict between the right wing (with the military), and the *zaibatsu*. This conflict was purely superficial or at least temporary. If the solutions to the economic crisis were the suppression of the peasant and labour movements, and the diversion of the existing frustrations into a war of aggression, the fascists and the *zaibatsu* were obliged to minimize differences and to develop common interests.

Therefore, after the mid-1930s, the *zaibatsu* were most anxious to gain a compromise with the fascists. Japanese ideology and the myth of Imperial divinity were useful for both groups' purposes. Traditional symbols were manipulated to mobilize the war effort: the Japanese who would not fight abroad for Mitsui or Mitsubishi would fight for the Emperor. It seems naive to suggest that Japan rushed headlong into war because its people lacked individuality and there was no civilian control over the military. If that were so, how can the similar aggression of other modern countries (where individualism was held to be a virtue) be explained?

During the war the emperor system, the family system, Shinto and so on, were presented as unique features of Japanese culture and society. These features were unique to Japan, and yet at the same time were universal models which other nations should voluntarily adopt. The principles of Japanese culture were the foundations on which the Asian 'Co-prosperity Sphere' was later built; the slogan of the time was *hakkō ichiu* – under the Emperor, the whole world is one family.

Appendix

A Chronology of Publications and Events 1915–1930[1]

1915 Sakae Ōsugi, *Shakaiteki Kojinshugi* (Social Individualism). Tongo Tatebe, *Toshi Seikatsu to Sonraku Seikatsu* (Urban and Rural Life).

9.1   Toshihiko Sakai, Motoyuki Takabatake and others published the periodical *Shinshakai* (New Society).

1916 Ryūkichi Endō, *Shakairyoku* (Social Forces).
Soukichi Tsuda, *Bungaku ni Arawaretaru Waga Kokumin-shisō no Kenkyū* (Studies on Japanese Intellectual History in the Light of Literature). 4 vols. – 1918.

9.1   Factory law enforced. It prohibited work of children under twelve years of age and limited the working day to twelve hours for women and for those under fifteen years of age.

9.11   *Binbō Monogatari* (A Story of Poverty) by Hajime Kawakami was serialized in the Osaka *Asahi Shinbun*.

10.10   Kenseikai formed, with Kōmei Katō president.

1917 Kitarō Nishida, *Gendai ni okeru Risoshuki no Tetsugaku* (Philosophy of Idealism in Our Times).
Kiichirō Souda, *Keizaigaku no Shomondai* (Problems of Economics).
Sakuzō Yoshino, *Shina Kakumei Shōshi* (A Short History of Chinese Revolutions).

5.1   The periodical *Shichi* (the predecessor of *Shisō*) founded by Iwanami Shoten.

1918 Sen Katayama, *The Labor Movement in Japan*.
Hajime Kawakami, *Shakaishugi Kanken* (My View on

---

[1] The dates listed on the left are the month and day of the event. For example, 9.1 means September 1.

29

Socialism).

Yasuma Takada, *Shakaigakuteki Kenkyū* (Sociological Studies).

Odo Tanaka, *Tetteiteki Kojinshugi* (Radical Individualism).

Tongo Tatebe, *Futsū Shakaigaku*, vol. 4, *Shakai Dōgaku* (General Sociology, vol. 4, Social Dynamics).

8.1   The Siberian expedition.

8.3   Beginning of a rice riot.

9.3   Saneatsu Mushakōji and others establish 'new village'.

9.29   Kei Hara organizes Seiyūkai Cabinet and becomes prime minister.

12.   Shinjinkai organized by the students of Tokyo Imperial University.

12.23   Sakuzō Yoshino, Tokuzō Fukuda and others organize Reimeikai.

1919 Shōji Anezaki, *Shūkyō Seikatsu to Shakai Mondai* (Religious Life and Social Problems).

Tsugurō Kawada, *Shakai Mondai oyobi Shakai Undō* (Social Problems and the Social Movement).

Yasuma Takada, *Shakaigaku Genri* (The Principles of Sociology).

Shōtarō Yoneda, *Bankin Shakai Shisō no Kenkyū* (Studies on the Recent Social Thought).

Shōtarō Yoneda, *Gendai Chishiki Kaikyū to Narikin to Demokurashii* (Contemporary Intellectual Class, Upstart Millionaires, and Democracy).

Sakuzō Yoshino, *Futsū Senkyoron* (Arguments on Universal Suffrage).

1.20   Hajime Kawakami publishes the periodical *Shakai Mondai Kenkyū* (Studies on Social Problems).

2.9   Ōhara Institute of Studies on Social Problems founded.

2.11   Nyozekan Hasegawa, Ikuo Ōyama and others publish *Warera*, the social science magazine.

3.6   Shinjinkai publishes the periodical *Democracy*.

3.8   Voting right for House of Representatives expanded, qualification reduced from males paying direct national taxes more than ten *yen* to males paying more than three *yen*.

4.1   Motoyuki Takabakate and others publish the periodical *Kokka Shakaishugi* (State Socialism).

5.1   Sakai, Yamakawa and others publish the periodical *Sin Shakai* (New Society).

6.1   Reimeikai publishes the periodical *Kaihō* (Liberation).

8.30   Yūaikai changes its name to Dainihon Rōdō Sōdōmei Yūaikai (The Japan Federation of Labour) at seventh annual congress.

9.10   The Department of Sociology founded in the School of Humanities of Tokyo Imperial University.

9.18   Workers of Kobe-Kawasaki Shipbuilding Co. demand wage rises and engage in a go-slow.

1920 Shinzō Koizumi, *Shakai Mondai Kenkyū* (Studies on Social Problems).

Nihon Shakaigakuin Chōsabu (Research Committee of Japan Sociological Society) (eds), *Gendai Shakai Mondai Kenkyū* (Studies on Contemporary Social Problems).

Tongo Tatebe, *Gendai Shakai Bunmei* (Contemporary Social Civilization).

Shōtarō Yoneda, *Gendai Shakai Mondai no Shakaigakuteki Kenkyŭ* (Sociological Studies on Contemporary Social Problems).

1.10   Tatsuo Morito, Associate Professor of Tokyo Imperial University, suspended from duties because of the publication of his article 'A Study on P.A. Kropotkin's Social Thought' in *The Bulletin of Economic Studies*.

2.5   A large strike breaks out in Yawata Iron Manufacture.

2.11   Large demonstration for universal suffrage in Tokyo by 111 associations.

3.28   Raichō Hiratsuka, Fusae Ichikawa and others found Shinfujin Kyōkai (New Women's Association), and from October publish the periodical *Josei Dōmei* (Feminism League).

5.2   First May Day demonstration in Tokyo.

5.16   Yūaikai, Shinyūkai and other labor unions which participated in the May Day demonstration organize Rōdō Kumiai Dōmeikai (League of Labour Unions).

12. Foundation of Nihon Shakaishugi Dōmei (Japan Socialist League).

1921 Nyozekan Hasegawa, *Gendai Kokka Hihan* (Critique of the Modern State).

Hajime Kawakami, *Yuibutsushian Kenkyū* (Studies on Historical Materialism).

Hyakuzō Kurata, *Ai to Ninshiki no Shuppatsu* (Toward Affection and Cognition).

Manabu Sano, (ed.), *Nihon Kokuminsei no Kenkyū* (Studies on the Japanese National Characters).

Shōtarō Yoneda, *Gendai Bunkajin no Shinri* (Psychology of Modern Civilized People).

2.1 Ōmi Komaki, Yōbun Kaneko and others publish the periodical *Tanemaku Hito* (People Who Sow Seeds).

4.2 Workers of Ashio Copper Mine Co. strike to demand the right to organize.

4.11 The amendment of laws of the organization of government of cities, towns and villages. Under the former laws, those qualified for citizenship were males of twenty-five years of age and over who had resided at the city, town or village and paid taxes to the city, town or village and paid land tax to the central government or paid national taxes of more than two *yen*. The new legislation qualified males of twenty-five years of age and older who paid taxes to the city, town or village. Under the old laws, voters were classified into two classes in towns and villages and three classes in cities according to land ownership or property. The new law created two classes in the cities and removed the classifications in towns and villages.

4.12 Abolition of the county assembly system (county head and office became administration units of central government).

5.24 Second annual congress of Japan Socialist League; the conflict between anarchism and Bolshevism becomes serious.

7. Workers of Mitsubishi and Kobe-Kawasaki Shipbuilding Co. engage in strikes.

10.1 *Shisō* (Thought) was published by Iwanami Shoten.

11.4 Assassination of prime minister Hara.

1922 Ryūkichi Endō, *Shakaigaku Genron* (The Principles of Sociology).

Tokuzō Fukuda, *Shakai Seisaku to Kaikyū Tōsō* (Social Policies and the Class Struggle).

Nyozekan Hasegawa, *Gendai Shakai Hihan* (Critique of Modern Society).

Manabu Sano, *Tokushu Buraku Kaihōron* (Arguments on the Liberation of *Buraku* People).

Yasuma Takada, *Shakaigaku Gairon* (General Theories of Sociology).

Yasuma Takada, *Kokka to Shakai* (State and Society).

Kyoson Tsuchiya, *Shakaikaizō no Tetsugaku to Bunka-shugi* (The Philosophy of Social Reforms and Culturism).

3.3 Foundation congress of Zenkoku Suiheisha (National Levelling League), publishes the periodical *Suihei* (Leveller) beginning in July. This was the first national association for the liberation of *buraku* people.

4.9 Foundation of Nihon Nōmin Kumiai (Japan Farmers' Association).

4.20 Amendments of law of organization of prefecture government. Qualification for election and the right to vote expanded to persons who paid direct national taxes.

7.15 Japan Communist Party founded illegally.

10.1 Dainihon Rōdō Sōdōmei Yūaikai changes its name to Nihon Rōdō Sōdōmei (Japan Federation of Labour).

1923 Hajime Kawakami, *Shihonshugi Keizaigaku no Shiteki Tenkai* (Historical Development of Capitalist Economy).

Ikki Kita, *Nihon Kaizō Hōan Taiyō* (An Outline of Laws for Remodelling Japan).

Shinzō Koizumi, *Kachiron to Shakaishugi* (Value Theories and Socialism).

Tatsukichi Minobe, *Kenpō Satsuyō* (A Compendium of the Constitution).

Ikuo Ōyama, *Seiji no Shakaiteki Kiso* (Social Foundations of Politics).

Eikichi Seki, *Shakaigaku Kenkyū* (Studies in Sociology).

Yasuma Takada, *Kaikyūkō* (Considerations on Classes).

Kyoson Tsuchiya, *Shin Shakaigaku* (New Sociology).

Shotaro Yoneda, *Gendai Bunka Gairon* (General Theories

of Modern Culture).

Senji Yamamoto, *Sei Kyōiku* (Sex Education).

1.27 Formation of the Women's Suffrage League.

3.13 Workers of the Japan Federation of Labour engage in strikes at Noda Soy Sauce Co.

3.30 Promulgation of amendments to factory law. The law now prohibited work by children under fourteen (previously twelve) years of age and work over twelve hours by those under sixteen (previously fifteen) years of age. (Enforced July 1926.)

4.28 Tenancy dispute, Gunchiku village, Kumamoto prefecture.

6.9 Takeo Arishima commits suicide.

9.1 Kantō earthquake.

9.2 Tokyo, Chiba, Saitama and Kanagawa prefectures placed under martial law. Persecution of Koreans spreads.

9.4 Kameido incident. Labour union leaders, Gitora Kawai, Keiichi Hirai and others killed by the army.

9.16 Gendarme captain Masahiro Amakasu murders the anarchists Sakae Ōsugi and his wife Noe Ito.

1924 Hatsunosuke Hirabayashi, *Nihon Jiyushisō Hattatsushi* (Developmental History of Japanese Liberalism).

Eijirō Honjō, *Nihon Shakaishi* (Social History of Japan).

Konan Naitō, *Nihon Bunkashi Kenkyū* (Studies on Japanese Cultural History).

Kō Nasu, *Nōson Mondai to Shakai Rinen* (Rural Problems and Social Ideas).

Jikei Sakurai, *Nōgyō Keizaigaku* (Agricultural Economy).

Masamichi Shinmei, *Kenryoku to Shakai* (Political Power and Society).

Ganjirō Suekawa, *Nōson Hōritsu Mondai* (Rural Legal Problems).

Hitoshi Yamakawa, *Musankaikyū no Seiji Undō* (The Political Movement of the Japanese Proletariat).

1.10 Members of Seiyūkai, Kenseikai and Kakushin Club move to defeat Kiyoura Cabinet. (The second pro-Constitution movement. The first was in 1912.)

3.28 In the tenant dispute in Kizaki village, Niigata prefecture, landlords close their land against tenants.

4. Shūmei Ōkawa, Seitoku Yasuoka and others found

the right-wing association Kōchikai (later in February 1925 it changes its name to Kōchisha).

4.27   Isoo Abe, Kesaya Yamazaki, Sanshirō Ishikawa and others found the Japan Fabian Society. From May they publish the periodical *Sakaishugi Kenkyū* (Studies on Socialism).

9.14   Formation of the Students' Federation of Social Science.

11.30   Tenants of Fuseishi *buraku*, Ōta village, Kagawa prefecture are arrested for mowing rice plants to prevent their distraint by landlords.

1925   Abe, Yamakawa, and Sakai (eds) *Shakai Mondai Sōsho* (Social Problems Series), 3 vols. –1926.

Katsumaro Akamatsu, *Nihon Rōdō Undō Hattasushi* (Developmental History of the Japanese Labour Movement).

Yoshitarō Hirano, *Horitsu ni okeru Kaikyutoso* (Class Struggles in Law).

Tsunao Inomata, *Kinyū Shihonron* (Theories of Financial Capital).

Tsuguro Kawada, *Shakai Mondai Taikei* (System of Social Problems), 3 vols. – 1926.

Kō Nasu, *Kōsei naru Kosakuryō* (Fair Rent for Tenancy).

Mō Osatake, *Ishin zengo ni okeru Rikkenshisō* (Constitutional Ideas in the Era of the Meiji Restoration).

Ikuo Ōyama, *Gendai Nihon no Seijikatei* (Political Processes in Contemporary Japan).

Sakae Sugiyama, *Shakaigaku Jūnikō* (Twelve Lectures on Sociology).

Yasuma Takada, *Kaikyū oyobi Daisanshikan* (Social Classes and the Third View of History).

Kyoson Tsuchiya, *Shakai Tetsugaku Genri* (Principles of Social Philosophy).

Kikue Yamakawa, *Fujin Mondai to Fujin Undō* (Feminist Problems and the Feminist Movement).

Kunio Yanagida, *Kainan Shoki* (Essays on Southern Islands).

Kunio Yanagida, *Kyōdo Kai Kiroku* (Documents of a Folklore Study Group).

4.15   Foundation of Dainihon Rengō Seinendan (Japan Federation of Youth Associations).

5.2	House of Representatives legislates for universal suffrage (applying to males of twenty-five years of age and older).
5.7	House of Representatives legislates for maintenance of the public peace.
5.25	Left-wing separates from Rōdō Sōdōmei and organizes Nihon Rōdōkumiai Hyogikai (Council of Japan Labour Unions).
7.11	Shibaura Manufacturing Co. strike, workers demand reinstatement of eighteen fired men.
11.	Kunio Yanagida publishes the periodical *Minzoku* (The Nation).

1926 Kazuo Fukumoto, *Shakai no Kōsei narabini Henkaku no Katei* (Social Structures and Change Processes).

Kazuo Fukomoto, *Keizaigaku Hihan no Hōhōron* (Methodology for a Critique of Economy).

Tsunao Inomata, *Gendai Nihon no Burujoajii no Seijiteki Chii* (Political Status of the Bourgeoisie in Contemporary Japan).

Takeo Ono, *Nihon Sonraku kō* (Thoughts on Japanese Villages).

Soichi Oya (ed.), *Shakai Mondai Kōza* (Social Problems Series), 23 vols.

Gantarō Suehiro, *Rōdōhō Kenkyū* (Studies on Labour Laws).

Etsuji Sumiya, *Yuibutsushikan yori mitaru Keizai Gakusetsushi* (History of Economic Theories Examined from the Perspective of Historical Materialism).

Yasuma Takada, *Shakaikankei no Kenkyū* (Studies on Social Relationships).

Teizō Toda, *Kazoku no Kenkyū* (Studies on Families).

1.19	Workers of Kyōdō Printing Co. strike against reduction of operations. Factory lock-out by company.
3.5	Formation of Rōdō Nōmin Tō (Labour-Farmer Party).
4.7	Establishment of Nihon Shinri Gakkai (Japan Psychological Society). It publishes the periodical *Shinrigaku Kenkyū* (Studies on Psychology).
4.26	Workers at Nihon Gakki (Japan Music Instrument Co.) strike to demand pay rise.

5.5 Tenants' disputes in Kizaki village become aggravated.

7.1 Abolition of county office.

8.6 Establishment of NHK (Nihon Hōsō Kyōkai).

9.3 Hamamatsu city assembly election – first election under universal suffrage.

1927 Kazuo Fukumoto, *Hōkō Tenkan* (A Change of Direction).

Seikyō Gōndo, *Jichi Minpan* (Common Rules of Self-Government).

Hajime Kawakami and Ikuo Ōyama (eds.) *Marukusushugi Kōza* (Study Series on Marxism), 13 vols – 1929.

Junichirō Ōtsu, *Dainihon Kenseishi* (Constitutional History of Japan). 10 vols – 1928.

Kōjirō Sugimori, *Shakaigaku* (Sociology).

Tongo Tatebe, *1,164 Ōyō Shakaigaku Jukkō* (Ten Lectures on Applied Sociology).

Takao Tsuchiya, *Hōkenshakai no Hōkaikatei no Kenkyū* (Studies on the Dissolution Process of Feudal Society).

Sakuzō Yoshino, (ed.), *Meiji Bunka Zenshū* (Collected Works on Meiji Culture), 30 vols – 1930.

3. Beginning of financial panic.

4.29 Foundation of Dainihon Joshi Seinendan (Japan Female Youth Association).

6.1 Kenseikai and Seiyūhontō form new Party, Rikken-minseitō.

12.6 Hitoshi Yamakawa and others publish the periodical *Rōnō*.

1928 Tetsuji Kada, *Shakaigaku Gairon* (General Theories of Sociology).

Hajime Kawakami, *Shihonron Nyūmon* (An Introduction to Marx's *Capital*).

Iwao Kokushō, *Hyakusho Ikki no Kenkyū* (Studies on Peasant Uprisings).

Kiyoshi Miki, *Yuibutsushikan to Gendai no Igi* (Historical Materialism and Its Significance to Contemporary Society).

Masamichi Shinmei, *Keishiki Shakaigakuron* (Theories of Formal Sociology).

Sakae Sugiyama, *Shakaikagaku Gairon* (General Theories of Social Science).

Kunio Yanagida, *Seinen to Gakumon* (Youth and Scholarship).

Marukusu-Engerusu Zenshū (Collected Works of K. Marx and F. Engels) 27 vols – 1936.

2.1   Communist Party publishes the newspaper *Akahata* (Red Flag).

2.20   General election, first under universal suffrage.

3.15   Members of the Communist Party arrested.

4.18   Hajime Kawakami resigns from Kyoto Imperial University.

4.23   Yoshitarō Ōmori resigns from Tokyo Imperial University.

4.24   Itsurō Sakisaka and others resign from Kyushū Imperial University.

6.29   Amendments of law for maintenance of the public peace. Penalties supplemented by a death sentence and penal servitude for life.

10.1   Kiyoshi Miki, Gorō Hani and others publish the periodical *Shinkō Kagaku no Hata no motoni* (under the Flag of the Newly Risen Sciences).

1929   Gorō Hani, *Tenkeiki no Rekishigaku* (The Science of History in Transition).

Shirō Hattori, *Meiji Ishinshi* (History of the Meiji Restoration).

Rikuhei Imori, *Nōsōn Shakaigaku* (Rural Sociology).

Tsunao Inomata, *Gendai Nihon Kenkyū* (Studies on Contemporary Japan).

Hajime Kawakami, *Daini Binbō Monogatari* (The Second Story of Poverty).

Kyochokai (ed.), *Saikin no Shakai Undō* (The Recent Social Movement).

Kiyoshi Miki, *Shakaikagaku no Yobigainen* (Preparatory Concepts in the Social Sciences).

Shinobu Origuchi, *Kodai Kenkyū* (Studies on Ancient Ages), 2 vols.

Masamichi Shinmei, *Shakaikagaku Jiten* (Dictionary of Social Sciences).

Seijirō Takigawa, *Nihon Shakaishi* (Social History in Japan).

Jun Tosaka, *Kagaku Hōhōron* (Methodology of the Sciences).

3.5   Senji Yamamoto assassinated.

4.16   Members of the Communist Party arrested.
7.4   Tanaka Cabinet resigns, Hamaguchi Cabinet organized.
7.   Shinobu Origuchi and others form the Folklore Society.
10.1   Crash of the New York stock market (Black Thursday).
11.1   Formation of Rōnō Tō (Labour-Farmer Party); with Ikuo Ōyama as president. It was dissolved on the following day.
1930   Eitarō Noro, *Nihon Shihonshugi Hattatsu Shi* (The Developmental History of Japanese Capitalism).
            Heitarō Ōishi, *Gunshŭ Shinrigaku* (Mass Psychology).
            Eitarō Sugiyama, *Shakai Kagaku Jūnikō* (Twelve Lectures on Social Science).
            Shirō Koike, *Kaikyū Ron* (Theories of Social Classes).
            Kōtoku Unno, *Shakai Jigyōgaku Genri* (Principles of Social Work).
            Shŭzō Kuki, *Iki no Kōzō* (Structure of *Iki*).
            Iwao Takayama, *Nishida Tetsugaku* (Philosophy of Nishida).
5.20   Professors of Tokyo Imperial University and of Hōsei University (Mōritarō Yamada, Yoshitarō Hirano, Kiyoshi Miki and others) arrested for their support of the Communist Party.
11.14   Prime Minister Hamaguchi shot.
In this year the economic depression became serious.

3 Sociology and Socialism in the Interwar Period

Introduction

During the interwar period Japanese intellectuals experimented with the use of imported methodologies. They intended to understand and analyze the often dislocating processes their culture was experiencing. Disenchantment with traditional thought was great in every field of endeavour, and nowhere more so than in the field of sociology. The traditional concept of social order and its purpose changed. The traditional assumptions that were the basis of the European nineteenth and twentieth century social thinkers' theories were no longer relevant. An examination of the development of social theory in Japan during this period and of the relationships between theory and practice could serve as a model for similar challenges in other areas of modern Japanese thought.

During the late Tokugawa era Western scholars studying Japan began to introduce European philosophy and social thought into Japan. At that time, Japanese scholars had difficulty with the concept of modern civil society. When sociology was first introduced to Japan in the 1870s by Amane Nishi, he barely understood its basic concepts. The explanation of the term 'society' in Nishi's article *Hyakugaku Renkan* (An Encyclopedia) clearly illustrates the antiquated understanding of Western sociology:

> Society is to be translated as the cooperative way of life. The term society is literally applicable to the Japanese *sha* [group] but it seems to correspond better to the Japanese *to* [clique] . . . The way of life of human beings means communal life within which people must be interdependent. Society, i.e. clique, refers to the life of clannishness that preceded the formation of the state or government (Nishi, 1870–71, p. 239).

According to Nishi, the formation of the state and establishment of government was based on the collective nature of human beings. Thus there could be no clear distinction between state and society. Although society or social life may arise first, the existence of the state or government was equally a product of the collective nature of human beings. In Nishi's schema the natural state of human beings was based on collectivity not individuality.

In 1882 Nagao Ariga published the first Japanese book which used the term sociology in its title. He criticized Western individualism in volume three of his *Shakaigaku* (Sociology) (1884). He cited the *New Testament* gospel according to Matthew, Chapter 10:

> For I have come to bring division, a man against his father,
> a daughter against her mother, a daughter-in-law against her
> mother-in-law; and a man's enemies will be those who belong
> to his own household. He who loves father and mother more
> than Me is not worthy of Me, and he who loves son or
> daughter more than Me is not worthy of Me.

In Japan society was analogous with the family and Ariga was therefore surprised by these words. He wrote:

> It is natural for Western people who believe such a creed not
> to treat their father as their natural father, mother as natural
> mother, children as natural children. North American
> societies have had a history of about three hundred years,
> and during that time families which have the same origin and
> same name would number more than a dozen. But they do
> not have any contact with each other, as if they are strangers.
> There exists no close relationship between main and branch
> families in the West. People always are eager for wealth. To
> be rich, husbands and wives, fathers and sons, mothers and
> daughters, brothers and sisters quarrel with each other (Ariga,
> 1884, pp. 281–2).

In Japan the basic society unit was the household, not the individual. Religion had close connections with the household and even modern industrial organizations were regarded in familial terms. Thus all members of a business organization were expected

41

to obey its head as if he were their father. The traditional Japanese notion of society differed markedly from the notion of Western civil society.

Under such conditions sociology in Japan would not become a popular discipline if the phenomena of civil society was the sole object for study. In Japan because the concept of civil society was undeveloped the meaning of sociology was often distorted. Within Japanese sociology the study of the state in order to justify the emperor system took precedence over the study of civil society. The recognition of this manifestation of the concept of sociology originated from the government. The official acceptance of sociology by the academic world occurred when Tokyo Imperial University established courses in the field and created a standard curriculum. In a country where the people saw government officials as their masters not as their servants, the state universities (i.e. Imperial universities) were far more prestigious than the private universities. In the academic world as in other fields, the lamentable custom of *kanson minpi* (making much of the government and nothing of the people) remained.

There were two sociologies in Japan: one, a discipline which served to support the ideology of the Emperor system, the other, an authentic sociology which independently sought to analyze civil society. Whereas the 'government-school' sociologists relied on the German theories such as Hegelian thought and tried to establish state-science, sociologists without ties to the government introduced American sociology and aligned themselves with socialism. Therefore at the turn of the century sociology was influential in the attempt to establish labour and socialist movements in Japan by intellectuals who had studied in the United States. One of the founders of the Japanese labour and socialist movements, Sen Katayama, claimed that the modern labour and socialist movements began in the summer of 1897 after the war with China. In 1897 the *Rodo Kumiai Kiseikai*, a labour association organized with the purpose of forming trade unions, was formed by iron workers employed in the government arsenal and in railway workshops. In December 1897, the first Japanese trade union, the Iron Workers' Union was organized, it had over one thousand members. At the same time rising interest in social reform meant labour and socialist movements were eagerly discussed by intellectuals and progressive workers. Workers attempted to increase wages, shorten working hours, and create better working conditions. In the agricultural sector tenants fought against landlords to lower land rents. Concurrently social- ists and liberals organized an association which demanded uni- versal suffrage. Such trends were favourable for the development of sociology.

Sociology in the Early 20th Century

During the first phase of the development of sociology, the need for an understanding of social theory and for social action, was recognized by both scholars and social activists. Initially the two impulses seemed to work in tandem; but by the beginning of the First World War the streams of theory and practice had, inevi- tably perhaps, moved apart. This schism was permanent.

The *Shakai Gakkai* (Sociological Society), Japan's first socio- logical society was founded in 1896. In April 1897 it commenced publication of a monthly journal, *Shakai Zasshi* (the title in trans- lation: *The Sociologist*). This association was established by non- academic sociologists: journalists, ministers, social reformers and socialists. Its constitution declared the society's purpose was to study the principles of sociology, socialism and social problems. The society's prospectus stated:

Sociology is the foundation of all social sciences. It studies the laws of the historical development of mankind and of the evolution of society in general. It researches the actual social life of people and shows the course of social reforms in the future. In the Western countries, sociology has paid much attention to current issues, and it is said that in the social sciences social problems are the main concerns. In Japan the gulf between rich and poor has come to be serious, and the poor are now confronted with serious problems. The problems of land ownership arise from conflict between landlords and tenants, and labour problems arise from the struggle between capitalists and labourers. Under such conditions it goes without saying that we must study the principles of sociology and research actual social life to prevent or control social problems. Regarding social policies

we must study the rise of socialism and the development of
socialist parties . . . Being abreast with the times, we establish
the Sociological Society and begin to discuss sociological
problems scientifically.

The interest in socialism and social reform resulted from the
increasing social problems which accompanied the development
of capitalism in Japan. During the late 19th century Japanese
sociology was influenced by American liberal sociology and by
the reformist ideas connected with Christian socialism and the
social gospel.

Sen Katayama

The early career of Sen Katayama provides a good example of
the influences upon early Japanese sociology. Katayama was born
of peasant parentage in 1859 and at the age of twenty-five went
to study in the United States where he stayed for twelve years.
In 1889 he entered Grinnell College where he studied liberal
theology and sociology. After graduation in 1892, he spent two
years at Andover and one year at Yale studying social problems.
When he returned to Japan in 1896 he was a socialist or social
reformist, as well as being a sociologist. He wrote an article
which appeared in the first and second issues of *Shakai Zasshi* in
1897 entitled 'The Relation of Sociology to Social Reforms'. This
article was a translation of a chapter of A.W. Small and G.E.
Vincent's book *An Introduction to the Study of Society* (1894).
Katayama failed to mention his article was actually a translation
and was eventually criticized for plagiarism. The article included
the following passage from Small and Vincent:

Sociology must be distinguished from Socialism. Socialism is
a programme. Sociology is both science and philosophy.
Socialism is related to Sociology somewhat as the platform of
either of our national parties to the Constitution [of the
United States] . . . Socialism assumes that which Sociology
investigates . . . In relation to immediate social issues the
sociologist is rather a referee, while the socialist is an
advocate. In contrast with the eagerness of Socialism, the
policy of Sociology is to make haste slowly (see Small and
Vincent, 1894, pp. 71–7).

This passage is especially interesting when one is made aware that Katayama later became a member of the presidium of the executive committee of the Comintern. As a Marxist-Leninist he made great efforts to destroy 'bourgeois sociology'.

Katayama's article also included Small and Vincent's view that

in so far as the labour problem is the wealth problem . . . Sociology is concerned for the labourer in the solution of the problems . . . This fact makes Sociology the ally of any class which is temporarily at a disadvantage against any other class. Hence Sociology looks to the equalization of social relations (Small and Vincent, 1894, pp. 78–9).

Katayama and other Japanese sociologists and socialists learned the relationships between sociology and socialism from Small and Vincent's book. They concurred with the insistence that socialism made sociology a necessity:

Systematic Socialism has both directly and indirectly promoted the development of Sociology. In this proposition, the reference is to all modern criticism which has attacked constituent principles of contemporary social order, and has proposed to remove inequalities by reorganization in the spirit of more inclusive and secure democracy (Small and Vincent, 1894, p. 40).

In August 1898 the *Shakai Gakkai* was dissolved and in turn *Shakai Zasshi* was discontinued. The dissolution of the society was closely related to the establishment of the *Shakashugi Kenkyūkai* (Association of Socialist Studies, ASS) in October 1898. Its most influential members were Sen Katayama, Tomoshi Murai, Isoo Abe, Shūsui Kōtoku and Naoe Kinoshita; many were Christian socialists who had studied in the United States. This association stated their 'purpose is to examine whether principles of socialism can be applied to Japanese society or not'. It ruled that membership of the association was open to all persons who agreed with their purpose, regardless of their attitude to socialism. Therefore, some liberal sociologists and social reformists became members of the Association of Socialist Studies. After the establishment of the ASS the academic sociologists who were not interested in socialism sought to establish a new association.

Sociology and Society of Japan

Hiroyuki Katō

In this context the *Shakaigaku Kenkyūkai* (Association of Sociological Studies) was established in November 1898. Hiroyuki Katō, Masayoshi Takagi and Yūjirō Motoyoshi were among its influential members. Katō who was born in 1838 was president of the association. In his youth he had studied Dutch and German. After serving as an official for the feudal government, he became a highly ranked official in the Ministry of Education of the Meiji government. As one of the scholars of enlightenment, he (with Yukichi Fukuzawa and others) formed a society called Meirokusha in 1873. During the early Meiji period he had advocated the theory of representative government and equal rights for all people, but he rejected this position after he became president of the University of Tokyo (later Tokyo Imperial University). He also attacked the doctrine of the natural rights of man with the weapon of social Darwinism, insisting there were no equal rights in the jungle. Katō resigned as president of the Tokyo Imperial University in 1893. In the same year a chair of sociology was established at the University, to which professor Shōichi Toyama was appointed.

When the Spencerian Professor Toyama became president of the University, Masayoshi Takagi succeeded as the lecturer of sociology. Takagi was influenced by Columbia University scholars (especially by F.H. Giddings), and tried to introduce psychological sociology to the discipline in Japan.

Yūjirō Motoyoshi

Yūjirō Motoyoshi was born in 1858 and graduated from Tokyo Imperial University in 1881. After two years of teaching English at Aoyama Gakuin College, he travelled to the United States and studied psychology and sociology at Boston University and from 1883 to 1887 studied the same at John Hopkins. He became a professor of psychology at the Tokyo Imperial University in 1888.

Thus members of the Association of Sociological Studies were more or less professional sociologists who held positions at Tokyo Imperial University. The Association published the periodical *Shakai* (Society) from January 1899. The title of *Shakai* changed to *Shakaigaku Zasshi* (The Journal of Sociology) in February

46

1902. The Association's constitution stated that its purpose was to study the principles of sociology, social problems, and policies of social reform. It should be noted that the word 'socialism' had disappeared and was replaced by the term 'social policies'. In the first issue of *Shakai*, the journal's editorial policy was announced:

> We would like to organize discussion of the ways to study and lead society. We can study society. Though the changing process of society is extremely complicated and many social events are appearing and disappearing one after the other, once we attain insight into the essence of phenomena we can find the immutable laws according to which society is moved or changed. Thus society can be studied through scientific methods. We can lead society. Once we find the immutable laws of society we can predict the movement and the changing process of society. Thus society can be led by sociologists.

The difference in character between the Sociological Society and the Association of Sociological Studies is clear. Whereas the former insisted on close relationships between sociology and socialism, the latter tried to exclude socialism from sociology. Against the journalistic aims of the former, the latter insisted on academic perspectives in the study of sociology and social policies.

In January 1900, the *Shakaishugi Kenkyūkai* (Association of Socialist Studies) was reorganized and renamed the *Shakaishugi Kyōkai* (Association of Socialists). The purpose of the association was now to study principles of socialism in order to apply them to Japanese society. Therefore non-socialist members who were merely interested in the academic study of socialism resigned, and only socialists remained.

The spring of 1900 saw the enactment the Public Peace Law. This law outlawed the organization of the working class into unions and effectively prohibited industrial workers and tenant farmers from agitating (in relation to in their own interests) against employers and landlords.

In May 1901 the Social Democratic Party (the first Japanese socialist party) was formed by Shūsui Kōtoku, Sen Katayama, Isoo Abe, Naoe Kinoshita and others. They published a Socialist Manifesto and a party platform. In part the Manifesto states:

How to abolish the gulf between rich and poor is one of the great problems of the 20th Century. The ideas of people's rights and freedoms which spread in the West, especially in France, contributed to the realization of political equality. However, the development of productive forces created new class antagonism between rich and poor instead of aristocracy and plebeian. In the first place, economic equality is primary and political is secondary. Therefore even if we could realize representative government and democratic polity, the majority of the people would still be unhappy if we failed to eliminate economic inequality. This is why our party devotes all its efforts to solving economic problems (see Kawamura, 1973–75, Vol. I, p. 243).

This passage illustrates the standard understanding of socialism and the Socialist Party at that time. The party was suppressed by the government after which, the conflict between sociology and socialism became more evident.

When the Russo-Japanese war began in 1904 socialists stood against it and advocated world peace. Sociologists such as Hiroyuki Katō and Tongo Tatebe supported the war demanding the government take drastic measures against Russia.

As mentioned earlier Hiroyuki Katō had abandoned the theory of people's rights and freedoms and had adopted the ideas of social Darwinism. At the turn of the century he also relinquished the doctrine of the right of the strongest. His fear of socialism and communism distorted his interpretation of evolutionist ideas. In the theory of the struggle for survival the conflict between classes or groups is emphasized, yet Katō's theoretical emphasis was on harmony within society. In this context, Katō adopted the theory of social organicism and modified it to mean state organicism in order to justify the status quo. To maintain the stability of the organ of the state, Katō stood against socialism, communism and also all liberal thought. He wrote:

I support utilitarianism but I do not support the doctrine of the greatest happiness of the greatest number. In the first place the state is not a simple aggregation of individuals like a small hill of gravel, but an organic unity in which every institution and agent has organic and harmonious relations . . .

If the state is regarded as needing to pursue the greatest

happiness of the greatest number, as in Bentham's theory, this proposition has to rest on the individualistic assumption that the state should be regarded as a mere aggregation of individuals like a small hill of gravel (Katō, 1900, p. 240).

Thus the welfare of society was considered to be equivalent to the wealth of the state, and patriotism was identified with loyalty to the emperor. If the Japanese state was like a natural organism, the emperor was its nerve centre. Since the emperor was a crucial organ of the state, he was to be protected at the sacrifice of the state's 'hands' and 'legs'.

When the Russo-Japanese war began Katō published *Destiny of Japan and Russia in Light of Evolutionary Theory*, in which he predicted a Japanese victory based on the theory of the 'survival of the fittest'. In Katō's view Japan was stronger than Russia because its society was firmly integrated under the emperor system (Katō, 1904, p. 85). Ironically however when Katō's theory of the organic state was elaborated, the basic infrastructure of the theory collapsed. Yet it should be noted that the weaker the basis of the theory became, the more strongly it was promoted as an ideology.

Tongo Tatebe

Tongo Tatebe who was born in 1871, graduated from the Tokyo Imperial University in 1896. As an undergraduate Tatebe majored in philosophy. After two years' study in Europe (subsidized by the Imperial government) he became a lecturer in sociology at the Tokyo Imperial University and a colleague of Masayoshi Takagi. In 1901 he became a professor at that university and after the opening of its Department of Sociology (in 1903) served as the department's chairman until 1922 when he resigned. As a sociologist he styled himself the Comte of the Orient. Tatebe believed society was the organic integrated body made up of the cooperative lives of the people. He published *An Introduction to Sociology* as volume one of *General Sociology* in 1904 and remained convinced of the principle of the organic integration of Japanese society. Tatebe described his position as 'sociocracy'; however, it was no more than a desire to justify the construction of a powerful nation under the reign of the emperor.

Similar to Katō, Tatebe was strongly opposed to Russia. Following the war, in 1906 he wrote a book of sociological studies of the war. In it he attacked pacifism and socialism, and supported Japanese imperialism as a sociological fact (Tatebe, 1906, pp. 305–7).

Socialists organized anti-war propaganda and began a socialist weekly called the *Heimin Shinbun* in November 1903. The following is a translation of their announcement:

It is said that liberty, equality and fraternity are three cardinal principles of human life.

In order to secure liberty amongst men, we support the principle of democracy, and desire to destroy all class distinctions and oppressions which grow out of the existing order.

To bless men with equality we insist upon socialism, and we desire to make all the means of production, distribution and exchange the common property of men . . .

To favour men with fraternity, we adhere to a policy of peace and endeavour to bring about disarmament, to stop bellicose attempts without race distinctions, and political divisions. We shall make every attempt, in realizing this idea, to rouse public opinion, and to allow all to act in conformity with the majority of men, provided our law will admit it; and we absolutely condemn man's rash attempt to satisfy his lust for power by waging war against neighbouring countries.

When the Russo-Japanese war broke out the socialists redoubled their efforts to bring about an early peace. On 20 March 1904 at a meeting in Tokyo the socialists passed a vote to send a message of mutual comradeship to the Russian socialists. In this letter they stated that as Social Democrats they were neither nihilists nor terrorists, they absolutely objected to the use of military force and advocated the resolution of conflict through peaceful means.

The *Heimin Shinbun* was suppressed in January 1905. The *Shakaishugi Kyōkai* (Association of Socialists) which had been founded in 1900, was also suppressed and dissolved in 1905. In February 1906 the Socialist Party was formed. At the first anniversary meeting of the party in 1907 heated debate concentrated on questions of party tactics. Radical and fundamental change was advocated by Kōtoku (and others) through a resolution which called for direct action. There was also a suggestion that the clause 'we advocate socialism within the law' be struck out of the party constitution. Universal suffrage and adoption of a policy of parliamentalism were proposed by Sen Katayama, Tetsuji Tazoe and others of a so-called less radical group. These differences proved unresolvable and the Party eventually split into two antagonistic factions.

In May 1910 the government began arresting socialists accused of plotting the assassination of the emperor. In a notorious show trial Kōtoku and twenty-three others were convicted of treason. Kōtoku and eleven others were executed. The so-called 'era of winter' began and socialists were severely suppressed. In October 1908, an editorial in the *Bulletin of the Institution of Sociological Studies* entitled 'On the Differences Between Socialism and Sociology', pointed out that sociology was not based on radical ideas held to be dangerous to the body social, but was a discipline for studying society without prejudice. According to this article because people had confused sociology with socialism, prior to the Russo-Japanese War sociologists had been seen as dangerous people standing against the government and national polity. After the war the sociologists who advocated a close relationship between sociology and socialism were severely restricted and lost influence within academic circles (see Kawamura, 1973–5, Vol. I, p. 271).

European-Derived Ideas of Liberal Sociology and Taisho Democracy

During the period following the end of World War I Japanese academics made a concerted attempt to introduce the discipline of sociology. By that time a number of young scholars had travelled to Europe, where they became aware of the significance of the continental example (particularly the German). The effort to bend European theory to the reality of Japanese specifics was in many ways courageous. Yet, because the European theories did not fit well into the Japanese situation, they were used to support a number of doctrines (including those of the nationalists) never intended by their original authors.

In 1913 Tongo Tatebe and some colleagues established the *Nihon Shakai Gakuin* (Association of Japanese Sociology). Tatebe was the association's first president and chief editor of its yearbook, *Nihon Shakaigaku Nenpō*. In 1914 at the second congress of the association Tatebe presented a paper entitled 'The National Policy of Our Empire and the Disturbance of World War'. According to Tatebe, the Japanese national polity was characterized by the idea that the prosperity of the Imperial Throne had to be as eternal as heaven and earth. To maintain the prosperity of the Imperial Throne in the face of severe international competition, Japan should become a powerful nation. For Japan to achieve superiority the Japanese population had to be increased to more than one billion. Thus Tatebe insisted that Japanese expansion must be one of the nation's priorities.

In 1916 the research committee of the Association of Japanese Sociology published an article entitled 'The Fundamental Policy of Education in Japan', in which they promoted the view that education's purpose was to establish a strong nation. The article proposed an educational program which emphasized fostering respect for the emperor and maintaining the prosperity of the household. Individualism was declared a threat which could undermine the solid base of national polity. In Tatebe's words 'the values of society always oppose the values of the individual, therefore if the values of individuals increase then the values of society will decrease' (Tatebe, 1916, p. 35). Tatebe condemned scholars who assumed that promotion of individual values would result in an increase in social values, and those who praised recent thought advocating democracy. In academia a nationalistic sociology which emphasized the unique national polity of Japan became dominant. The conservative sociologists who occupied positions in universities and institutions became the leading faction of the Association of Japanese Sociology.

Shōtarō Yoneda

However, several sociologists did take a liberal position. One of the most prominent liberal sociologists was Shōtarō Yoneda. In 1893 he was born to an outcaste family. After completing a study course of English at a college in Nara prefecture, he went to the

United States and Western Europe to study sociology. In the United States he studied the sociological theories of L.F. Ward, A.W. Small and F.H. Giddings. Yoneda was also influenced by G. Simmel's formal sociology. He returned to Japan in 1902 becoming a lecturer at the Kyoto Imperial University. But due to his outcaste background he remained a lecturer for a considerable period of time. He finally became the university's first professor of sociology. He criticized Tatebe's organic theory of sociology and defined the social as mental interaction between individuals, an idea first put forward by Simmel. Yoneda accepted Simmel's theories of formal social relationships. Following Simmel, he defined the object of sociology as *Formen der Vergesellschaftung* and focused on *seelische Wechselwirkung* among individuals. It is important to note that Yoneda perceived social relationships as form (not content) which was a result of Simmel's influence.

In 1919 Yoneda published 'Democracy and Japan'. In this article he argued that the emperor's sovereignty over Japanese national polity was incompatible with the people's sovereignty under democracy, but that *minponshugi* as a political system could be introduced without touching on the problem of sovereignty. According to Yoneda, a democratic political system should be realized in the form of universal suffrage and social policies. He insisted that a political movement which pressed for more than these two goals was as dangerous as one which aimed for neither. Accordingly, he rejected both socialism and conservatism (Yoneda, 1919b, p. 135).

Yoneda's position on the national polity and democracy was almost parallel to Sakuzō Yoshino's. Yoshino was one of the most prominent leaders of the Taisho democracy movement, and had already published an article on 'the politics of the people' in 1914. He rebutted the argument that 'the politics of the people' was incompatible with the concept of Japanese national polity, or that democracy was contrary to the Japanese Constitution. He specified the conditions which he believed were necessary to develop a 'politics of the people': the expansion of voting rights, the establishment of fair boundaries for voting districts and the formation of government by political parties rather than oligarchs (Yoshino, 1914, pp. 212–3).

In 1916 Yoshino wrote 'The True Meaning of Constitutionalism' in which he distinguished *minponshugi* from democracy.

Whereas democracy implied that sovereignty rests with the people, *minponshugi*, as Yoshino saw it, meant that a sovereign, must value the will and welfare of the people. Therefore, *minponshugi* not democracy should be developed in Japan. Yoshino saw socialism and republicanism as dangerous doctrines incompatible with the concept of national polity, but *minponshugi* was not. Yoshino believed that *minponshugi*, as a manifestation of constitutional monarchy, was necessary for Japan: it was government for the people, but not by the people (Yoshino, 1919, pp. 260–3).

Yoneda contributed to the development of Japanese sociology not only in the area of general theory but also in more specialized fields. As a sociologist he was the first scholar to study social problems. In his book *Gendai Chishiki Kaikyū Undō to Narikin to Demokurashii* (The Modern Intellectual Class Movement, the Upstart Millionaire and Democracy) published in 1919, Yoneda focused on the problems of the new middle class. He defined the intellectual class as people who did not own property and gained their income through technical skill or knowledge. Yoneda believed the intelligentsia was almost the same as the new middle class, but it was not independent and was either reliant upon the bourgeoisie or the proletariat. Previously, the bourgeoisie and aristocrats had protected intellectuals, assimilating them into their classes. However, this situation changed with an increase in the number of intellectuals. By 1920 intellectuals had difficulty finding employment because the bourgeoisie could no longer assimilate them. Yoneda saw this phenomenon as one of the greatest social problems of his day. Some intellectuals had begun to identify with the proletariat. The leadership and assistance of intellectuals would be needed if the working class movement was to develop in strategy and organizational areas. Thus, Yoneda recognized the value of the intelligentsia's commitment to the development of the working class movement (Yoneda, 1919a, pp. 106, 134–5).

Yasuma Takada

Yasuma Takada who was born in 1882 graduated from the Kyoto Imperial University in 1910. His supervisor at both undergraduate and graduate school was Yoneda, and accordingly Tadaka adopted almost all of the important sociological ideas supported by his teacher. In his undergraduate days socialist thought influenced Takada. Until Yoneda dissuaded him from becoming involved in socialism, Takada had been attracted by Kōtoku's *Shakaishugi Shinzui* (The Quintessence of Socialism) published in 1903 and believed that his enthusiasm for socialism could be satisfied by studying sociology. In his early academic years Takada wrote some significant theoretical articles including: 'On Social Laws' in 1911; 'Nature of Theories of Social Evolution' in 1912; 'Theories of Social Laws' in 1913; and 'Nature of Social Laws' in 1914. He tried to discover the universal laws of society and to exclude social evolutionary theories from the field of sociology. Takada focused 'sociological laws' and was not interested in the laws of social development or 'historical laws'. These ideas formed the basis for his theory of 'the third view of history' (the sociological-historical view), which he expounded in 1925. Attacking both idealistic and materialistic views of history Takada placed more emphasis on conscious social relations rather than on productive or economic relations (see Takada, 1925).

In 1919 Takada published a large volume entitled *Shakaigaku Genri* (The Principles of Sociology). In this work he accepted Yoneda's theories and defined the social as mental interaction between individuals. Takada's approach is a formal sociology like Simmel's, in the sense that the form or structure of society is the most significant element for theoretical analysis. In the era of Taisho democracy Takada could freely define the social as the mental interaction of individuals detached from the state and household. However, in comparison with Simmel, Takada placed more emphasis on the unity or bond between individuals than on their interaction. Takada belied society was far more than mental interaction, it was the mental unity of individuals. Even though mental interactions among individuals exist, unless each individual desires to live cooperatively within the social unit, the society cannot exist. The will to coexist was crucial: society could only exist when people decided to live together. According to Takada, society logically consisted of individuals but was not a mere aggregation of individuals. Individuals not only interact with each other but are bound by external social forces. The forms of unity or bond are objective facts: society is not merely interaction but is in essence a unity.

In his *Shakaigaku Gairon* (General Theories of Sociology) (1922), Takada expounded two laws of social change. The first, the 'law of *Vergesellshaftung*' was the tendency for social change to proceed along an axis from *Gemeinschaft* to *Gesellschaft*. Here he distinguished between two societies, one based on primitive natural ties and the other based on secondary cultural ties. The second, the 'law of constant quantity of social bond' holds that in any society the amount of total social bond is constant. Therefore, the more individuals come into contact with others, the less dense each social interaction will be. This law is also called the diffusion of social interactions.

In a 1938 article entitled *Nihon no Tsuyomi* (The Strength of Japan) Takada argued that the spiritual strength of Japan had its roots in the social ties of the rural community. Accordingly, to protect the village community was to protect the strength of Japan. Takada said 'I am a child of the village, and a child in spirit of nostalgia' (Takada, 1934, p. 21). Takada believed the Japanese should not despise nostalgia. Nostalgia reminded Takada of the importance of Japanese folk which was why he reconsidered his former position of cosmopolitanism. In *Nihon no Tsuyomi* he emphasized the peculiar *gemeinschaftlich* character of Japanese society. Takada wrote:

> Japanese society is still young because of its *gemeinschaftlich* character. People are simple and honest by nature and not selfish. Individualism is not yet strongly ingrained, and the individual is able to absorb himself in the collective of the social whole . . . Because of this communal character, the Japanese can throw away his life for his country in complete earnestness. All Japanese, not only professional soldiers, are willing to sacrifice themselves for the sake of their country (Takada, 1938, pp. 192–3).

Takada also recalled his younger days and wrote:

> When I was writing my *Shakaigaku Genri* there was nothing but the concept of class in my mind. I was so influenced by the thought of cosmopolitanism at that time that the concept of folk was insignificant for me. However since then I am aware of the meaning of folk (Takada, 1940, p. 21).

It is surprising that such a prominent scholar of Western sociology could become aligned with the ideology of 'Japanism'.

In the sociological world Takada predicted the direction of *Vergesellschaftung* as the course of social development. Yet in the spiritual world he was a child of the rural community: in the years he spent living in an industrial urban area he yearned for rural life and sought *Gemeinschaft* in spirit.

Teizō Toda

Teizō Toda was a leading scholar in the field of family sociology. He was born in 1887 and graduated from Tokyo Imperial University in 1912. While he was lecturer in sociology at his alma mater, he went to the United States and Europe where he studied the theories and methods of social research and sociological positivism. He became an associate professor of the Department of Sociology in 1920 and was made a full professor in 1929.

Toda published *Kazoku no Kenkyu* (Studies of Family) in 1926. For this book he had analysed data from the 1920 census (Japan's first modern census) and conducted a positivist study of families. He predicted the transition of family from institution to companionship in modern Japan. He analysed the familial relationships from two perspectives: relationships between spouses and between those parents and children. He paid little attention to the traditional household institutions (*ie*). He pointed out that in the 1920 urban family the power of the family head was diminished, and the continuity of family line was no longer strongly emphasized. Of course, the *ie* institution remained a living concept among those families with large amounts of land or property. However, he insisted that the poor urban families had nothing to do with the *ie* institution in their actual family life.

Toda acknowledged that parent-child relationships in Japanese families were much stronger than those between husbands and wives. He also affirmed that within a family the male maintained a privileged position and in so far as the remaining prevalence of primogeniture, the eldest son also held a privileged position. However, Toda criticized the traditional pressure of the *ie* institution and supported civil freedom and independence for all members of the family. He concluded that the free self-realization of all family members (regardless of sex) could occur through changes in relationships within the conventional family life.

In the 1920s Takada, Toda and other leading Japanese sociologists tried to establish a liberal sociology. However, they did nothing more than introduce modern Western sociological theories to Japan.[1] When crisis came in the 1930s they readily converted to positions obedient to the ideology of Japanese nationalism or 'Japanism'.

Toda's perspective altered drastically during the Second World War. For example, in his book *Ie no Michi* (The Way of the Household) (1942) he emphasized the importance of the patrilineal family. He wrote that every *ie* in Japan had the Emperor's household as its main family, therefore filial piety could consist of loyalty to the Emperor. Each household could trace its line back to an ancestral father who was at the same time a god of Japanese folk. The Emperor could trace a direct line to an ancestral father through primogeniture. Toda emphasized that the expansion of the way of the household (*ie*) was to establish the mutual prosperity sphere in Asia which was to be directed by the Emperor. The peaceful order of Asia should be established against the aggressive acts carried out by Western countries under the mask of freedom, and be maintained like a large household.

Socialism and the Labour and Peasant Movements

In April 1910 Naoya Shiga, Saneatsu Mushakoji, Takeo Arishima and others published a magazine called *Shirakaba* (White Birch). After the magazine's launch, the group became known as the *shirakabaha*. In their writings this group emphasized the self-realization of the individual; optimistically believing that a new society could emerge if each individual did their best according to their own conscience. Most members of the group came from rich families and enjoyed a liberal life style which was tolerated

---

[1] Major sociological works translated into Japanese in the 1920s included: in 1921, G. Simmel's *Grundfragen der Soziologie* and C. H. Cooley's *Human Nature and the Social Order;* in 1922, Cooley's *Social Organization*; in 1923, L. H. Morgan's *Ancient Society* and J. G. Tarde's *Les lois de limitation*; in 1924, E. Durkheim's *Sociologie et Philosophie*, and Tarde's *Les lois sociales*; in 1925, W. McDougall *An Introduction to Social Psychology*, and *The Group Mind*, F. H. Gidding's *The Elements of Sociology;* in 1926, M. Weber's *Wirtschaftgeschichte*; in 1927, *The Complete Writings of K. Marx and F. Engels*; Simmel's *Uber soziale Differenzierung*; in 1928, R. M. MacIver's *The Elements of Social Science*, Tarde's *L'opinion et la foule*; in 1929, Giddings's *The Principles of Sociology* and C. Bougle's *Qu'est-ce que la sociologie?*

only within the upper classes. Some members of *shirakabaha* had been sympathetic to socialism in their youth, but most disliked socialists and any radical movement. However, immediately after the treason trial of 1910 many socialists expected the *shirakabaha* to play a positive role during the ensuing 'era of winter'. When the young anarchists Sakae Ōsugi and Kanson Arahata published *Kindai Shisō* (Modern Thoughts) in 1912, they tried to use the liberal ideals of the *Shirakabaha* as socialist propaganda. *Kindai Shisō* at best had a circulation of few thousand. As there were no socialist periodicals at that time, people of socialist sympathies were inclined to read it. Because socialist propaganda was severely restricted Sakae Ōsugi and others utilized individualism as a substitute for socialism. In his 1914 article 'Sei no Sōzō' (Creation of Living) published in *Kindai Shisō* Ōsugi stressed that under the prevailing conditions almost all institutions were ready to oppress the free creation of living, and the only way to achieve self-realization was to revolt against these institutions. In this context, his assertion of radical individualism came close to anarchism. By free creation of living was meant repudiation of mental slavery. Ōsugi believed that the constraints imposed upon individuals by social institutions should be destroyed, in order to allow the development of the free inner drive of the self.

At the same period of time the labour movement was rigidly controlled. In 1912 the *Yūaikai* was founded, it was a 'union' organized under governmental auspices, and included capitalists, professors, and government officials on its governing council. *Yūaikai's* chief activity was the publishing of a paper to spread anti-labour propaganda. Bunji Suzuki, the first president of *Yūaikai*, changed his strategy in 1916 after returning from the United States where he had attended a conference of the American Federation of Labour. *Yūaikai* started to demand the right for workers to organize and to strike as a union. Socialists, who expected the rise of the labour movement, were encouraged by the 1917 February and October Russian revolutions. In Japan nationwide rice riots began in 1918; their spread led to the overthrow of the Terauchi Cabinet. Following the resignation of the Terauchi Cabinet Kei Hara president of the *Seiyūkai*, organized the first party Cabinet in Japan.

In 1918 Ōsugi moved to the workers' district of Kameido in Tokyo and began publishing a paper called *Rōdō Shinbun* (Workers Daily). Arahata parted from Ōsugi and with Hitoshi

Yamakawa commenced publication of *Shin Shakai* (New Society). Yamakawa who was born in 1880 in the Okayama prefecture, became associated with the Socialist Party in 1906 and supported Kōtoku's advocacy of direct action. After the Kōtoku trial in 1910, he went back to Okayama. In 1916 he saw his return to Tokyo where Ōsugi became an anarcho-syndicalist, denying the validity of politics and political parties. However, in 1922 he participated in the founding of the Communist party, which he left in 1927 when he founded the magazine *Rono*.

At the seventh congress of the *Yūaikai* in 1919 the name of the organization was changed to *Dainihon Rōdō Sōdōmei Yūaikai* (Japan Federation of Labour). As a labour union the *Yūaikai* demanded: the right to organize workers, the abolition of child labour, the creation of a minimum wage system, and an eight-hour work day. Among its national policies were demands for universal suffrage; the amendment of the Public Peace Police Law, and the democratization of the education system.

After World War I, labour disputes became more frequent and strikes broke out in many of the large factories and mines. In 1915, 64 labour disputes involving 7,800 workers were recorded; in 1917, there were 398 disputes involving 57,300 workers; in 1919, 497 disputes involving 63,000 workers, and in 1925 the number of disputes increased to 1,260 with 127,000 workers participating. Labour unions were forming rapidly. Their number increased from 107 in 1918 to 432 in 1923. (See Table 2–1 in Chapter 2.)

However, there were serious antagonisms among the socialists. At the second congress of the Japan Socialist League in 1921, there were heated debates between socialists, anarcho-syndicalists, and Bolsheviks. The anarchists (led by Ōsugi) emphasized direct action. After Ōsugi's assassination by police in the disturbance following the 1923 Kanto earthquake, the anarchists planned a terrorist campaign in retaliation for the death. However, their terrorist strategies lost them influence among the working class. Concurrently, the so-called Bolshevik group (led by Yamakawa) which had ousted anarchism, supported the Russian October revolution and actively opposed the Allied Siberian expedition in 1918. They believed that any near future Japanese revolution should be of the Bolshevik socialist type. As they had been attracted by the theories of proletarian dictatorship and dreamed of establishing a soviet power-base comprised of workers, farmers and soldiers, they accordingly denied the importance of universal suffrage.

Thus, Yamakawa wrote a 1920 article on universal suffrage in which he insisted that the Japanese labour movement need not have as its goal the achievement of the privilege of voting; it could remain free from the illusions of parliamentary democracy which had hampered the development of labour movements in advanced Western countries. In 1922, in his article 'Futsū Senkyo to Musankaikyū no Senjutsu' (Universal Suffrage and the Tactics of the Proletariat) Yamakawa also warned that the proletarian movement could be emasculated by parliamentalism (Yamakawa, 1922, p. 212). In line with this Yamakawa criticized Yoshino's theories of democracy. He pointed out that Yoshino paid little attention to the problems of sovereignty and only demanded the expansion of voting rights. According to Yamakawa, democracy was closely related to class struggle, and bourgeois democracy and proletarian democracy were quite different matters (Yamakawa, 1918, p. 199). Parliamentary government was an institution of bourgeois democracy. The proletariat had to destroy parliamentary government and replace it with free association in which small scale self-government could be fully realized (Yamakawa, 1917, p. 69).

The Japanese Communist Party, which was illegally established in 1922, outlined the needs of democracy in its draft platform. Its chief aims included: 1) abolition of the Emperor system; 2) abolition of the House of Peers; 3) universal suffrage for males and females over the age of eighteen; and 4) freedom of association for labour unions, labour parties, and all other labour organizations. The communists did not have much influence among the workers when the draft was tabled. In 1924 the leaders decided to dissolve the Party. The Communist Party was reorganized in December 1926, and in 1927 passed a resolution in which it defined the revolution confronting the Japanese people as one based on bourgeois democracy. However, this resolution was rejected by a group which seceded from the party and formed a faction called the *Ronoha* (the 'Worker and Peasant Faction'), so called because the group included supporters of the magazine *Rono*.

In 1925 the government passed a law granting universal suffrage to males who were twenty-five years of age and older. Yet, it was not the socialist and labour movements, but the liberal elements of the bureaucracy, political parties and big business who took up the initiative on universal suffrage. Before universal suffrage, the basis for qualification to vote had been tax-paying ability. Thus, prior to 1919, males who paid direct annual taxes of ten *yen* or more were eligible to vote for the House of Representatives. In 1919 this financial requirement was being reduced to three *yen* or more annually paid in tax. Similarly, prior to the 1921 amendments to the laws regulating local government, those who qualified for citizenship were males over twenty-five years old who resided in the cities, towns or villages, and who paid both resident taxes and land taxes to the central government, or who paid national taxes of more than two *yen*. Voters were classified into three divisions in the cities and two in towns and villages. In towns and villages the voters who paid higher taxes were placed in the first class division and the remaining taxpayers were placed in the second class. Each class elected half of the total representatives to local assemblies. Absentees had voting rights, if they did not meet the age and residential qualifications, they could still vote if their taxes were paid at the local level and if the amount they paid ranked within the highest third of all taxes paid. Following the 1921 amendments males of twenty-five years of age and older who had paid taxes at the local level, were divided into two classes in the cities, and the classification system was abolished in the towns and villages. Absentee voting rights were also abolished. In 1921 the county assembly system was abolished, and in 1922 laws governing the organization of prefectures were amended, expanding the election qualifications to people who had paid direct national taxes.

When universal suffrage for males of twenty-five years of age and over was proclaimed, the first test of the new law occurred with the city assembly election in Hamamatsu city in 1926, and at the national level in 1928. However, even after universal suffrage had been introduced socialists exerted little influence on real policies at both levels. This was in part due to oppressive government legislation which controlled the socialist and labour movement. Such laws as the 1925 Law for the Maintenance of Public Peace, and the 1926 Violence Control Law, were a part of the oppression.

In 1918, the tenant disputes over high rents in rural areas, which were closely connected with the urban rice riots, arose. The number of such disputes increased from 256 in 1918 to 1,680 in 1920. After 1923 these disputes were longer in duration and more frequently involved litigation. (See Tables 2–2 and 2–3 in Chapter 2.) It was in such conditions that the first national tenant organization the Nihon Nōmin Kumiai (The Japanese Farmer's Union), was founded in April 1922.

At first tenants requested temporary rent reductions but later their demands changed to permanent reductions in rent regardless of crop yield. The high rate of rice rent was maintained through the communal regulation of *buraku*. The payment of rice rent had been considered a community rule. With the growth of tenant disputes this traditional practice changed. The traditional status hierarchy was weakened and landlords' social and political privileges were diminished. The 1925 proclamation of universal suffrage also affected tenants' thinking. After 1925 the customary method of election of the *buraku* head, secretary and councillors, was reformed in many places.

For example, the Obaden *buraku* of Ojigawa village in Niigata prefecture, retained the *omodachi* system until 1925. In Obaden, there were twenty privileged households called *omodachi*, each of whom owned more than 1.3 *cho* of arable land. The *omodachi* had special meetings to decide community affairs. The *buraku* head and secretary were elected by *omodachi* and by *tochimochi* who owned less than 1.3 *cho*. But households with no land (*komae*) had no voting rights.

In 1923 the tenants organized a union and through it demanded that the *omodachi* grant voting rights to all non-landowners for the election of the *buraku* head and secretary. In 1925 the landlords finally met this demand. Encouraged by this success, tenants asked for the right to be elected as *buraku* head or secretary. The *omodachi* refused this demand. This resulted in the tenants boycotting the 1925 *buraku* head election and the tenants also began to campaign against the *omodachi* system. Later in that year they demanded that the *omodachi* meeting be abolished, and in 1926 it was finally reformed. Under the new agreement all authority of the *omodachi* meeting was transferred to the newly established *buraku* council meeting. Irrespective of landholding every household had one vote in the election of local officers at the *buraku* council meeting.

After universal suffrage in 1925 some tenants were elected to the town and village assemblies. Through their recurrent collective efforts tenants attained rights. It was often said: 'These tenant disputes are caused not only by the high rate of rent but also by tenants' consciousness of their rights as equal human beings'.

In general, at the initial stage of the tenancy movement its leaders were almost always wealthy tenants or owner-tenants engaged in large scale cultivation of land. The different orientations and objectives of the movement were stated in the tenant disputes. Large rent reductions made it possible for tenants to accumulate funds and to engage in increased cash crop agriculture. As might be expected, wealthy tenants received greater advantages from the concessions made by landlords than poor tenants. Affluent tenants who had an opportunity to buy land became less aggressive in the movement, and in turn, the poorer tenants became more radical in their demands.

All tenants demanded rent reductions regardless of the scale of their land cultivation. But the decline of the landlord system had different effects on the wealthy and the poor tenants. At that time socialists' only clear policy was the promotion of the capitalization of agriculture. The socialists stood against capitalization from 'above', which they believed would ensure the long-term survival of the semi-feudal system. Instead they supported capitalization from 'below' and tried to change it to socialization at an early stage. Socialists believed that abolition of the landlord system should be all tenants' first goal; on gaining it the poor farmers could then fight the upper stratum of farmers who pursued further capitalist development of farming. Yet the socialists did not recognize that the condition of Japanese agriculture itself rendered capitalist development difficult. In an economy dominated by large industrial capital, even the upper stratum of farmers had little chance to develop a capitalist agriculture.

In fact, in the 1930s the old rural middle class who directly cultivated their own land and were active in producers' cooperatives, supported the right-wing groups and young military officers who claimed to speak for the peasants. Farmers of the upper and middle strata opposed capitalism because they thought it would produce a crisis and destroy rural life. Cooperation between the upper and the lower strata and the maintenance of peace and solidarity, were stressed in order to strengthen national unity under the emperor. Agrarian fundamentalism was seen as a solution to the crisis. However, it was in reality merely a revival of traditional values.

The Development of Indigenous Scholarship: Kunio Yanagida and Kizaemon Aruga

In the same period of time new considerations which had a bearing on sociological theory (often involving evidence drawn from the specifics of Japanese society) were gaining influence. Drawing on history and the realm of traditional Japanese beliefs and social practices, a number of influential thinkers developed theories which grew out of what they understood was the bedrock of national experience. Their attitudes were often influential and their example has continued to be held in high regard in postwar Japan. Yet their conceptions were also fraught with difficulties and dangers, some practical, some inadvertently ideological.

Kunio Yanagida, the most influential 20th century Japanese scholar of folklore, was born in 1875 in Hyōgo prefecture. He graduated from the faculty of law at the Tokyo Imperial University and after graduation became an official in the Ministry of Agriculture. In his youth Yanagida was a poet and man of letters. Among his close friends at that time were Tōson Shimazaki, Katai Tayama and Doppo Kunikida. Yanagida began his studies of agronomy around 1900. He published volumes entitled *Nōseigaku* (Agronomy) in 1902–1905 and *Jidai to Nōsei* (The Age and Agricultural Administration) in 1910. In *Jidai to Nosei* he stressed the importance of the continuity of households (*ie*). Skeptical as to whether imported theories such as Marxism could explain Japanese society's dynamics, he argued that indigenous theories were necessary for the explanation of indigenous social phenomena. For example, he criticized the modern Western theories of land rent including the Marxist. He uncovered and categorized the emic terminology and stressed its significance.

According to Yanagida, the relationships between *oya* and *ko* were social. He distinguished between concepts such as *oya* (one who takes the role of the fictive parent) and *umi no oya* (biological parents). Although the term *oya* is now used in a more limited sense, primarily to indicate blood or family ties, Yanagida emphasized the fact that the terms originally indicated a leader-follower relationship within a social unit in which labour was organized. This social unit used to be a large household – the extended family. Yanagida demonstrated out that the fictive kinship ties played an important role in household social relationships. Within the network of fictive kinship lineage groups existed as important social units. Thus the internal relationships within each household dictated the character of external relationships between households.

Because of the complex background of social relationships Yanagida believed Japanese folklore would provide a rich source of inspiration for the development of indigenous theories. His research on local customs in various parts of Japan led him to evaluate the ability the Japanese household had to perpetuate itself. Yanagida had identified individualism as a deviant form of behaviour which only served to undermine the value placed on lineage; furthermore, individual desires were seen as being unrelated to, or at least as existing in a sphere totally separate from the needs of the nation. In *Jidai to Nosei* he argued that the unique nature of Japanese culture was rooted in the fact that the Japanese people had lived according to tradition and served the emperor as an institution for almost two thousand years. If no household system existed in Japan, people would not understand the essential nature of being Japanese (Yanagida, 1910, p. 39).

Despite taking a very conservative ideological stance Yanagida believed that modernization was imperative. He believed that continuity of the household, including the continuity of the Imperial Household, was very important even after the Meiji Restoration. Yanagida realized that the social landlord's character had changed and they had lost their traditional power over tenants. Yanagida saw that tenants' demands for the reduction of rice rent and the abolition of feudalistic practices of landlords as inevitable. In *Toshi to Nōson* (Urban and Rural Society) in 1919 he supported the farmers union's demands. But at the same time he criticized the union because it had been organized only by tenant farmers. He pointed out that even if the present rice rent were to be totally abolished and tenants became owners of the land they farmed, they would still be no better off than the small landowning farmers who had significant debts. Yanagida therefore believed the union should include owner-cultivators and endeavour to find employment for farmers (Yanagida, 1919, p. 345).

Yanagida insisted that communal ownership of land was a traditional Japanese custom. Cooperation by farmers engaged in agricultural production did not originate in Western communist ideas, but in the traditional practices of peasants who survived through mutual assistance in village communities. He believed that new capitalist forms of agriculture would not be realized in Japan (Yanagida, 1919, p. 378). This was because the capitalization of agriculture realization would require the expulsion of poor peasants from the land without creating social unrest. Yet Yanagida also maintained that the minute size of most family holdings could not be maintained in the future of agriculture. Therefore, in order to establish stable family farming in Japan some farmers needed to voluntarily transfer to other occupations. The farmers who remained in the village would be expected to spontaneously cooperate with each other, finally bringing to reality a cooperative system of farming based on the communal ownership of land (Yanagida, 1919, pp. 355- 7). This was Yanagida's plan. For Yanagida opposition to landlords' control did not mean the promotion of the capitalist development of agriculture. He paid much attention to the communal way of life of common people in both rural and urban areas.

As Yanagida indicated, the significance of ancestor worship links social structure with religious values. The religious authority of a household head is based in his status as a direct lineal descendant of the *ie*. In his article 'Tamashii no Yukue' (The Abode of the Departed Souls) (1949) Yanagida wrote that in Japan the ancestors' souls do not travel far from their native abodes. They stay on the hills of their homeland and watch over their descendants' lives. Respect for one's ancestors naturally requires respect for the household head who is the link between the ancestors and descendants (Yanagida, 1949, p. 561). In his article 'Nōson Kazokuseido to Kanshū' (Rural Household System and Customs) (1927) Yanagida stated that a household head must continue to celebrate festivals and to integrate his household members. A head must do his best to ensure the prosperity of his descendants. Therefore, the head of the household will feel he has failed in his responsibilities to his ancestors if he loses his family's fortune. Yanagida believed it would be harmful if the Japanese people began to attach little importance to the continuity of their households (Yanagida, 1927, p. 356).

After World War I Yanagida shifted his attention from agronomy to folklore. He combined folklore with history, and elaborated an indigenous discipline of social history. His concept of folkloric studies was well expressed in a lecture entitled 'Seinen to Gakumon' (Youth and Scholarship) (1925):

> The goal of studying the social history of our own country is to solve the problems of the common people. To understand the reason why we, the common people, still have to suffer miserable conditions in our lives, we must study the history of our own country and clarify the relationships of ourselves to our own society, i.e. to Japan. To study history makes man wise. Heedless undertakings of the people would be dangerous in these days when people who have stood outside of political life now have voting rights. They have been left unlettered and have nothing to do but pray to the gods for mercy. Under the system of universal suffrage, public education should be emphasized. New scholarship should play an important role in enlightening the people to promote their better understanding of their present and future situation (Yanagida, 1925, p. 16).

On the subject of women's liberation, Yanagida expressed a unique opinion in his 1934 lecture 'Josei Shigaku' (The History of Japanese Women). He predicted the realization of female suffrage in the near future and stated that:

> as with men's suffrage, the assertion that woman should have the right to share in decisions regarding national affairs is not refused by anyone in so far as the theory itself is concerned. One could object to it only on the pretext that it is still premature to talk about it or that the procedure has not been examined closely. Women today should be prepared to participate in national politics and undertake social services which could be done by women alone (Yanagida, 1934, pp. 253–4).

Yanagida pointed out the significant role of women in the traditional household which required that all members participate in the communal way of life. Historically the household status of an *okata* or *toji* (a wife of the head) was very high. If becoming the head of a household was a goal for young men, then becoming an *okata* was a goal for young women. In the traditional household the work of the housewife was not simple: she was required to make decisions regarding the management of cooperative labour within a large family group. Specific aspects of family affairs were for her alone to make decisions, and in such matters even her husband could not intrude with an opinion. Yanagida therefore expected in the communal epoch of the future, a reactivation of the traditional role of women.

In regard to the education of women Yanagida indicated in his *Daikazoku to Shokazoku* (A Large Family and a Small Family) (1940) that it was difficult to bring up the traditional *okata* type of woman in the modern education system. Nor was it easy for parents to raise their daughters to become a docile and modest *anesan* (new bride), and to later develop into a gallant and dignified *okata*. Being a bride is not the same as being a household head's wife. As a new bride a woman is expected to obey her mother-in-law, but as an *okata* she is expected to manage many household affairs, such as the distribution of household produce. Yanagida saw Japanese women as living in an age requiring unforeseen cooperative activities. Women were expected to perform important roles in a community which resembled a large extended family (Yanagida, 1940, pp. 144–5). If we are to see the revival of communal society in a broader context in the near future, we should not disparage Yanagida's prediction of the coming large extended family as reactionary.

Yanagida, as a folklorist, conducted considerable research into the lives of common people but he was relatively indifferent to the construction of new theories. Kizaemon Aruga (who was much influenced by Yanagida's folklore) was a sociologist ambitious enough to create new indigenous Japanese theories. He was born in 1897 in Nagano prefecture and graduated from the department of art history at the Tokyo Imperial University in 1922. He began his studies as a folklorist and then switched to sociology. As the son of a wealthy landlord he had no need to take up employment at any of the universities or institutions until the end of the war.

Aruga wrote an article entitled 'Nago no Fueki' (A Corvée of the *Nago*) in 1933. At that time there was a debate centred around the feudal land rent issue, within the Marxist camp. Members of the *kōzaha* faction so-called because most were contributors to the *Nihon Shihonshugi Hattatsushi Kōza* (Lectures on the Developmental History of Japanese Capitalism), characterized the rent paid to landlords as feudal rent. Members of the *rōnōha* faction, so-called because most were writers for the magazine *Rōnō* (Labourers and Peasants), characterized it as a form of modern capitalist rent. The *rōnōha* insisted that high rents were caused by competition among small peasants who were eager to lease land. The *kōzaha* pointed out that the landlord system after the Meiji Restoration was still a semi-feudal system. Based on their reading of Marx's *Das Kapital* the *kōzaha* Marxists believed that in Japan the forms of feudal rent (developed in sequence as labour rent, product rent, and monetary rent) were evident. Therefore, the Marxists in Japan defined the corvée of the *nago* (a kind of *kokata*) as labour rent. A *nago* was a serf who worked for a *myoshu* (a kind of *oyakata*) and a *nago's* labour services could be defined as feudal labour rent. Aruga refuted such assertions and pointed out that the *nago's* labour was not a form of feudal rent but a form of household labour by the *kokata* for the *oyakata* within the extended family system.

In *Ninon Kasokuseido to Kosakuseido* (The Japanese Family System and Tenant System), Aruga argued that the origin of the relationship between landlord and tenant in Japan was similar to that which existed between the *oyakata* and *kokata* in the pre-feudal period. Originally they were not separate relationships but formed one *Interessengemeinschaft* in which each had different roles for conducting the cooperative management of agriculture. When he attacked the Marxists in relation to this matter, Aruga maintained that the independence of subordinate *nago* or *kokata* was a characteristic of the feudal Tokugawa period (Aruga, 1943, p. 631). He demonstrated that the *oyakata-kokata* relationship within the large extended family was an historical carry over and had existed before the small landholding family gained independence.

During the Tokugawa period, overlords (*ryōshu*) collected land taxes directly from the peasant. In the Tokugawa period the former *nago* or *kokata* became the *honbyakushō* who had a duty to pay taxes directly to overlords. The independence of the *nago* and *kokata* from the *myōshu* and *oyakata* caused the dissolution of the large extended families. In the course of nearly one hundred years – from the latter half of the 16th century when Hideyoshi's cadastral survey was first conducted, to the beginning of Tokugawa feudal system – the *honbyakushō* increased in number because of the progressive dissolution of *myōshu* farming, which was accompanied by the important increase in the number of independent *nago* and *kokata* households. In addition, the equal partitioning of arable land increased the number of *honbyakushō*.

However, by the end of the Tokugawa period the differentiation of *honbyakushō* had brought serious problems. Their upper classes began to accumulate arable land, and became landlords, while the lower classes lost their land and became tenants. Thus a new set of landlord-tenant relationships were established. Aruga particularly emphasized that these new relationships were again influenced by lineage relationships. As we saw earlier, social relationships between landlords and tenants were like those of parents (*oya*) and children (*ko*). Their relationship was one of mutual obligation and service. Tenants believed that they could make a living under the landlord's favour, although almost half of their rice harvest was paid in rent. They also expressed their personal subordination to the landlord through the performance of certain services. In the case of corvée, domestic and ceremonial services were assigned as much as labour services. For example, Aruga described the surviving relationship between the *oyakata* and the *nago* of the Saitō family in Ishigami village, Ninoe county, Iwate prefecture in 1935. He observed services performed by the *bekke* (branch families) and *nago* at *o-bon* (All Souls' Day):

> The celebration of the festival began on the fourteenth of the seventh month. However, on the thirteenth day preparations were made for the arrival of the souls of the deceased by sweeping ancestral graves, and repairing and sweeping the roads that passed through the village and led to the graves. The graves of the *oyakata's* ancestors were swept by the *bekke* and *nago*. Early in the morning of the fourteenth, the *bekke* and *nago* went to the *oyakata's* to do *suke* (labour services) – the *nago* cleaning the ground and the *bekke* decorating the altar. When this work was finished, all went together to the grave, carrying offerings . . . Each night during the celebration, a faggot of pine was left burning in front of the gate as a welcome to the returning souls. On the sixteenth the souls were seen off (Aruga, 1943, pp. 638–9).

Such *oyakata* as family heads were not typical after the feudal period. The landlords in the Meiji period were usually neither *oyakata* nor heads of main families. The relationships between main and branch families did not always coincide with the relationships between a landlord and tenant in the Meiji period. But the ideological use of genealogical relationships by landlords was a different matter. The landlord could control tenants through traditional relationships between the main and branch families. In cases where genealogical status did not correspond with land-ownership status and where landlords were not actually from main families, the records were often manipulated. For landlords in the Meiji period, the longer they had been established the better; however, this was not a necessary condition as the rule of the landlord was based upon land ownership. Lineage relationships were simply an important means to legitimate the landlords' power and evoke a spontaneous will to follow their dictates. However, even if there had been no landlords the concept of the lineage group and the continuity of the household would have remained, especially in owner-cultivator households.

In short, Aruga recognized a peculiar characteristic of the Japanese: the social hierarchy is legitimated by lineage relationships. For instance, he noted that vertical relationships in Japan were characterized by paternalism, and as the relationships between members of the family were hierarchical, so too were relations between main and branch families, or between the emperor and 'his people' (Aruga, 1943, p. 726). According to Aruga, the major structural feature of Japanese society was its familial principles of organization. These principles were not only applicable to the community, but to the state and all other organizations. Aruga's conservative stance could be easily criticized. But his arguments around to the national character of the Japanese have useful implications for the further study of the Japanese people, their culture and society, as do Yanagida's views.

Aruga massed a considerable amount of empirical evidence to demonstrate that the *oyakata-kokata* relationship within the large extended family was a carry over from earlier times and existed before the small landholding families gained their independence. But he also exaggerated the nature of *oyakata-kokata* relationships before the feudal Tokugawa era, and sought to give ideological support to such relationships claiming they were the essence of Japan's unchanging national character. In taking this stance, he became aligned with ultra-nationalism as it existed in the peculiar intellectual milieu of the 1930s and early 1940s.

If we can say that the essential character of family relations does not necessarily have a hierarchical basis, we can also describe familial organization as involving horizontal relations. When faced with a choice between egalitarian relationships and hierarchical ones, there is little question that the former would be chosen. Groupism and communalism have nothing to do with vertical social relationships; nor do vertical social relationships necessarily result from groupism. The emphasis on vertical, rather than horizontal relationships is merely an ideologically biased use of traditional values. It is unlikely that in Japan, or in other non-Western pre-industrial societies, complete personal independence could emerge first, followed by some kind of solidarity between individuals. Such mechanical distinctions between two stages of development do not seem relevant to the Japanese experience.

In 1908, the editor of a socialist journal for women's liberation in Japan wrote an editorial entitled 'Kyosanshakai no Kazoku' (Families in Communist Society), describing that in the future 'affections between husband and wife and between parents and children will be the central forces in the family', but 'in present society love for one's sons, parents, spouse and oneself is made to conflict with one's love for others and for society'. It continued, 'if one can love oneself, one's family members and relatives without weakening one's love for others and for society, then all these different loves can develop as the admirable, beautiful and true sentiments of all human beings' (Arichi, 1977, p. 170). This remains true. In that era the revitalization of horizontal relationships or the development of solidarity among common people in traditional groups, was seen as an important task.

The story of the conflicting demands of theory, history and culture during the interwar period in Japan is thus a complex one. A sense of the struggle in the areas of both academic social theory and social action must remain paramount in the minds of those who review the confusions and successes of an historical period. However, in retrospect, it can be said that the struggles of Japanese intellectuals and socially-concerned citizens alike did allow each in their own way, to reach an important level of self-awareness both personally and with regard to the roles in which

their society had cast them. In this very important sense, much
was accomplished.

PART II

Part II consists of three chapters devoted to discussion of the theoretical and empirical problems of rural and urban community studies. By the 1950s sociological studies in Japan tried to focus on rural, rather than urban communities. Japanese sociologists who took this approach included Eitarō Suzuki, Kizaemon Aruga and Tadashi Fukutake. In the neighboring field of folklore studies, Kunio Yanagida sought to establish indigenous scholarship. Yanagida advanced an ahistorical ethnographic approach, whereas Fukutake focused on the problems the development of Japanese capitalism produced.

Chapter 4 critically examines the works of Tadashi Fukutake, the most representative post-war Japanese sociologist. Fukutake's work deserves attention because of his considerable influence on Japanese sociology and for the regard this work (when published in English) has received outside Japan.

The theoretical frame of reference employed in Part I is retained for the critical perspective. It is first noted that Fukutake saw the developmental process of rural Japan according to the schema of modernization from *Gemeinschaft* to *Gesellschaft*. He related this approach to the transition from the vertical-extended-family type of village to the horizontal-associational type. The latter would become more predominant in accordance with the development of capitalism in agricultural Japan.

Fukutake made a major theoretical error in assuming that a smooth development of capitalism in agriculture was possible for Japan. According to Fukutake, modernization from 'above', in which many semi-feudal remnants are necessarily preserved, was to be avoided and modernization from 'below', along with smooth development of capitalism in agriculture, should be welcomed. Until the end of the 1950s, Fukutake saw a significant problem in rural overpopulation. However, from the 1960s the situation altered, as the agricultural population rapidly decreased. Many people left rural areas for Tokyo, Osaka and other industrial cities. But with the overpopulation problem removed, the smooth development of capitalism in agriculture that Fukutake expected did not eventuate. He underestimated the communal relationships within Japanese families and villages. I criticize Fukutake's account for not providing the perspective of a postmodern society where conflicts and contradictions between rural and urban communities are dissolved.

In Chapter 5 I analyse the concepts of community and power. This is done with specific reference to the power structures of two local communities. Both theoretical and empirical analyses of community power structure are undertaken. The differences between community power structure in the U.S. and Japan, are my main theoretical concerns.

Since the Meiji Restoration (which is regarded as the beginning of the modern period) communities of the *Gemeinschaft* type have persisted in Japan. It is generally believed that since the modern period, the closed nature a community has disappeared, supplanted by the emergence of an open society in which individuals enjoy freedom and equality. This modern society is analytically and functionally divided into two spheres: civil society and political society.

American research into the power structures of local communities, defines power empirically not as political power or force but as some kind of leadership or authority among people within the community. In the U.S. community is independent from state power and is self-governing. However, in Japan the community is an administrative subunit of and subordinate to the state; thus there is no clear cut distinction between political society and civil society.

The research on community power structure in Japan was undertaken in Shimoda city in Shizuoka prefecture and Yokoshiba town in Chiba prefecture in the 1980s. We made a list of leaders in the community by asking informants to name an important person. These leaders were then asked to select other leaders from the list. The eventual group of priority leaders was made up of professional politicians – Diet members, governors, mayors, town managers, members of the prefectural assembly, members of city and town assemblies, etc. – and not business leaders.

Chapter 6 focuses on pollution in Japan specifically in the late 1960s and the early 1970s. The movement against environmental destruction first arose as a community-defending movement, then developed into a community-reconstructing movement. They were known as citizens' movements or residents' movements, again the main focus was the community. An extensive anti-pollution movement arose in the latter half of the 1960s for a number of reasons: the damage caused by pollution was widespread but residents also had been oppressed by community political leaders and for the first time asserted their sovereignty against corporations' unchecked pursuit of profit. The community needs to take control of production and consumption of goods for its own people's sake. I argue that the citizens' movement was not a defensive movement, but a reality-reconstructing movement.

The main thesis of Part II is that the scheme of development from traditionalism to rationalism, from particularism to universalism, and from hierarchical status relationships to egalitarian contract relationships, is not directly applicable to the Japanese experience. It had been assumed that industrial development following the Western model required a social setting radically different from pre-industrial relationships, a system fundamentally akin to that which did develop in the West. This assumption, however, is untenable when examining Japan.

As James C. Abegglen pointed out in his book *The Japanese Factory*, the development of industrial relationships in Japan had occasioned much less alteration of preindustrial social relationships than would be expected in the Western model of industrial growth. The rise of industrial relationships in the West is generally attributed to the development of an impersonalized and rationalized view of the world and others. But in Japan social features such as the principles of family loyalty and cohesion have been important sources of energy and motivation for the transition to industrialization.

Perhaps this was also a cause of industrial pollution. Yet the remedies sought for this problem do not involve the dissolution of communal relationships or the development of individualism. The process of development initially involving the establishment of rational relationships between individuals and followed by the free association of individuals, is not expected to occur in Japan.

4 A Critical Evaluation of the Sociological Thought of Tadashi Fukutake, Rural Sociologist of Postwar Japan

Introduction

Tadashi Fukutake who was born in 1917 is one of Japan's leading sociologists. After graduating from the University of Tokyo in 1940 he conducted a wartime survey of a Chinese village community. The results of this study were published in his first major book, *Chūgoku nōsonshakai no kōzō* (The Social Structure of a Chinese Village Community) in 1946. In 1948 Fukutake became assistant professor at the University of Tokyo, and in 1960 was promoted to professor. Thereafter he published many books including some in English, of which *Man and Society in Japan* (1962), *Japanese Rural Society* (1967), and *Japanese Society Today* (1974) were especially significant.

Because Fukutake became a representative figure of the postwar Japanese sociology, a close examination of his work is instructive. Significantly the end of World War II marked the commencement of his sociological studies, and his main concern has been the democratization of Japanese society. As a rural sociologist he was primarily concerned with the liberation of the tenant farmers who had suffered domination by landlords. Although he criticized the semi-feudal system and supported the modernization of the family and rural lifestyles, he did not believe that Japan's social problems would be solved by capitalist modernization.

When analysing Japanese society one must first acknowledge that since at least the turn of the century Japanese society has been shaped by capitalism. Japan is still the only non-Western society to have a highly developed capitalist system, though other countries have achieved some success in this direction. Yet studies emphasizing the unique aspects of Japanese society (such as

Chie Nakane's) tend to treat the traits of Japanese society, culture
and personality, as if they were ahistorical phenomena, existing
outside of the influence of history, geography and social class
(see Nakane, 1968 and 1970). In contrast Fukutake's used an
historical perspective in his study of the modern capitalist stage
of Japanese society.

Unlike the advanced forms of Western capitalism, Japanese
capitalism retains many traditional or pre-modern elements. In
Fukutake's scheme of explanation the 'distortion of modernization in Japan' arose from its timing: Japan's 'capitalistic modernization commenced at a time when capitalism in other parts of
the world was about to enter the stage of imperialism' (Fukutake,
1962, p. 6). In Japan there has been neither a tradition of freedom for citizens nor an economic ethic of capitalism supported
by religion, as experienced in the West. Fukutake noted that
Japanese modernization could not proceed in the same manner
as in the West; that is toward what was regarded as a typical
civil society. He wrote:

> from the first, Meiji government policies promoted
> industrialization and greater production, national wealth,
> and military strength . . . That this growth was protected and
> fostered from the very beginning by the national government
> meant that no truly liberal tradition developed with it
> (Fukutake, 1974, p. 3).

Fukutake was correct in emphasizing the survival of semi-feudal
elements in modern Japan. What characterized early Japanese
capitalism was its industrialization 'from above', through the centralized power of national government. Village communities were
still prevalent and landlords dominated peasants through traditional privileges in these communities. At the time of the Meiji
Restoration, conditions had not yet matured to a stage where the
dissolution of feudalism and the development of capitalism would
spontaneously proceed.

Fukutake observed that Japan embarked on a process of
forced-draft capital accumulation and as a result capitalism
advanced at great speed. The Meiji government introduced the
modern factory system from the West and established government enterprises. These were later transferred to the control of
privileged merchants who formed *zaibatsu*, giant family-con-

trolled enterprises. The first burst of industrialization after the Restoration produced industrial goods for military use. This sector utilized imported modern equipment. The second stage brought the development of consumer goods industries, mainly textiles. The third stage came with the expansion of heavy industry in general, this occurred during the Russo-Japanese war of 1904–1905. As Jon Halliday noted, 'the extent to which the development of heavy industry was government-led and arms-oriented cannot be exaggerated' (Halliday, 1975, p. 58).

Fukutake focused on the backward and distorted nature of Japanese capitalism. He considered prewar Japan a pre-modern society resting on its 'old-fashioned' rural foundation. Fukutake pointed out that Japanese agriculture did not essentially differ from that of the feudal period, and 'it is hardly surprising that the farmers who made agriculture their livelihood, and the rural society which these farmers created, should have been of an old-fashioned character' (Fukutake, 1967, p. 8). The astonishing development of Japanese capitalism supported by the mechanism of maintaining the low cost of rice and low wages, conferred no fringe benefits, but kept Japanese agriculture and 'Japanese villages firmly entrenched in their old-fashioned mould'.

As capitalism developed changes did occur in rural society. With the spread of a higher stage of commodity-based economy, the contradictions between capitalist production and the landlord system became visible. The relationship between landlord and tenant began to change from around the time of World War I. Beginning in 1915 and proceeding into the 1920s tenant disputes spread throughout Japan. In 1916 and 1917, when they were particularly numerous the government responded with repression; later it combined repression with attempts to adjust rents and the establishment of schemes in which tenants could purchase the land they worked. The Taisho era (1912–1926) saw the rise of a movement for reform involving labourers, farmers, students and women, called the 'Taisho Democracy Movement'. The extension of universal suffrage in 1925 (as mentioned in Chapter 3) was one of its most significant results. By undermining the basis of the landlords' domination of the village increased enfranchisement changed the traditional power structure in rural areas.

By the mid-twenties (late Taisho and early Showa) the position of landlords had declined within the ruling bloc and monopoly capital had become dominant. Thereafter the landlord was steadily relegated to the background. After the Meiji Restoration the ruling bloc had consisted of government leaders descended from the lower echelons of the former warrior class, privileged merchants (who later formed *zaibatsu*), large landowners, the new peerage, and the court supported by the Emperor system. In the Taisho period the *zaibatsu* increased their power and party politicians and bureaucrats appeared as new elements of the ruling elite. As Japanese capitalism approached the monopoly stage, the political power of landlords also declined.

In Japan party politics and party cabinets were not products of mass movements from below. Rather, they resulted from the initiative of big business, although parliamentary politics received its main impetus from the introduction of universal suffrage in 1925. The 1926 abolition of county offices symbolized the rationalization of administration in the hands of the liberal elements of the *zaibatsu* and politicians. In the rural areas, farmers of the upper stratum (not landlords) played a major role in reconstructing the village's social order. In the 1920s the reformist elements in big business and the government attempted to resolve from above, contradictions in the semi-feudal landlord system.

'Japanism' and the myth of the Emperor system had the support of military officers right-wing groups, and also monopoly capital. Traditional and revered symbols were manipulated to mobilize the people for Japan's great war. Those who would not fight abroad on behalf of monopoly capital were encouraged to do so for the Emperor. Monopoly capital also took the initiative in building up the myth of the Divine Emperor, profiting from its use. Shortcomings in the work of Fukutake is now clear: he failed to both perceive and explain the decisive role that monopoly capital played before the war. He also overlooked the manner in which the 'old-fashioned' system functioned to enhance the political power of monopoly capital. Fukutake oversimplified the situation by asserting that all Japanese had a feudal outlook, and that Japanese society was more or less held together by its traditional culture. It seems incredibly naive to suggest that Japan rushed headlong into the war only because of a lack of individualism, civilian control, or civic social order. If this were so, how can we explain the similarly aggressive wars of other modernized countries where individualism was held to be a virtue?

The Question of Feudal Influence on Rural Social Structure

Japanese imperialism was defeated in 1945 and great changes took place under the American occupation after the war. The main reforms were the introduction of a new Constitution, a purge of undesirable personnel from public office, dissolution of the *zaibatsu* (the rebuilding of Japanese capitalism) and land reform. The promulgation of a new Constitution demythologized the emperor, categorically denying he had supernatural attributes and relegating him to serve as a 'symbol of the state and of the unity of the people'. Land reform undercut the foundation of the semi-feudal relationship between landlord and tenant, and also undermined the family system which had been regarded as a uniquely Japanese institution.

Under these conditions the major theoretical focus attention was the democratization of Japanese society. Along with other social scientists, Fukutake engaged in fieldwork in rural Japan. In 1949 he published his first book on rural Japan which emphasized the importance of democratization for the rural family and community. 'Unless Japanese village society can move toward being truly democratic,' he wrote, 'Japanese society will never become a stable democracy' (Fukutake, 1949, p. 1). Later, during the rapid growth of the Japanese economy in the 1960s, he also pointed out that 'unless Japanese villages can somehow in the course of their transition move towards a solution of these contradictions, Japanese village society will never become a truly democratic society'. Fukutake believed the rural sector was cause for considerable concern because 'at present one cannot hold out bright prospects for Japanese agriculture and Japanese villages' (Fukutake, 1967, p. 27). However, although he continued to use the expression, 'a truly democratic society', its implications changed over the course of time, as we shall see later.

Fukutake believed that the major obstacle to democratization of rural Japan was the minute size of family holdings. The postwar land reform had merely transferred the ownership of land and had not affected the actual size of holdings, leaving the problem of atomized holdings, the cancer of Japanese agriculture untouched. Yet at that time, Fukutake believed that Japanese capitalism had already reached the monopoly stage, and that a

movement away from small holdings could be achieved by socialist cooperation (Fukutake, 1949, p. 235).

Immediately after the war Takeyoshi Kawashima published an
essay entitled *Nihonshakai no kazokuteki kosei* (The Familial
Structure of Japanese Society) (1946), in which he argued that
democratization of Japan would fail unless the Japanese family
system was revolutionized (Kawashima, 1950, pp. 24–25). Hisao
Ōtsuka also wrote an article in 1946 entitled 'Kindaiteki ningen
ruikei no sōshutsu' (The Necessity of Creating the Modern Civic
Type of Person). He too was afraid that the institutions of democracy would be like a skeleton lacking flesh and blood, unless
people changed their values and gave voluntary support to
reforms. Ōtsuka believed that the democratically inclined person
would only emerge when tenants were liberated from the
oppression of the landlords and a full-scale domestic market was
created (Ōtsuka, 1968, p. 16).

Within ten years these two prerequisites for democracy were
realized, but matters did not move in the direction Ōtsuka had
predicted. He later claimed that he had not visualized early
modern European societies as a model for contemporary Japan.
His earlier writings, he argued, were meant to suggest how the
Japanese people could assimilate new ideas and incorporate them
into their own actions (Ōtsuka, 1963, p. 108). Nonetheless, mis-
understandings resulted from Ōtsuka's failure to address the
problem of class contradictions in modern Japanese society. He
did not fully comprehend the implications of the presence of big
business interests in Japan. Nor did he understand the ability of
monopoly capital to subordinate state agencies while at the same
time continuing to use a prewar vocabulary on the uniqueness of
Japan and the Japanese.

Fukutake's failure lay in overemphasizing the feudal elements
of modern Japanese society. He argued that 'individuals can
no longer be prevented from having desires of their own, but
nevertheless *"ie"* and the "hamlet" which required the suppression of such individuality are still living concepts' (Fukutake,
1967, p. 212):

> The hamlet is still the hamlet. Just as that other important
> social unit, the *ie*, has not disappeared, so the hamlet too,
> though headed for disintegration, has still not arrived at that
> point. We have not reached that happy state in which free

individual farmers can cheerfully co-operate with each other, spontaneously and voluntarily, not as a result of the pressures of the 'village community' (Fukutake, 1967, p. 87).

In this context the *ie* is the household community (*Haus-gemein-schaft* in German), the hamlet (*mura* in Japanese) the village community (*Dorf-gemeinschaft* in German). The continued exist-ence of the *ie* and the hamlet does not result from semi-feudal social relationships. The *ie* and hamlet of today are not those that existed in the prewar landlord system, for after the war farmers owned land and sold their own produce. As Fukutake noted, Japanese agriculture was carried out by family labour; capitalist farm management by means of hired agricultural labour-ers never really developed. In such conditions the *ie* and the hamlet will continue to survive until capitalist agriculture reaches an advanced stage of development. The communal characteristics of the *ie* and the hamlet will remain while small-scale family holdings still exist. Hence, the goal is not to encourage the further capitalist development of agriculture, but to encourage the free cooperation of farmers against the oppressive power of monopoly capital.

In his 1949 book on the social characteristics of rural Japan, Fukutake drew a distinction between the *dōzoku* type of village and the *ko* and *kumi* types of village, contrasting their respective principles of organization. The former is based on lineage relationships and the latter on neighbourhood relationships of purposeful association (Fukutake, 1949, p. 34ff). The *dōzoku* is a lineage of male descent comprised of branch families and the original parent family.

Exploring in detail the structure and functions of the *dōzoku*, Kizaemon Aruga developed many of Yanagida's themes. In par-ticular, he made the following distinction between the internal and external relations of the family:

The system of the extended family is characterized by both an internal structure of relationships in which each family member is connected subordinately to a patriarch and an external structure according to which each extended family is connected subordinately to the head of the lineage group (Aruga, 1943, p. 722).

84

According to Aruga, the major structural feature of Japanese society was its familial principle of organization, which applied not only to the family, but even to the community and the state. The overriding principle of 'concentric hierarchies' meant that each group had its own subunits of organization, while also being part of some larger organization. The Japanese state or nation was seen as the ultimate unit of organization, the Emperor serving as patriarchal head of the national family. Just as relationships between members of the family were hierarchical, so too were relations between main and branch families, and between the Emperor and 'his people' (Aruga, 1943, p. 726).

Aruga's belief in the importance of a peculiarly Japanese national character can be seen in the following passage:

> Though I do not deny the existence of social classes in Japan, I believe that the Japanese have a consciousness somewhat different from that found in the West. Western social organization is based on the individual and has developed along horizontal lines. For example, the political system revolves around the interaction among representatives from each social class. Japanese social organization, however, is based upon the vertical or hierarchical links between *oyakata* and *kokata* or between main and branch families within the *dōzoku* (Aruga, 1943, p. 323).

After World War II, Chie Nakane, adopting Aruga's theories, described Japanese society as follows:

> The overall picture of [Japanese] society . . . is not that of horizontal stratification by class or caste but of vertical stratification by institution or group of institutions . . . Even if social classes like those in Europe can be detected in Japan, and even if something vaguely resembling those classes that are illustrated in the textbooks of Western sociology can also be found in Japan, the point is that in Japanese society this stratification is unlikely to function and does not really reflect Japan's social structure. In Japanese society it is really not a matter of workers struggling against capitalists or managers but of company A ranked against company B (Nakane, 1970, p. 87).

According to Nakane, Japanese social cleavages occur not between horizontally defined groups but between vertically defined groups. Accordingly, struggles between workers and capitalists do not exist. Instead antagonism develops between company A and company B.

With such an historical background, and on the assumption of coincidence between ranking based on descent and that based on economic standing, Fukutake argued that the *dōzoku* type of village developed into the *kō-kumi* type (Fukutake, 1949, p. 40). The *dōzoku* had only significance when the ranking of its descent relationships was supported by economic power, and paralleled by landlord-tenant relationships. Only in this case could the original family be able to exert strong control over other members of the group. But even in the feudal era, this was rarely the case. More often the original family would fall into decline as its branches became more powerful.

Fukutake later modified his model, noting that 'the *dōzoku* group centred around a cultivating landlord could hardly be said to be typical of the modern period when Japanese agriculture was characterized by the parasitic landlord system'. But he continued to argue that, 'the *dōzoku* group is, however, undeniably important as a basic pattern for the social structure of the Japanese villages' (Fukutake, 1949, p. 40). Fukutake also admitted that the *dōzoku* groups had developed along with the cultivating-landlord system at the end of the feudal era and not with the 'parasitic landlord' system of modern Japan. As noted earlier, the typical *dōzoku* groups were not found in the feudal era when the *oyakata*'s extended family had dissolved and most *kokata*-peasants became independent. The *dōzoku* groups of the cultivating landlord system were not a prototype, and were only seen in the later-developed areas where a cultivating landlord happened to maintain his agricultural labour force through *oyakata-kokata* relationships. So Fukutake admitted that 'even where they were typically found it was, in fact, fairly rare for there to be an orderly pyramid of an original stem family, stem families and branch families left intact' (Fukatake, 1949, p. 60). Therefore, in the more developed areas the absence of such *oyakata-kokata* relationships was typical by the Meiji era.

In relation to Fukutake's typological dichotomy, Susumu Isoda tried to draw a distinction between the family-status type and the non-family-status type village (see Isoda, 1955, Chap. 2). The two types were held to be contemporaneous rather than success-ive. Under the landlord system in modern Japan, the determinant of family status was not descent, but land ownership. Therefore the non-family-status type village was usually exemplified by mountain and fishing villages where the differentiation of arable land ownership was undeveloped and large landholding landlords were absent. Unless the village communities were hierarchically structured, the direction of development from *dōzoku* to *kō-kumi* would be very doubtful. *Dōzoku* and *kō-kumi* type villages could actually exist in the same historical period.

Fukutake on Japan's Postwar Democratization

As previously mentioned, immediately after the war Fukutake argued that the democratization of rural Japan would only be possible through socialistic co-operation between farmers. Await-ing socialist democratization, he was skeptical of capitalist mod-ernization. Yet in his later books he altered his position and supported the government policies designed to promote the 'mod-ernization' and 'rationalization' of agriculture with the removal of part-time farmers.

Under rapid industrial economic growth, agriculture ceased to be the main area of economic development. Farmers who could no longer maintain their livelihood solely with agriculture became part-time farmers, and the agricultural labour force increasingly consisted of women and old men. In order to rescue agriculture Fukutake demanded structural reform:

> If a decline in the agricultural population means a decrease
> in the number of farms and an expansion in the average size
> of holdings, this is something very much to be desired from
> the point of view of agricultural development (Fukutake,
> 1967, p. 198).

Fukutake believed the main problem was that a decrease in the agricultural population did not necessarily imply a decrease in the total number of farming households. Accordingly he sup-

ported the Basic Agriculture Law of 1961, the preamble of which
states:

> It is a duty springing from our concern for the public welfare,
> and a necessary complement to the mission of agriculture and
> agriculturalists in our society, to ensure that those
> disadvantages resulting from the natural, economic and
> social limitations of agriculture are corrected, to promote the
> modernization and rationalization of agriculture while
> respecting the free will and initiative of those engaged in it,
> and to ensure that the nation's farmers can enjoy a healthy
> and cultured livelihood not inferior to that of other members
> of the population (The Commission, 1961).

In line with the Basic Agriculture Law the government also
implemented the Structural Improvement Program. Poor farmers
and part-time farmers protested, believing the program to be a
'policy of wiping out the poor farmer'. Fukutake did not see it
that way. According to Fukutake, even if the part-time farmers
with small holdings had farmed cooperatively, little progress
would have been achieved. The Structural Improvement Program
was open to criticism because it contained no provisions to aid
the migration of poor farmers. 'What is necessary,' Fukutake
stressed, 'is that the poor part-time farmers should be, not wiped
out, but made able to transfer to some other occupation without
hardship or insecurity' (Fukutake, 1967, p. 199).

Fukutake failed to consider whether in fact the capitalist system
was able to transfer these poor farmers to other occupations
without the creation of hardship. The ideal of a smooth transition
contrasts sharply with the reality of the lives of *dekasegi* (seasonal
workers from poor agricultural households). Clearly, it was no
longer a socialist but a capitalist form of cooperation which Fukutake believed was necessary. He rejected the possibility of cooperation among poor farmers, and considered cooperation among
the upper stratum of farmers (after the poor part-time farmers
have been 'transferred' to other industries), the only remedy for
stagnation in agriculture.

However, the changes which actually occurred differed from
Fukutake's expectations. For example, the number of farm
households decreased from 6,176,000 in 1950 to 4,661,000 in
1980, and in the same period the ratio of agricultural workers

A Critical Evaluation of the Sociological Thought of Fukutake

Table 4–1 Numbers of farm households by full-time and part-time
status

Year	Full-time (%)	Part-time		Total (%)	Number of households (1,000)
		1st class (%)	2nd class (%)		
1950	50.0	28.4	21.6	100.0	6,176
1955	34.8	37.7	27.5	100.0	6,043
1960	34.3	33.6	32.1	100.0	6,057
1965	21.5	36.7	41.7	100.0	5,665
1970	15.6	33.6	50.8	100.0	5.402
1975	12.4	25.4	62.1	100.0	4,953
1980	13.2	21.5	65.1	100.0	4,661

Cited from *Nōrinsuisantōkei* [Agriculture Forestry and Fisheries statistics]
(Tokyo: Nōrintōkei kyōkai, 1982), p. 123.

(including fishing and forestry and workers) as a percentage of
the total work force decreased from 44.6% to 9.8%. But such
changes did not create favourable conditions for agriculture. Statistics show that the number of part-time farming households
increased from 50% in 1950 to 86.6% in 1980, and in particular
that those who chiefly engaged in other occupations (the second-
class part-timers) increased from 21.6% in 1950 to 65.1% in 1980
(see Table 4–1).

Thus most of the farmers who were unable to maintain their
livelihood in agriculture, did not abandon farming but became
part-time farmers. Of course some small farmers did leave agriculture. As shown in Table 4–2, the number of farmers cultivating
land of less than one hectare decreased from 4,420,000 in 1950
to 3,157,000 in 1980, while the total number of farmers decreased
from 5,931,000 to 4,496,000 in the same period (the Hokkaido
district is excluded from these figures because of its specific agricultural conditions). The number of farmers cultivating more than
three hectares increased from 27,000 in 1950 to 105,000 in 1980.
However, one cannot conclude from these data that a real tendency towards a capitalist agriculture exists in Japan. Although,
during the 1950s the number of farmers who cultivated less than
one hectare decreased while the number of cultivators of between
1.0 and 1.5 hectares increased, in the 1960s and 1970s the latter
began to decrease. In the 1970s the only increase was in the
number of farmers cultivating holdings larger than 2.5 hectares.
On the other hand, the ratio of farmers who cultivated less than

89

Table 4.2 Farm households by scale of cultivated land

(Hectares)	1950	1955	1960	1965	1970	1975	1980
	Numbers (1,000)						
Under 0.5	2,468	2,285	2,275	2,096	1,999	1,984	1,848
0.5–1.0	1,952	1,955	1,907	1,762	1,604	1,436	1,309
1.0–1.5	945	981	1,002	945	868	727	660
1.5–2.0	363	376	404	407	404	349	327
2.0–2.5	176	132	147	156	170	162	163
2.5–3.0		48	54	59	71	74	82
3.0–5.0	26	28	34	36	55	67	90
5.0–	1	1	2	2	5	9	15
Total	5,931	5,806	5,823	5,465	5,174	4,818	4,496
	Percentages						
Under 0.5	41.6	39.3	39.1	38.4	38.6	41.2	41.1
0.5–1.0	32.9	33.7	32.7	32.2	31.0	29.8	29.1
1.0–1.5	15.9	16.9	17.2	17.3	16.8	15.1	14.7
1.5–2.0	6.1	6.5	6.9	7.4	7.8	7.2	7.3
2.0–2.5	3.0	2.3	2.5	2.8	3.3	3.4	3.6
2.5–3.0		0.8	0.9	1.1	1.4	1.5	1.8
3.0–5.0	0.4	0.5	0.6	0.7	1.1	1.4	2.0
5.0–	–	–	–	–	0.1	0.2	0.3
Total	100.0	100.0	100.0	100.0	100.0	100.0	100.0

Cited from *Nōrinsuisantōkei, op. cit.*, p 125.

one hectare only decreased from 74.5% in 1950 to 70.2% in 1980. Thus, in 1980, a mere 4% of all farm households – only 187,000 out of a total 4,496,000 – had favourable conditions for the development of farming, and there was little opportunity for expansion through the purchase or leasing of land from the smaller farmers.

Fukutake believed that the problems experienced by Japanese agriculture are derived from the small scale of family farming. Therefore he supported policies which promoted the migration of small farmers. He considered that further capitalist development of agriculture could solve the present agricultural crisis in Japan. But as we have seen above, under the control of big business which supports liberalization policies with regard to agricultural products, agriculture itself faces great difficulties. The agricultural crisis in Japan is a crisis of the small family enterprise. If, as Fukutake thought, the smooth transfer of small farmers to other occupations was possible, then the development of upper stratum farmers might occur regardless of cooperation. But if it is impossible for them to transfer they should not be 'wiped out', but protected and guaranteed as stable small farming enterprises. Through the stabilization of their production, they would cooperate spontaneously and move toward non-capitalist large-scale farming.

From such a standpoint, Fukutake has attacked the left-wing parties' policies: 'the left-wing parties have succeeded in making only a very weak impact on the farmer and their policies are highly formalistic and lacking in appeal'. Fukutake claimed that the so-called 'poor-farmers' of Japan are far worse off than the poor farmers in advanced countries, and that even the upper stratum of farmers must cooperate if they are to have any future (Fukutake, 1967, p. 221). Thus he placed priority on the cooperation of upper stratum farmers over that of 'poor farmers'. Fukutake advised the left-wing parties that:

> when it becomes clear that the hopes of progress by individual
> management are illusory and if, at that time, the radical
> parties can offer concrete plans to substitute for that illusion,
> then and only then can one expect any new developments
> in the farmer's political attitudes (Fukutake, 1967, p. 221).

Fukutake concluded that the right to cooperate was to be reserved for farmers of the upper stratum. In *Japanese Society Today*, he argued that agriculture could not be saved unless measures were taken to assist people in leaving agriculture, and to develop a system promote cooperation among the families remaining (Fukutake, 1974, p. 50). Once again he succumbed to the illusion that a policy of transferring farmers to other occupations (without risk of unemployment) could be successfully implemented. Thus, to take a further example, he criticizes the Socialist Party for its weak response to the needs of farmers, and for its protests against the conservatives' policy of discarding poor farmers, but he fails to offer any practical alternatives. He merely writes that:

> the socialists should have foreseen changes in the structure of
> rural society, and should have assured farmers that, unlike the
> government party, they would find ways to create employment
> opportunities for farmers so that even if they left the farms

Table 4–3 The class structure of Japan (%)

	1950	1955	1960	1965	1970	1975	1980
Capitalists	1.9	2.0	2.7	3.6	3.9	4.2	4.7
Persons in security services	0.9	1.1	1.1	1.2	1.2	1.4	1.4
Self-employed proprietors	58.9	53.2	45.7	38.3	34.8	29.4	27.3
Agriculture, forestry and fishing	44.6	37.7	30.6	23.0	18.1	12.7	9.8
Mining, manufacturing, transportation and communication	6.2	6.2	6.2	6.2	7.3	6.8	6.7
Sales	6.2	7.0	6.2	5.9	6.0	6.1	6.7
Services	0.9	1.5	1.6	1.9	2.3	2.6	2.7
Professionals and specialized technicians	1.0	0.9	1.0	1.2	1.1	1.2	1.4
Working class	38.2	43.6	50.5	56.9	60.1	65.0	66.6
Salaried employees	11.9	12.5	14.2	17.0	18.7	21.9	23.3
Productive workers	20.0	22.4	27.8	29.2	29.6	28.7	28.5
Nonproductive workers	4.3	6.8	7.8	9.3	10.5	12.2	12.4
Unemployed	2.0	1.9	0.7	1.4	1.3	2.3	2.5

Source: Cited from Fukutake, 1974, p. 26. Data of 1975 and 1980 are added from the *Census* of each years.

they could get jobs without having to worry (Fukutake, 1974, p. 143).

According to Fukutake, the reformists' 'conservatism' is far worse than conservatives' 'reforms'.

Fukutake acknowledged that government agricultural policies were fundamentally adapted to the interests of big business. He pointed out that although the Liberal Democratic Party had been at great pains to speak of the need for farmers and for the modernization of agriculture, there was always a proviso: 'in so far as this does not clash with business interests or hinder their development' (Fukutake, 1967, p. 195). Fukutake on the other hand, in emphasizing the need to modernize agriculture, called on the national government to 'wipe out' the poor farmers from rural areas, not in the interests of big business but for the sake of the farmers themselves.

Fukutake described the modern Japanese class structure as comprising a handful of capitalists, an old middle class of independent proprietors (mainly farmers and shop owners), the new middle class (consisting of a those in small number of services, and specialized technicians), and finally the working class which includes salaried workers. Table 4–3 clearly reveals a steady decline in self-employed proprietors. However, the working class has come to occupy two thirds of the total. From the point of view of class rule, the capitalists' domination of the working class is equally clear. In Japan, as in other industrial societies, the capitalists and top managers of large corporations who ally themselves with politicians and high-ranking bureaucrats, have become the ruling class. Thus Fukutake wrote:

> the roughly 100 Japanese corporations capitalized at one billion *yen* or more constitute no more than 0.1% of all enterprises, but own half the total capital. Moreover, the greater part of industry is virtually controlled by a few giant enterprises. The large number of small enterprises and the high degree of monopoly control are two striking features of Japanese industry. It is those who control the giant enterprises that run Japan (Fukutake, 1974, p. 27).

As Fukutake admitted, the national government is controlled by the power of monopoly capital, and the dictates of capital are given priority over social welfare. The 'miracle' of rapid economic growth since 1960 has depended upon such things as immense environmental destruction. The serious problems of pollution, traffic congestion, population imbalance, income inequality, destruction of agriculture and small enterprises, and social tension were the direct results of deliberate government policy. The policies were adopted for the purpose of capital accumulation, and not to gain the unavoidable 'by-products' of technological development. In fact economic policies catering to big business have increasingly destroyed livelihoods, and national and local 'development' plans have threatened the survival of communities and exploited the land, labour and lives of their members. If this is true, how could Fukutake look so favourably on the conservatives' 'reforms'?

In the period immediately after the war, 'modernization' was considered equivalent to democratization, although the conservative government and big business were opposed to a 'modernization' that was aimed at the expansion the civil liberties and rights. Since the early 1960s the term 'modernization' has been appropriated by conservative ideologues in order to sell their own economic development policies. In Fukutake's case, 'democratization' initially meant the movement toward socialism or 'socialization', but it later came to mean the process of 'capitalization' and, in this sense, 'modernization' in its more recent usage. This corresponded with a national policy dedicated to the development of an extraordinarily high rate of economic growth. As the original goal of 'democratization' was buried, Fukutake's own definition also changed.

Fukutake altered his position once the tension generated by the AMPO[1] demonstrations of 1960 had receded. At that time a growing concern with 'modernization' was evident. While serving as the American Ambassador to Japan, Edwin Reischauer was active in propagating a 'modernization theory' to counter the influence of Marxism and socialism. The 'modernization theory' created by an ideological competition in which two parties claimed that they were the true interpreters of the Japanese experience. Within this framework it is not surprising that Reischauer's activities have been referred to by Japanese intellectuals on the left as the 'Reischauer offensive'.

Three basic characteristics of the 'modernization' approach stand out: the belief in progress, the belief in rationality, and the normative judgment that mechanization or industrialization is good. Scholars adopting this approach tried to sum up Japan's experience in terms of a model of gradual, non-revolutionary development along capitalist and even 'democratic' lines. Japanese sociologists of the functionalist school were quick to adopt this approach. For example, in 1964 Ken'ichi Tominaga wrote *Shakai hendō no riron* (Theories of Social Change), in which he used the vocabulary of Parsonian 'system theory' to criticize Marxist theories of social change. The various social problems and contradictions resulting from Japan's rapid development here dismissed as minor and temporary aberrations which simply represented the 'time lag' by which 'social development' followed economic development (see Tominaga, 1964).

In *Japanese Society Today* Fukutake stressed the importance of social welfare and wrote that 'the level of social welfare must rise even at the sacrifice of growth in the economy'. He concluded that 'Japan must become a society which truly guarantees to everyone, whether he can work to his fullest capacity or is unable

---

[1] AMPO refers to the U.S.-Japan Security Treaty. In 1960 there were many demonstrations against the revised Treaty; these mass demonstrations brought down Prime Minister Nobusuke Kishi's government.

to work, "a healthy and cultured life" ' (Fukutake, 1974, p. 153). The goal is admirable, but how can it be attained without controlling the immense power of big business? The overall defect of Fukutake's sociological theories was an underestimation of the oppressive power of monopoly capital. The basis of the anti-democratic elements in Japan is big business. To truly democratize of Japanese society it is more important to fight the capitalist economic and social development designed to promote the profits of big business, than it is to remove the pre-modern elements that survive in families and villages.

Conclusion

Today Japanese society is a capitalist society; Japan is no less a capitalist country than the United States or Germany. Every modern capitalist society has its own national character, its own historical traditions, its own political process, and indigenous elements which are neglected when we discuss capitalist society in general. Modern Japanese society has different cultural traditions from modern Western societies. As historical fact, the capitalist society first emerged in the West in countries which had common cultural traditions and initially modernization theories tended to ignore the experience of non-Western societies. This resulted in a tendency to confuse modernization and Westernization. In Japan indigenous elements have often been regarded as deviations (or aberrations) and have meant that the Japanese situation has not followed the accepted course of modernization.

On the other hand, Japan as a late-developed capitalist country has retained many pre-modern and communal relationships within its families and communities. Traditional values which emphasize communal interests have been preserved in the everyday life of the common Japanese. This cultural tradition has originated from centuries of communal living in small household enterprises. One might claim that further capitalist development should be encouraged, and might encourage Japan to strive towards the idealized model of Western advanced industrial societies; but further 'modernization' or 'rationalization' in Japan will not resolve the contradictions and problems of Japanese society. Japan in common with many Western countries has faced difficulties which the capitalist system itself has initiated. The dominance of monopoly capital has sometimes had disastrous consequences for the Japanese people. 'Modernization' policies do not aim to dissolve feudal or semi-feudal relationships but to reorganize them and facilitate the rule of monopoly capital. However, the main obstacle to democratization in Japan is not the existence of small household enterprises but vast monopoly capital. In order to realize a new egalitarian society in which each individual can freely develop his or her potential and attain self-realization, the power of monopoly capital must be abolished. This is exactly what Fukutake ignores in his theoretical frame of reference.

X Modernization in Japan has not meant the dissappearance of feudal ~~traditions~~ values, but rather the reorganization and accomodation of traditions into the modern setting

5 Tradition and Community Power Structure in Japan

Historical Background

In Japan the term 'community' generally refers to a *Gemeinschaft* type of social organization. Traditionally, a community was a village made up of fifty to one hundred households, based on living under a system based on of communal land ownership and irrigation. The village was the lowest administrative unit of Tokugawa feudal government, and its basic components were households. There have been two types of village communities. In one, private landownership was recognized and households were accordingly ranked in a hierarchical order. The other was based on an age grading system, with males or females of younger age groups living in one large household.

In contrast, in the West the term 'community' usually referred to a *Gesellschaft* type of social organization. The formation of these urban communities occurred after the dissolution of the traditional village and household communities. This 'community' functions as a local organization in modern society. In the West, such communities began to surround industrial cities in the process of urbanization, emerging after the disappearance of rural hamlet and pre-industrial merchant quarters.

A new urban community is composed of independent individuals, their independence being the result of the breakdown of the traditional communities. In the pre-modern era individuals were submerged in the community, for example, upon marriage the bride was assimilated into her bridegroom's household. The family was not a temporary group, but a permanent community into which individuals were born, or assimilated and in which they remained until death.

One of the most peculiar features of modern Japan is that capitalism has developed without the complete destruction of traditional communities. The village, as an administrative unit of the feudal era, was bestowed the right to use irrigation and common land. The village's arable land was partitioned and measured by overlords so that a land tax could be calculated. In 1873 after the Meiji Restoration the new government abolished the feudal rice tax, and private land ownership was fully recognized. Tax was then assessed on the value of land, and the village community was no longer the unit of rice-tax collection. Although these measures disrupted the old system of village community, the communal regulation of farming and communal solidarity both remained intact.

In 1888 a new set of regulations for the structure and administration of cities, towns and villages was promulgated. Under this municipal code several old towns and villages were incorporated into new and larger entities. The former village had its status downgraded to that of hamlet (now called *buraku*), and several *burakus* formed a new village or town. For example, Suye village in Kumamoto Prefecture in 1935 comprised eight administrative units (called *ku*), most of which contained two or more hamlets (*buraku*). But communal problems pertaining to agricultural and local affairs continued to be settled at the *buraku*, or village level. The communal ownership of water (irrigation), waste land, forest and roads was an important basis for community life.

Kunio Yanagida, a renowned scholar of Japanese folklore, supported the demands of the unions in the 1920s, saying:

It is a natural development in Japanese rural villages that the farmers' unions try to realize gradually a cooperative way of life in the community through the promotion of economic cooperation. Anyone who is surprised at this union strategy must be an ignorant person unaware of the historical development of Japanese peasant society. One might have reason enough to criticize such naive socialist ideas which lack reality for the Japanese people. But one who denies the historical fact that Japanese peasants could make a bare living only through mutual aid within the community, is neither conscientious nor compassionate (Yanagida 1919, pp. 211–12).

After World War II, a new civil code was enforced and the old family system was dissolved. The SCAP program to 'democratize' Japan proscribed the community-type organizations called *buraku-kai* and *chōnai-kai* and aimed to root out the remnants of 'feudal' and military elements in Japanese society. However, despite the legal dissolution of the old family system, the prohibition of *buraku-kai* and *chōnai-kai* by the Allied Occupation, and Japan's rapid economic growth since the 1960s, the communal way of life and the common people's sense of belonging to the group has still survived in rural and urban areas.

Social Reconstruction of the Community

During the 1920s and early 1930s, (especially after the Kantō earthquake in 1923), new neighbourhood associations were formed and a feeling of community identity developed in the urban areas of Tokyo. The neighbourhood association as a form of community was newly reconstructed from traditional aspects of community life. People had constructed new communities, but retained constituents of communal life which already existed as Japanese tradition. The pattern of the 'social reconstruction of a community' did not intrinsically change after the war. Thus Theodore C. Bestor described the communal way of life in a contemporary urban Tokyo community as follows:

> When death occurs in Miyamoto-chō, the *chōkai* notifies residents, helps at the funeral and makes the *chōkai* meeting hall available for the wake. The *chōkai* cooperates with the police in traffic safety campaigns and inspects children's bicycles. Together the volunteer fire brigade and the *chōkai* sponsor safety meetings and patrols and aid the professional fire department in extinguishing blazes and disaster relief. The *chōkai* maintains street lights on back alleys, and during the summer, *chōkai* work crews spray the entire neighbourhood with pesticides (Bestor, 1985a, p. 127).

Immediately after the war, leftist politicians and intellectuals agreed with the SCAP view that community-type organizations were remnants of the pre-modern and feudal past. They tried to disrupt communal relationships and to establish a society based on Western individualism. But intellectuals such as Yanagida predicted the long-term survival of feelings of community. In 1954 he wrote:

After the war I was visited by a famous socialist and we were discussing the problems of family which were the current topics at that time. I asked him what one should do when faced with situations such as where children lose their parents or elderly parents lose their children on whom they are dependent. His reply was that there will be no such problems when perfect homes for the aged and fine orphanages are established and each person can enjoy his or her life as an independent citizen. Since then almost ten years have passed, but the progress of society is still slow and society still does not take care of the poor and the weak. Under such conditions, how could liberals and socialists promote reforms of the family and realize a society based on individualism in Japan? (Yanagida, 1954, pp. 35–6)

It is desirable that the modern nuclear family be established in Japan. However, because of the fragility and vulnerability of the nuclear family, the modern community as a whole should take care of every member's education and social welfare. Yanagida believed that to encourage the establishment of a new type of community, the traditional family relationships needed to be revitalized.

In the U.S. Daniel Bell predicted a future post-industrial society in which knowledge and information would become predominant over industry. Alvin Toffler predicted the emergence of societies based on the 'third wave', as contrasted with 'second wave' societies which were based on industrialization. He argued that the 'third wave' would pave the way for the establishment of a new code of behaviour, overcoming the restrictions of the 'second wave' which included: standardization, centralization, subjugating the concentration of energy, wealth and power. The 'third wave' civilization was described as a society with institutions contrasting to those of the nuclear family, standardized mass education, large corporations, large labour unions, the centralized nation-state and pseudo-representative systems of politics. The characteristics of the 'third wave' were similar to those of the 'first wave': non-centralized production, use of regimentative energy, non-urbanization, medium scale organization, domestic labour, and highly integrated production-consumption.

In Japan arguments concerning the post-industrial society are often closely related to the arguments by nationalists and conservatives on the 'conquest of modernity'. An emerging 'age of [Japanese] culture' is predicted with occurrence of the end of the modernization. Nationalists and conservatives believe that any arguments in favour of an 'age transcending modernity' are congruent with the theme of a 'return to Japanese tradition'. On this point, a study group organized by late prime minister Ohira made the following suggestion in a report entitled 'The Age of Culture' (1980):

> Post-Meiji Japan has defined itself as being backward and underdeveloped in all respects and has made every attempt to Westernize, modernize and industrialize by patterning itself after Western advanced industrial countries . . . However, new demands (i.e. 'demands for culture') are now called for in pursuit of better conditions in the future.

Ohira also asserted that:

> material civilization based on modern rationalism has arrived at the point of saturation. We are now shifting away from the modern age to the age which transcends it – away from the economy-centered age to the culture-centered age.

According to Ohira, the 'age transcending modernity' is the age in which Japan achieved full modernization and ranks with Western advanced countries while retaining elements of pre-modern community structures and values.

As a late-developing capitalist nation, Japan does have some underdeveloped aspects. These form a social basis of 'grass-roots conservatism' in local politics. Conservatives and large corporations take advantage of the remnants of communal relationships in their pursuit of profit. They believe the 'age of post-modernization' is also the 'age of culture' as well as the 'age of local communities'. In Japan political conservatism differs from traditional American conservatism. In the U.S. it aims to preserve the capitalist system, but in Japan its goal is to preserve the emperor system and promote modernization from above. Japanese conservatism favours the traditional hierarchy with the emperor at its apex. Japanese conservatives believe that the social Darwinist doctrine of the survival of the fittest and the free market system are dangerous elements which undermine central-ized power which is based on traditional patriarchy.

Opposing the arguments of conservatives and nationalists, reformist elements see the prospect for communal relationships to facilitate the formation of a new communal society. In this regard it should be noted that Japanese political culture has an indigenous potential for direct democracy, that is, democratic self-government within local communities.

Ruling Elite Model vs Pluralistic Model

In the U.S. the study of community power structures has a long history. The reputational method Floyd Hunter employed seems to be based on the assumption that power in a local community is seldom independent of power in the wider sphere. His theory shares similarities with Marx's class rule theory. Hunter assumed that an economically dominant group is also a politically domi-nant group, having political power within the local community. However, he overlooked the difference between national and local levels. Men with power in the local communities are not necessarily members of the economic ruling class at the national level.

C. Wright Mills denied the concept of a ruling class (even at the national level) because he believed it relied too heavily on Marx's assumption of economic determinism. However, he ack-nowledged the existence of a power elite in three realms of contemporary American society – economic, political and mili-tary. Talcott Parsons criticized the power-elite theory as a zero-sum concept of power. He maintained that power was in fact a desirable resource in highly organized societies, and criticized Mills' standpoint as being based on romantic and anarchic assumptions that power in itself is an evil.

In the following discussion the term 'political power' will refer to the power of government, its elected officials and their appointees. The term 'civil power' will refer to non-governmental power.

We can argue against Parsons that power is always zero-sum in political society, where each member has equal legal rights and issues are decided by the majority. However in civil society, there is no such power. It could be said that Parsons focused on personal influence in the private sphere, whereas Mills was concerned with compulsion in the public sphere. In civil society influence, not compulsion, is the only effective means for integration. People have to persuade each other to reach consensus. As regards community power structure, power, correctly speaking, means influence. In a modern sense, the community is independent from political power. It is a realm of self-government by citizens.

Mills' power elite model is valid at the national level, but cannot be applied at the community level. Thus, there is reason for Robert Dahl to insist on a pluralist model of the decision making process in a local community. In a survey of New Haven, Dahl demonstrated there were different decision-makers for different community issues. However, as G. William Domhoff pointed out, Dahl's discovery of 'pluralism' at the local community level is not incompatible with the idea of a ruling class and/or power elite at the national level. Domhoff admitted the existence of governing class based on property ownership, he also used the concept of a power elite which was defined as persons co-opted by the governing class from the mass. Equality of opportunity promoted by meritocratic scales in the co-option process does not necessarily lead to the democratization of society. Democratization of co-option criteria is imperative so that no portion of the function of government is allotted to the less talented persons.

However, admitting of the existence of a national governing class, need not prevent one using a pluralistic model to analyse local communities. In a local community, an economically dominant group is not always politically dominant. Although there are dynamic power relationships between the owners and managers of companies and their workers, capitalists as a class of the community do not necessarily hold the power.

At the national level capitalists must be organized as a ruling class to hold political power whether they undertake the function of rule or bestow it upon others is irrelevant. Since people have equal voting rights to elect assembly members, to secure their rule over the working class, capitalists must establish their hegemony in civil society. Furthermore, the property-owning class must co-opt talented members of the ruled classes so that

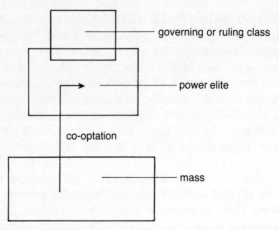

Chart 5–1 Relationship among governing class, power elite and mass

the latter do not use their ability on behalf of their own classes. Separation between political society and civil society is not a favourable condition for the ruling class.

Japanese people as members of political society have equal political and legal rights. They have the right to elect members of the Diet, and the majority party in the Diet can elect its party president to the position of prime minister. The prime minister then organizes a Cabinet, and under the control of government bureaucracy functions as the ruling apparatus. Administrative staff are co-opted from citizens according to ability. The bureaucracy is accepted as a legitimate part of the legal order; and administration by bureaucrats has legitimacy because a political party with a majority in the Diet can organize executives and access governmental power.

The separation between civil and political societies is a major contradiction of the modern regime in the West. But it is also a great achievement and positive result of the Western type of modernization. However, were participatory democracy or self-government fully realized the distinction between the two would become meaningless. In the U.S., studies of community power structures following Hunter have focused on the realm of civil society. Power in the community has nothing to do with state power or political power in society, but is authority or influence in the private sphere. It is hegemony, or the ability to create consensus.

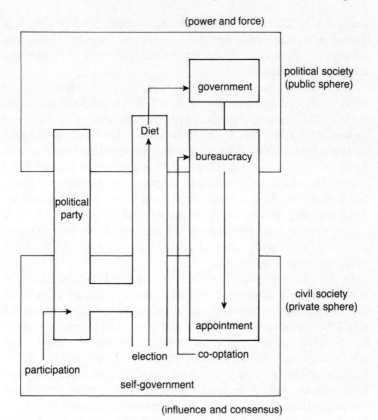

(power and force)

Chart 5–2 Relationship between political and civic societies

As will be shown in the analysis offered below, the power of the community to some extent relies on traditional legitimacy. In Japan the community is the real power base of grass-roots conservatives.

Community Power Structure: Case Study I

To examine the Japanese local community power structure we conducted research in two communities. The first was Shimoda city in Shizuoka prefecture, located about 80 miles east of Tokyo in the southern part of the Izu peninsula; the other was Yokosh-

iba town in Chiba prefecture, located about 50 miles west of
Tokyo near the Narita international airport. We conducted our
surveys in Shimoda city in September 1985 and in Yokoshiba
town in June 1986.

Shimoda city was originally a town that was established in
1896. In 1955 it was amalgamated with five neighbouring villages
and in 1971 Shimoda city was born. Its population was thirty-one
thousand in 1980, this figure included ten thousand in the area
of the original town. In each former village there were several
hamlets which were old villages during the feudal period. Each
hamlet (*buraku*) was divided into several *kumi* consisting of about
ten households. Young males aged from fifteen to thirty formerly
lived together in one large house in each hamlet. They were
expected to become members of the fire brigade, to help villagers
in case of emergency, and to assist in the funeral and marriage
ceremonies of villagers.

In the old Shimoda town there was a good harbour, and the
town became a centre for marine transportation in 1636 when
the Tokugawa government was in office. In the Edo period the
ship building business developed and employed many carpenters.
In the Meiji period rail transportation became dominant, and
after completion of the Tokaido line from Tokyo to Osaka, the
harbour gradually became less important. However, the transition
from wooden sailing vessels to steamers in the Meiji period saw
the establishment of new ship building businesses using new technology and financed by local capital. Ship-building and related
industries were predominant in Shimoda town around 1898.

Before the rail link between Ito and Shimoda was established
in 1961, transportation was mainly provided by a privately owned
bus line whose head office was located in Shimoda town. In the
northern part of the city there is a hot spring from which hot
water is drawn, and hot spring hotels and inns were centrally
located in the town. There were 32 such hotels and inns in 1960.
The population of Shimoda town by household and by industry
in 1954 is shown in Table 5–1. The industries in which most
households in Shimoda town were engaged were services
(22.7%), wholesale and retail (22.1%), and manufacturing
(17.5%). This was the economic base upon which political conflicts developed prior to the construction of the Izukyū railroad.
Those of the old established families deemed the most privileged
were: 1) families of the main traditional ship agencies; 2) families

Table 5–1 Household members by industry 1954 in Shimoda city

Industry	Household members
All industries	100.0% (8920)
Agriculture	1.6
Forestry and hunting	0.2
Fisheries and aquaculture	60.3
Mining	0.0
Construction	8.5
Manufacturing	17.5
Wholesale and retail	22.1
Finance and insurance	1.5
Real estate business	0.1
Communication and public utilities	8.4
Services	22.7
Government	6.7
No jobs	4.6

owning and managing the main hotels and inns; 3) families owning and managing a ship building company; and 4) families owning and managing a bus company. In particular, the presidents of two large companies in Shimoda town at that time had considerable economic influence.

When the Izukyū line was opened in 1961, the industrial structure of Shimoda city changed. The city's population by industry from 1960 to 1980 is shown in Table 5–2. In 1965, four years after the opening of the railroad, the proportion of the population in agriculture, forestry and fisheries declined from 35.5% to 23.9%, while the proportion in services increased from 17.5% to 25.6%, and in wholesale and retail from 16.8% to 20.3%. These trends have continued. In 1980, the population engaged in agriculture was 6.2%, and in fisheries 3.0%, while those engaged in services had risen to 33.1% and in wholesale and retail the figure was 26%.

The opening of the railway resulted in the rapid increase of tourism to Shimoda. People came for sea bathing in summer and hot spring bathing in the other seasons. The Izu Peninsula had also been a honeymoon resort before it was supplanted by Hawaii. In 1962 the number of tourists visiting Shimoda was double that of 1961, and in 1970 it had increased to 6.5 times the 1961 level. As tourist numbers increased so did the provision of tourist facilities. The number of hot springs hotels and inns increased from 32 in 1960 to 61 in 1971, while the less elaborate

Sociology and Society of Japan

Table 5.2 Employed persons by industry in Shimoda city

	1961 13,339	1965 14,003	1970 16,037	1975 16,176	1980 15,522
All Industry	100.0%	100.0%	100.0%	100.0%	100.0%
Agriculture	28.4	18.7	14.0	8.2	6.2
Forestry & Hunting	2.3	1.0	0.3	3.2	0.3
Fisheries	4.8	4.3	3.3	2.8	3.0
Mining	1.1	0.7	0.3	0.2	0.1
Construction	9.2	8.5	8.5	10.0	9.1
Manufacturing	6.3	6.6	7.3	7.1	7.5
Wholesale and retail	16.8	20.3	23.3	24.3	26.0
Finance and insurance	1.1	1.4	1.6	1.8	2.2
Real estate business	0.1	0.2	6.0	7.5	6.6
Communication and transportation	7.0	8.5	8.5	7.3	7.1
Electricity, gas and water services	0.7	0.8	0.7	0.8	0.8
Services	17.4	25.6	28.2	33.1	33.1
Government	4.8	3.4	3.3	3.3	3.8

forms of accommodation (managed by ordinary householders), numbered 50 in the city area in 1960 and 230 in 1970.

The Izukyū Rail Company which constructed the new line developed Shimoda as a tourist city. This company belonged to the Tōkyū group which had extensive involvement in transportation and tourist operations. The company undertook the development of tourist, bus and hotel industries in Shimoda city and constructed resort facilities. The old families of the city were ruined by competition with the companies of the Tōkyū group. Consequently the owners and managers of hotels, and the original bus company, had their power and influence reduced. The families owning the only remaining ship building company transferred its management rights to a major national fishing corporation.

The so-called 'oil shock' of 1973 commenced the slowing of Japanese economic growth which had been sustained throughout the 1960s; and a series of earthquakes in 1974, 1977 and 1978 damaged the image of Shimoda as a tourist city. The city's population peaked at 32,040 in 1976, but has since declined and was down to 30,623 in 1985. The revitalization of Shimoda city is now being pursued, especially by the younger generation. Business in Shimoda has become dull, and Izukyū, which once held relatively important sway in the city's economy, suffered heavy real estate investment losses in the wake of the oil crisis, thus beginning a

Table 5–3 Members of the city assembly by party in Shimoda city

	1971	1975	1979	1983	1986	
Liberal Democratic Party (LDP)	21	20	21	19	20	A faction 8 B faction 8 Neutral 4
Democratic Socialist Party (DSP)	–	–	3	3	2	
Komei Party (KP)	2	3	3	2	2	
Japan Socialist Party (JSP)	–	–	1	–	–	
Japan Communist Party (JCP)	1	2	2	2	2	
Nonpartisan	5	5	–	–	–	
Total	29	30	30	26	26	

steady weakening of the economic position of the Tōkyū group on the peninsula. Another service-transportation conglomerate, the Seibu group, subsequently stepped in and brought with it the more fashionable seaside sports such as yachting, surfing and wind surfing.

Before examining the power structure of Shimoda city, we need some basic information about its political life. As shown in Table 5–3, the Liberal Democratic Party (LDP) forms the majority in the city assembly. Prior to 1979 the non-LDP members were conservatives whose political positions were almost indistinguishable from the LDP. However, in 1979, along with the Kōmei Party (KP) and the Japan Communist Party (JCP), the Democratic Socialist Party (DSP) and the Japan Socialist Party (JSP) all won the seats in the assembly. In 1984, a DSP member of the assembly, X, ran for mayor and won (in an off-year election, an LDP candidate won).

When X began his campaign there was a written agreement made between the JSP, the JCP and the local unions' association, which declared that:

Shimoda city faces great difficulties. Because of the numerous disasters and the depression, the city's economy has been greatly damaged, and since 1977 the population of the city has been declining.

Under such conditions we should strive to protect the lives of the people of Shimoda city. The present administrators who control the city government have been standing for the interests of a few rich people and against those of the ordinary people for a long time.

The present mayor has no concrete policy to overcome the depression and revitalize the local economy and culture, or to make Shimoda city attractive for its citizens, especially for the younger generation . . .

We demand as goals for the city government:

1. To establish self-government by the citizens and to protect citizens from illegitimate interference by the national and prefectural governments.

2. To develop indigenous industries such as tourism, commerce, agriculture, forestry and fishery.

3. To establish a peaceful Shimoda city that is able to declare itself 'a non-nuclear city' and to make the constitution useful in our everyday lives . . .

Candidate X accepted this agreement and expressed willingness to pursue its goals.

Concerned with finding solutions for the city's basic problems he called for a convention by 'an association to vitalize Shimoda city'. Thus a loose coalition was formed between candidate X and the reformists. X defeated the LDP's official candidate, Y, who was the incumbent mayor. X received 9,667 votes, only 486 votes more than Y. This indicated that some conservatives had to have supported X. His official program was to protect the interests of small and family businesses and the jobs of labourers, farmers and fishermen.

In order to discover who held power in Shimoda city, we gathered information from around three hundred people through interviews and documents. We then made a preliminary list of leaders, and these were ranked by respondents who were asked to select important persons. According to the scores obtained in this manner, a final list of leaders was made, to which were added the names of the following non-resident politicians: a governor, members of the prefectural assembly and Diet members.

Of the 134 leaders on the original list, 11 were deleted because they were either absent or had not responded by the time of the survey, and 10 were deleted because they were not nominated. Therefore, our final list of leaders contained 113 names. These leaders were then asked to choose between 20 and 30 persons from the list who had influence upon the affairs of Shimoda city, and they were then to name the top 12. The leaders who were listed in the top 20–30 were given one point, and those in the top 12 one additional point. Totalling these points, we found that top ranking was given to the present mayor (X) who had a score of 200 points. Then we calculated weighted reputation scores in the range 0.0 to 1.0. A leader has a weighted reputation score to the extent that he is given many rating points from other leaders who themselves have weighted reputation scores.

As we indicate in Table 5–4, there are 12 political leaders among the top 30. Of those, five are non-resident, four are members of the Diet and one is a governor. Of the other seven two are members of the prefectural assembly, two are members of the city assembly and the remaining three are the mayor, and two former mayors. Two progressive politicians are among the top 30; one is the present mayor from the progressive coalition and the other is a JCP member of the city assembly. These two politicians will have no power if they lose their official positions. All of the remainder are leaders in both the political and the economic spheres. They will continue to enjoy their leadership roles even if they lose their political positions.

The other 18 persons are pure economic leaders: there is no socio-cultural leader among the top 30. No. 2 is a female stock-holder of a major national pharmaceutical corporation, No. 4 is owner and president of the largest construction company in the city, No. 6 is president of the Chamber of Commerce, No. 7 is president of the Credit Union and No. 12 is the owner and president of a hotel.

On becoming mayor No. 1 faced difficulties in carrying out his policies as a progressive candidate. Many problems were inherited from the previous mayor. One, which we will shortly examine, was the conflict brought about by the renovation of a large downtown supermarket.

It is clear from the above data that those who have power and/ or influence in Japan's local communities do not necessarily also have economic power. Leaders ranked within the upper stratum are either politicians at the national level who have little to do with local community affairs, or politicians at the prefectural level, such as the governor and members of the prefectural assembly. This is a feature peculiar to the local community power structure in Japan. However, in Shimoda city, members of the property-owning class are still influential in local decision making. This demonstrates that to some extent economic structure can determine power structure even within a local community. For

111

Sociology and Society of Japan

Table 5-4 The list of the leaders ranked within the top 30 by reputation scores in Shimoda city

Rank	Reputation score	Remarks (*non-resident)
1	1.000	Mayor
2	0.865	
3	0.813	*Government
4	0.810	
5	0.774	Member of the Prefectural Assembly
6	0.776	
7	0.666	
8	0.629	*Diet Member
9	0.620	
10	0.585	*Diet Member
11	0.568	Ex-mayor
12	0.545	
13	0.539	*Diet Member
14	0.538	
15	0.536	Member of the Prefectural Assembly
16	0.429	
17	0.399	Former Mayor
18	0.392	
19	0.381	
20	0.364	*Diet Member
21	0.363	
22	0.352	
23	0.339	
24	0.337	
25	0.325	
26	0.319	
27	0.315	Member of the City Assembly
28	0.305	Member of the City Assembly
29	0.259	
30	0.290	

example, in Shimoda city two rival service transportation conglomerates have decision making power on important issues through some of the city's political leaders. When the interests of local entrepreneurs conflict with those of national big-business concerns, the latter usually have sufficient power to prevail.

We will discuss in detail the conflict between the Shimoda branch of a supermarket chain in the Shizuoka prefecture, and the local retailers of downtown Shimoda. Previously, a relatively large supermarket (built in 1977 by Tokyu) had caused some trouble between Tōkyū and the local retailers. In 1979 another supermarket affiliated with a prefectural bus company closed because of the economic slump. A department store company, Y, which already owned two stores in the town, bought the supermarket's stocks from the bus company and attempted to reopen it in January 1983.

An association of shopkeepers, consisting of unions of vegetable and fruit stores, fish shops, butchers, wine shops and restaurants (and others), formed a Citizens' Association to prevent the opening of a third branch of Y's store. A chronological history of events is as follows:

Feb. 28, 1983	The Y department store proposed negotiation with the Citizens' Association.
March 2	The Citizens' Association submitted a petition to freeze the reopening plan.
March 29	The resolution for freezing the plan was adopted in the City Assembly.
April 12	Sit-in movement to prevent remodelling construction.
April 20	A blockage by the Association of Shopkeepers.
May 9	Y store stated that it would commence negotiations with the Association of Shopkeepers. The blockade was resolved.
Feb. 29, 1984	The mayor, the chairman of the city assembly, and the president of the Chamber of Commerce presented a compromise plan, which proposed postponing the reopening until May 1985.
May 21	A decision was made by the mayor to postpone the reopening until April 1987.
July 2	The new mayor's inauguration.
Jan. 11, 1985	The mayor met the Y store executives. Y store declared that construction of the new supermarket would start in early February.
Feb. 16	Construction was started, the mayor's proposition was ignored, and Y store announced that it would reopen the supermarket on March 20th.
March 11	The mayor answered the assembly that it was impossible to postpone the reopening.
March 21	Y store reopens.

[handwritten margin note: example of corporate power]

On 19 February 1985, the president of the Citizens' Association, the president of the Fishmongers' Union, the president of the Union of Vegetable Shops, the president of the Butchers' Union, the president of the Japanese Liquor Shops' Union and the president of the Retail Association made the following statement:

> Dear president of Y store,
> The mayor will be arrested by the police because he said he would forcibly prevent the reopening of your store.
> From February 16, you began construction on the building ignoring orders to stop given by the mayor, the president of the Chamber of Commerce and the chairman of the City Assembly. The mayor asked Y store to obey the mediation that froze re-opening till April 30, 1987; and he declared that if Y store were to continue construction, he would take drastic measures, even to the point of risking arrest by the police . . .

This statement had little effect and the Y store prospered from the time it reopened. This was a matter that should have been politically decided. In reality the situation was an economic invasion by Y company under the guise of reopening an old supermarket. It should not have been an issue for the city assembly or mayor. One of the reasons it became a political issue was that both the mayoral and city assembly elections were being held, and the conservative politicians were forced to feign support for the demands of the small merchants. The Association of Citizens was mainly composed of merchants who did not necessarily represent the interests of all citizens. People living in the downtown area were, in fact, pleased that the department store was reopened. From this evidence we can conclude that in a free market, resolution of the reopening issue could have been reached spontaneously. Even if political leaders such as the mayor and the members of assembly mediated in the dispute, they could only postpone the reopening; they could not prevent it indefinitely.

Community Power Structure: Case Study II

In the case of Yokoshiba-town, as shown in Table 5–5, almost all of the leaders ranked within the top 20 were elected officials, or had been formerly. Using the same procedure as for Shimoda city, we arrived at a total of 62 leaders. First we gathered information from approximately three hundred persons; then we asked fifteen respondents to select the ten most important persons. According to the scores thus obtained, a list of leaders was drawn up. To it were added the names of politicians who lived outside the town. Of the 77 on the list, 11 were deleted because they were absent or unreachable, and a further four because they were not nominated, thus leaving 62 on the final list.

Of the top 20, twelve are active politicians. Above all it should be noted that the person ranked first is a non-resident Diet member. With that member included there were a total of five non-resident national and prefectural level politicians. The other seven active politicians are a town manager, an assistant town manager and five members of the town assembly. The leaders ranked within the top eight are all active political leaders. If we added retired or inactive politicians (one former member of the prefectural assembly and three former members of the town assembly) and leaders occupying public positions (a superintendent of education, a chairman of the board of education and a chairman of the board of agriculture), 19 out of 20 are political leaders in a broad sense. No. 20, a company owner, is the only pure economic leader.

The present town manager is a former chief of a section in the town office and has no economic power. However, among the political leaders are some who are also economic leaders. No. 5 is a member of the assembly and is also president of the Chamber of Commerce. No. 9 is a former member of the prefectural assembly, a timberland owner and a retired forestry manager. No. 12 is a professional and No. 13 is a company director. No. 15 and No. 19 engage in agriculture and No. 17 is a storekeeper. No. 18 is an ex-president of the Chamber of Commerce.

In Yokoshiba-town there were two factions of the LDP, one headed by the Diet member No. 1 and the other by the Diet member No. 3. Of the 15 town residents among the top twenty leaders, nine belong to No. 1's faction (Nos. 2, 5, 6, 7, 8, 13,

Table 5–5 The list of leaders ranked within the top 20 by reputation
scores in Yokoshiba town

Rank	Reputation score	Remark (*non-resident)
1	1.000	*Diet Member
2	0.973	Town Manager
3	0.866	*Diet Member
4	0.714	*Governor
5	0.689	Member of the Town Assembly
6	0.674	Assistant Town Manager
7	0.670	Member of the Town Assembly
8	0.576	Member of the Town Assembly
9	0.557	Former Member of the Prefectural Assembly
10	0.545	Superintendent of Education
11	0.510	*Member of the Prefectural Assembly
12	0.501	Former Member of the Town Assembly
13	0.400	Former Member of the Town Assembly
14	0.400	*Member of the Prefectural Assembly
15	0.389	Member of the Town Assembly
16	0.377	Member of the Town Assembly
17	0.362	Chairman of the Board of Education
18	0.358	Former Member of the Town Assembly
19	0.308	Chairman of the Board of Agriculture
20	0.289	

16, 17 and 19) and four to No. 3's faction (Nos. 12, 15, 18 and
20), while two are neutral (Nos. 6 and 10). Of the eighteen
assembly members in Yokoshiba-town, the only one from an
opposition party is the Komei Party member. All others are
either members of the LDP or are independent conservative
candidates who are indistinguishable from LDP members. When
the 62 leaders were asked to name their favourite parties (given
a multiple choice) 78.0% named the LDP, 9.2% the DSP, and
8.1% the KP.

Yokoshiba town's population is approximately fourteen thousand. It consists of two former villages and a former town, which
were amalgamated in 1955. Yokoshiba town is located in a long
slender area from the seashore to the mountains. The former
town is surrounded by a rural area. Each of the former villages
has several hamlets (*buraku*) which were old villages under the
feudal administration. More than 60% of the total population
lives in the former town areas, while the former mountain village
and the former fishing village regions have around 20% each.

Table 5–6 Numbers of farm households in Yokoshiba town

Year	Full-time	Part-time		Total	Number of
		*1st class	*2nd class		Households
1955	not available				1,542 (100)
1960	53.5%	25.4%	21.3%	100.0%	1,510 (98)
1965	34.5	28.3	37.2	100.0	1,434 (93)
1970	22.8	45.2	32.0	100.0	1,358 (88)
1975	18.2	37.4	44.4	100.0	1,255 (81)
1980	20.8	38.0	41.2	100.0	1,156 (75)

1st class part-timers are those who engage mainly in agriculture, and 2nd class part-timers are those who engage mainly in other occupation.

In some areas the hamlet still functions as a semi-formal local organization in which several neighbourhood groups (*ku*) are established. But in areas where the non-agricultural population has increased, the *ku* has become independent of the *buraku*, leaving the *buraku* purely agricultural.

Statistics indicate that since 1955 rapid urbanization and industrialization has occurred in Yokoshiba town. As shown in Table 5–6, the number of farm households has decreased from 1542 in 1955 to 1156 in 1980. The proportion of full-timers decreased from 53.5% in 1960 to 20.8% in 1980. The proportion of the population employed in agriculture and fishing decreased from 69.7% in 1955 to 30.1% in 1980. The urbanization and industrialization of this area has been accelerated by the construction and opening of Narita international airport. As Yokoshiba town is located near the airport, many development programs have been pursued by municipal governments with the subsidiary aid of the central government. The development of manufacturing and of the area surrounding the airport has been planned. In the latter category, golf links were constructed in Yokoshiba town near the airport.

With the influence of all of these factors the power structure of the town has changed. In the fishing communities the traditional power of boat owners collapsed with the decline of fishing in the early postwar period. But in the mountain village communities the power of timber owners persisted in the same era because the land reforms did not regulate the ownership of forest. Thus, before the airport was established in 1978, the town seemed to be controlled in the old town by the owners and managers of stores, and by landlords in the mountain areas. However, with

117

Table 5–7 Employed persons in Yokoshiba town

Year	Agriculture	Industry	Commerce	Total	
1955	69.7%	6.4%	23.9%	100.0%	(6,798)
1960	63.5	9.8	26.7	100.0	(6,664)
1965	55.4	14.5	30.1	100.0	(6,324)
1970	47.5	19.4	33.1	100.0	(6,596)
1975	35.7	24.7	39.6	100.0	(6,626)
1980	30.1	25.9	44.0	100.0	(7,059)
National (1980)	10.9	33.6	55.5	100.0	

the opening of the airport and initiation of related development programs, and also as the seaside area of the town was developed as a resort, owners and managers of construction companies and real estate businesses have entered the upper stratum and gained political influence and leadership. These people are interested in establishing connections with national and local politicians and administrators. Among them are new politicians who, supported by the centralized national and prefectural power of conservatives, have acquired power in the town. These facts explain why the 62 leaders when asked 'who are influential in the affairs of Yokoshiba town?' five non-resident politicians and seven active local politicians were nominated within the top 20. But this does not mean that traditional legitimacy has totally disappeared: it is an inevitable adjunct to the rule of bureaucratic administration through centralized national power.

The districts in which Yokoshiba town is located are called the 'kingdom of conservatives'. In Yokoshiba town two factions of the LDP have emerged. Their differences do not centre around policy issues, but are the result of a competition for power. It is under such conditions that plutocracy has been practised. Each faction spends a large sum of money buying votes in every election, at both the national and local levels. Among conservative candidates bribery is quite common and often involves police connivance.

In the 1984 election for town manager each of the two candidates was said to have paid $100 per vote. Thus a total of two million dollars was spent by the two camps. It was also claimed that in the Diet election of 1983 each LDP candidate paid $20 per vote. In the same year in a neighbouring electoral district the successful incumbent LDP candidate, Z, was arrested after the election and lost his seat in the House because of election irregularities. This was unusual because, as mentioned earlier, election bribery in these districts is normally overlooked. Successful candidates have seldom been arrested, although campaign workers often are. The reasons behind the winning candidate's arrest in this case, therefore deserve explanation.

Candidate Z's experiences in the previous election in 1981 led him to view the conventional method of buying votes as inefficient and irrational. Bribery in an election is usually carried out by campaign staff. They give money to experienced campaign workers who have useful connections in certain areas. These so-called 'distributors' distribute money to leading persons in the communities (*buraku*), and they in turn pass the money on to the heads of each family. It is common practice for persons at each stage of the process to pocket some of the money. Money given to the family head is never passed on to each family member. Thus half of the originally allotted money does not reach the voter. Z did not trust his staff's handling of bribery money. He appointed his brothers and relatives to be the 'distributors' and they themselves employed experienced people in the *buraku* to distribute the bribes directly to each voter, not to the family head. However, someone in one of the *buraku* was asked to hand the money in person to an old woman who was taking a bath. As a result, the bribery was very conspicuous and the police could no longer ignore these violations of electoral law. Thus Z's brother and relatives were arrested, which then led to Z's arrest.

Elections in which each adult has an equal vote undermine the basis of the legitimacy of traditional community rule. Paradoxically this is demonstrated by the case we described above. Candidate Z's downfall occurred because he bought all votes at an equal price. He violated protocol in failing to acknowledge the traditional hierarchy. Had he honoured traditional procedure even in bribery, the authorities would have overlooked the offence. Candidate Z failed to return to the House because he had practised democracy in plutocracy.

Conclusion

Our empirical research in the two localities allowed us to draw the following conclusions concerning Japanese community power structure: (1) In both communities, politicians at the national level, such as Diet members, are regarded as the most influential members of the community. (2) Politicians of both prefectural and county levels who live outside the community are also in the upper ranks of those holding power within the community. (3) At the community level, politicians such as the mayor, town-manager and members of city and town assemblies are ranked among the most influential persons in the community, on a par with owners and managers of companies within the community.

In Japan a local community power structure has existed in close relationship with both the centralized power of the national government and the traditional *Gemeinschaft* type of village and town communities. Thus political power cannot be separated from civil affairs. The merging of the private and the public, and the paternalism symbolized by the relationship between *oyakata* and *kokata*, are characteristics of both national and local Japanese power structures.

However, the foundation of such traditional patterns of power has been undermined in various ways. First of all, the introduction of modern democratic institutions has undermined the foundation of traditional paternalistic domination, nationwide. Of course the change has not been straightforward. In the postwar period, the 1970s reversal of the previous steady decline in conservativism seems to have been very important. In the late 1960s the reformist coalition won the major elections for heads of local governments against the LDP candidates. At that time also, many citizens' movements against environmental destruction allied themselves with reformist parties such as the JSP and JCP. But the majority of seats in local assemblies were still held by conservative elements, because of the strong foundation of 'grass-roots conservatism'. Furthermore, because of their failure to provide concrete alternatives, the heads of the reformist coalitions in major cities such as Tokyo, Osaka and Kyoto were defeated within ten years by conservative candidates. Parties such as the KP and SDP have adopted middle-of-the-road policies and in some cases have allied themselves with the LDP.

The 'conservatization' of local and national politics is in fact quite separate from the recurrence of the traditional pattern of community power structures, and it is no longer the general trend in Japanese politics. One view of the true nature of the triumph of conservativism is that it represents a widespread disassociation from political parties in general. The weakening of party identification, or depoliticization, means paradoxically the separation of private and public affairs. Yet in so far as it undermines the foundation of the traditional patterns of dominance as well as the interrelation of public and private affairs, it has some positive aspects. The enlargement of the realm of self-government by citizens, and the increased independence of private from public affairs, are signs of an emerging of post-conservative politics in Japan.

6   The Citizens' Movement against Environmental Destruction in Japan

Introduction

Since 1960 Japan has undergone rapid economic growth. The 'miracle' of such sustained growth has been tied to, and not incidentally resulted in, the toleration of immense industrial pollution. The problems of a deteriorating natural and social environment are neither an unexpected nor an unavoidable by-product of high economic growth. The impact of *kogai*, the general term for environmental pollutants, has exceeded tolerable limits. As government and business become more successful in establishing gigantic industrial complexes, the more *kogai* is produced. Consequently the health of the Japanese people and the natural beauty of the landscape are in jeopardy.

Although *kogai* is usually translated as 'pollution', the concept is unique to Japan and has a much wider meaning. *Kogai* can be divided into two main categories: industrial and urban. The first category includes: (1) air pollution and noxious fumes caused by soot, smoke and poisonous gases; (2) water (river, sea and lake) and soil pollution caused by liquid waste; (3) noise and vibration; and finally, (4) ground subsidence caused by the excessive industrial need for water and gas. The second category includes: (1) air pollution caused by car exhaust and house heating; (2) river pollution caused by inadequate domestic drainage and garbage facilities; (3) traffic and other miscellaneous urban noise; and (4) such problems as cramped housing, inadequate sunshine, traffic congestion, commuting etc. One might also distinguish another category, political *kogai*, which is produced by operations of the state, and includes: (1) noise and vibration produced by military bases; (2) water pollution caused by radiation from warships; and (3) air pollution caused by nuclear testing.

Residents' or citizens' movements originated with protests against *kogai*. About 70 per cent of such protests have concerned industrial *kogai*. The Japanese refer to protest movements involving the residents of a particular locality as 'residents' movements', but occasionally use the term 'citizens' movements'. However, the use of these concepts can differ: 'residents' movements' are smaller scale movements with specific goals, and 'citizens' movements' are those of larger scale with wider goals. I shall use the concept of citizens' movements to also include the residents' movements. Jun Ui, one of the most outstanding leaders of the citizens' movement in Japan, estimated that in 1974 there were more than ten thousand citizens' organizations whose goals were better living conditions or environmental improvements (Ui, 1974, p. 4). The world's major pollution-related diseases first appeared in Japan, either as a result of air pollution or the ingestion of polluted food and water over extended periods. By January 1979 over 73,000 Japanese people were recognized as *kogai* victims, and pollution-related diseases were directly responsible for hundreds of deaths.

Before I examine the various environmental protest movements, I would like to illustrate the pollution problem by citing American anthropologist Robert Smith's vivid comparison of his two visits to Kurusu, Kagawa Prefecture, in Shikoku, which were twenty-five years apart and his comments on the 'price of progress':

In 1951 the only way of reaching Shikoku was by the boat or
ferry lines that linked it to the main island of Honshu . . .
the view from the ferry as it swung out into the main channel
was of a succession of small islands of greatly varied shapes,
some graced with gnarled plum and pine trees, others so dry
that they were almost completely barren . . . The small
fishing boats were always much thicker here, but there were
almost no freighters such as could be seen occasionally
further out to sea. All along the shoreline up toward the great
headland of Yashima were extensive salt fields . . .
Twenty-five years later, the crossing of the Inland Sea
provides a vastly different prospect. Wherever the coastline
has proved suitable, land reclamation projects have been
carried out. On these great flat extensions of the land have
been built industrial and marine installations of all kinds –
petrochemical plants, oil refineries and storage tanks,
deepwater berths for tankers and freighters – all of which
discharge their wastes into the air and into the waters of the

sea. As a consequence, the Inland Sea has begun to die. On the very hot, humid and windless days of midsummer the view from the ferry is a nightmare. There are few fishing boats left, for most of the marine life that survives is inedible, but through the yellow-brown smog that blankets the entire passage on such a day one can see that there has been an enormous increase in the volume of commercial shipping. On a few islands the vegetation has died off completely, not from lack of water, but from the effects of pollution discharged by the industrial plants that are everywhere up and down the coast. Even the islands cannot be seen clearly any more, unless the ferry passes close by them . . . the greater evaporation beds of the salt field have long since been converted to landfills for industrial and marine use . . . In the perspective of twenty-five years, the crossing is an infuriating reminder of the heedlessness of those who have poisoned the air and the water (Smith, 1978, pp. 8–10).

The story of citizens' environmental protests begins at the local level. Local governments have encouraged regional industrial development under the control of the national government. In most instances pollution can not only be attributed to industrial activity but also to the government's stimulation of economic growth.

Ideology and Reality of High Economic Growth

In 1950 the government laid out the National Plan for the General Development of Land Act to aid recovery from war damage and to develop the national economy. The basic idea of the Act was taken from the TVA developmental model in the USA. It aimed to establish multi-purpose dams for the development of power resources, agricultural production and for the control of river systems. This development plan failed, however, because the corporate sector wanted the government to spend public funds developing industrial areas instead of the underdeveloped rural areas.

In 1955 the government established the Five Year Plan for

Economic Independence, in which the economic growth rate was predicted to be 5.0 per cent. Yet the actual growth rate was 9.5 per cent in 1955, 8.5 per cent in 1956 and eventually 17.3 per cent in 1959. From such a performance the planners affirmed that high economic growth was indeed possible. In 1960, prime minister Hayato Ikeda announced that the Plan would be used to double national income, with the further object of doubling the people's real income by 1970. In promising greater affluence and an end to both unemployment and poverty, the government proposed focussing on the following five areas: (1) increasing the service capacity of roads, harbours, industrial lands and waters, railroads, airports, etc.; (2) emphasis on heavy and chemical industries such as steel, electricity, petrochemical and engineering; (3) expansion of exports; (4) increasing human resources and skills, and developing scientific technologies; and (5) modernization of agriculture and small enterprise.

In 1962, a Plan for the Pacific Belt Industrialization was formulated, and in 1962 the Comprehensive National Development Plan was made public. Since the late 1950s the business world had been concentrating its capital and energy on establishing new plants in cities on the Pacific Belt. This development strategy was followed by the Strategic Point Development method under the Comprehensive National Development Plan. The basic philosophy of the Strategic Point Development method was to select a limited number of geographically strategic points, develop them as ideal industrial cities, and thereby extend the resultant economic benefits to neighbouring areas. The government also legislated for the construction of new industrial cities. Hiromi Hata believed that the object of the government initiated method was to set in motion the following chain of events in the newly developed industrial areas:

1. Local government expenditure to improve the industrial environment (land, water, roads and electricity);
2. Encouraging the establishment of heavy and chemical industries as key enterprises;
3. Developing associated industries after the introduction of heavy and chemical industries;
4. Development of cities;
5. Change of lifestyle, particularly diet (from a rice-centred diet);

6. Change in agricultural production in the surrounding rural areas (from rice production to diversified production);
7. Raising individual income in the area (urban and rural);
8. Increase of local government tax revenue;
9. More public investment in the living environment (schools, medical facilities, libraries, parks, etc.);
10. Improvement of social welfare in the area (Hata, 1976, pp. 5–6).

However the reality of the development plan was contrary to the planners' intentions. Though local governments competed to attract industry as a revenue-generating device, heavy and chemical industries were not easily convinced to migrate to these areas. Consequently, the local governments faced serious financial problems. Prior investments in industrial environment improvements suddenly became deficits. Where local government did succeed in inducing industries into their areas, the consequences were increased pollution and industrial disaster not increased financial solvency. With various tax exemptions given to the invited industries as incentives to migrate, local government revenue did not increase as expected. Moreover, the existing local industries, particularly fishing and agriculture, were undermined by the sale of rights to the use of land and sea.

For example, Kurashiki city in Okayama prefecture (one of fifteen cities designated as a New Industrial City) began purchasing paddy fields, upland fields and forest for industrial land development in the late 1950s. The municipal government promoted reclamation to establish the Mizushima littoral industrial belt by buying the fisheries' rights in 1960. It then granted a bounty equivalent to the fixed property tax of the enterprise. Total amounts of the bounty for enterprises by year were as follows:

In the three years from 1961 to 1964, the amount of municipal government investment in the preliminary works and purchases considered essential for the creation of an industrial base (roads, water, land, etc.) was 2790 million *yen*. When one considers the difference in annual municipal revenues between 1965 (1555 million *yen*) and 1970 (2969 million *yen*), it becomes immediately apparent that the benefits of these grants went to the industrial enterprises. For this reason, municipal finance operated at a deficit from 1967, and the cumulative deficit reached 657 million *yen* between 1967 and 1969. It was therefore an illusion that the

Table 6–1 The bounty for enterprises of Kurashiki city

Year	Amount of grant
1961	10.5 (million *yen*)*
1962	95.9
1963	123.3
1964	140.7
1965	172.6
1966	236.0
1967	255.0
1968	229.0
1969	208.0
1970	186.0

*Note: The average million *yen* equivalent at this time = US$41,000.00

New Industrial City designation could make municipal finance profitable and benefit residents. It became obvious that supporting corporations caused the exploitation of local residents and was also disastrous for the accommodating communities.

Another significant result was increased pollution. In June of 1965 a discharge of cyanic acid ions into Mizushima district's Yobimatsu Harbour poisoned large quantities of inland sea fish. Since 1965 rice plants and other grasses have withered, and nearly all of the area's agricultural products have been damaged by air pollution. In Yobimatsu town a victims' association of fruit growers was organized. One member of the association, an old man since retired from rice dealing, said in 1974:

> This place was once famous for its scenic beauty. Fishermen could make a good living from the ample marine life. But after the beginning of big enterprises, fisheries have suffered serious damage. Though I was a rice dealer, at the same time I cultivated an orchard. But since 1965, fruits did not grow well because of air pollution. Then we formed the victims' association of fruit growers and struggled against the enterprises, prefectural and municipal governments for five years. In the beginning, many peasants gave us the cold shoulder and treated us as madmen. My son succeeded a rice dealer who used to sell his product to the employees of big enterprises. Now however, most enterprises refuse him because of his father's affiliation with the anti-pollution movement. My son complains, saying that he has to take care of his children and asks me not to disturb his business.

Employees could better their position in big companies unless they made trouble with the locals. Consequently, they formed a kind of foreign community completely isolated from the local community. Such circumstances and ideas were, I think, the main sources of increased pollution. Though employees must also have been suffering from pollutants they refused to sign their names during any anti-pollution signature-collecting campaign (Saitō, 1974, pp. 34–35).

A sociologist who conducted intensive research in Yobimatsu town reported that all fish taken from the Misushima inland sea area had been barred from the market because of health risks. In 1967 a system of compensation in which fish from certain areas of Mizushima were bought for seventy per cent of market value was introduced. The cost of this scheme was covered by contributions from the prefectural and city governments and the implicated industries. After being bought the catches were then burned. When an old fisherman was asked why he no longer worked he replied, 'I do not want to take fish no one needs no matter how much money I can make from them'. It became obvious that pollution was not only destructive to the material, but also to psychological aspects of life; a life whose meaning had become irreparably altered.

The 'Corporate State' and the Emergence of Environmental Protest

Ken'ichi Miyamoto characterized the Japanese government as a kind of 'corporate state', in the sense that gigantic corporations subordinate the state to their will, running national finance for their own profit. A main feature of national Japanese finance is the public investment structure. As can be seen from Table 6–2 (Miyamoto and Shōji, 1975, p. 61), public investment is concentrated at the industrial base which accounts for 54.8 per cent of total investment. In contrast to this is the 26.1 per cent of public investment in the living base.

128

Table 6–2 Public investment in the 1960s

		(billion *yen*)	(%)
	Total	33,726.0	100.0
I	Production base (social means of production)	18,486.7	54.8
	1 Roads	6,915.3	20.5
	2 Harbours	748.6	2.2
	3 Airports	65.9	0.2
	4 Equipage of harbours (including reclamation)	753.7	2.2
	5 National railroads	3,809.2	11.3
	6 Telegram and telephone	3,453.7	10.2
	7 Industrial water	328.6	1.0
	8 Agriculture, forestries and fisheries	2,411.7	7.2
II	Living base (Social means of consumption)	8,799.8	26.1
	9 Urban planning	583.5	1.7
	10 Preparation of housing sites	508.6	1.5
	11 Environmental hygiene	360.8	1.1
	12 Water supply	1,303.9	3.9
	13 Social welfare	691.5	2.1
	14 Drainage	764.4	2.3
	15 Educational facilities	2,559.1	7.6
III	16 Conservation of national land	2,114.1	6.3
IV	17 All others	4,325.4	12.8

In 1973, the national government established the Socio-economic Basic Plan with the intention of constructing a 'welfare society'. It planned to raise public investment in the five year period from 1973 to 1977 to 90,000 billion *yen*. However Table 6–3 demonstrates that elements of the production base, such as industrial roads, etc. basically remained unchanged.

Miyamoto also pointed out that the 'corporate state' was supported by local governments acting as its 'agencies', and by the 'grass-roots conservatism' of local communities. As mentioned previously, local governments have become accomplices in the crime of pollution through their wooing of industry. Under 'grass-roots conservatism' discontented residents have become accustomed to being suppressed by the influential political leaders of local communities. The labouring class is controlled by the very enterprises for which they work. Japanese labour unions are generally enterprise specific. As a rule labour unions have been reluctant to support citizens' protests against pollution, because the unions share industrial management's interests for the expan-

Table 6–3 Plans and past records of public investment

	Proposed expenditure 1973–77		Actual expenditure 1968–72	
	Amount of money (billion *yen*)	%	Amount of money (billion *yen*)	%
Environmental hygiene	7,740	8.6	2,012	5.3
Public rental housing	6,080	6.8	2,388	6.3
Social welfare	1,820	2.0	1,027	2.7
Schools	4,370	4.9	2,535	6.7
Roads	19,000	21.1	8,370	22.1
Railroads	7,850	8.7	3,349	8.8
Airports	770	0.9	270	0.7
Harbours	3,190	3.5	1,101	2.9
Communications	6,510	7.2	3,730	9.8
Conservation of lands	5,830	6.5	2,340	6.2
Agricultures	5,550	6.2	2,263	4.0
All others	18,290	20.3	8,499	22.4
Adjustment	3,000	3.3	–	–
Total	90,000	100.0	37,884	100.0

sion of production and improved efficiency. Organized labour has largely taken a passive and occasionally obstructionist role in relation to the citizens' movements against pollution.

Until 1968 the local labour union of the Minamata Chisso Corporation had opposed the action taken by 'Minamata victims', who suffered from a neurological condition attributed to poisoning by mercury contained in the Chisso Corporation's effluent. The victims were regarded as 'those who would destroy labourers' rice bowls'. In another case, the Yokkaichi local union of Mitsui Kasei Corporation withdrew from the regional league of labour unions in 1967 when Yokkaichi asthma victims finally filed law suits against six of the enterprises including Mitsui. As a final example, a labour union from the Kanose factory of Showa Denko supported the company in opposition to the programs of the Niigata prefectural labour union council, which included a policy of support for victims of the Niigata Minamata disease.

Under such circumstances only local residents were inclined to join the citizens' movements against pollution, thus, only the potential victims of local pollution problems saw themselves as having an interest in citizens' movements. Those local residents who protested against pollution faced difficulties and considerable discrimination. Traditionally, people suffering such personally and environmentally destructive conditions, endured them by 'crying themselves to sleep'.

Four major cases will now be reviewed. In that of Minamata disease, which appeared in 1953 in Minamata city, Kumamoto prefecture, it took twenty years for the district court to order the Chisso Corporation to pay compensation to all of the victims. Minamata disease, which is a dysfunction in neurological coordination, originally appeared in cats that ate large amounts of discarded fish taken from Minamata Bay. Shortly afterward, similar neurological symptoms began to appear in human adults. In 1956 Dr Hajime Hosokawa began studying the disease and found that it was caused by heavy metals ingested via the consumption of contaminated fish. In 1959, a Kumamoto University team singled out methyl mercury as the probable cause of the disease and named Chisso Corporation as the likely source of the mercury. Chisso's management hired their own study team which not surprisingly argued mercury was not the cause. Thus, the real cause remained unidentified while the numbers of people contracting and dying of the disease continued to increase. During that same year, victims and fishermen tried to negotiate with the Chisso management for the complete purification of factory polluted water and for compensation for the loss of fishing rights. The negotiations failed, due to bad faith on the part of Chisso Corporation.

Then in 1965 a Niigata University team found that residents living along the Agano River in Niigata prefecture had the same neurological symptoms associated with Minamata disease. In March 1966 the Ministry of Health and Welfare concluded that Niigata Minamata disease was caused by methyl mercury which originated in the waste from the Kanose plant of Showa Denko (which used the same process as Chisso) on the Agano River. The further conclusion that the Minamata experience had been suppressed, permitting a second outbreak of the disease, caused local residents to rise up. In August, twenty-two separate local organizations including local unions formed the Minamata Disease Counter Measures Council of Democratic Groups and demanded a solution to the pollution problem. In December the victims themselves formed a group. In June 1967, when the Niigata victims sued Showa Denko, they filed Japan's first pollution lawsuit, which they subsequently won.

The third of the 'Big Four' pollution verdicts concerned *itai-itai* disease in Toyama prefecture. *Itai-itai* disease, now known to be a result of long-term cadmium poisoning, first appeared in peasants living on the Jintsu River in Toyama prefecture. Cadmium poisoning causes bone brittleness, such as experienced by a man who suffered successive pressure fractures of the spine and whose height was shortened by twelve inches as a result. *Itai* means 'aches and pains' and this disease was so named because its victims died crying '*Itai-itai*'. The contaminated water of the Jintsu River was used to irrigate the local residents' rice paddies. The cause of the disease was unknown prior to Dr Noboru Hagino's 1957 diagnosis that mineral pollution played a leading part. Unfortunately, Dr Hagino was treated as crazed and insensible and his diagnosis was therefore rejected. He had hypothesized that industrial waste containing cadmium, zinc and lead, which were released upstream by the Kamioka plant of Mitsui Mining and Smelting in Gifu prefecture, was the source of the mineral contamination.

Victims began petitioning the Kamioka smelter in November 1966, and decided to file suit in January 1968. As Dr Hagino had announced in 1957 that *itai-itai* disease was the result of long-term cadmium poisoning, protesters demanded that compensation be retrospective to that time. While victims were mobilizing and preparing to initiate litigation, the rest of the community's attitude to *itai-itai* disease began to change. Various groups within Toyama prefecture, including labour unions and leftist parties, formed the Prefectural Countermeasures Committee to support the victims and to publicize the cadmium pollution situation. In May 1968, shortly after the first group of plaintiffs filed suit, the Ministry of Health and Welfare released its conclusions regarding the origins of the disease, which supported all of Dr Hagino's major contentions. They named Mitsui Mining and Smelting as the most probable source of contamination. Thus *itai-itai* disease became the first pollution disease caused to be formally recognized by the government. The verdict in the lawsuit was delivered in June 1971. Although the *itai-itai* case was the third pollution suit filed, it was the first to arrive at a verdict in favour of the plaintiffs, and thus played a very important part in setting precedents for future pollution litigation.

The fourth case is that of Yokkaichi asthma in Mie prefecture. The Yokkaichi case had been filed prior to the Minamata verdict, but differed from the other three cases. Whereas the other three cases involved concentrated water pollution from a single sources, the Yokkaichi case involved air pollution from multiple sources. Yokkaichi was the area in which the first large group of heavy industries was established in a *kombinat* style of regional development. *Kombinat* is a Russian term for a massive complex of related manufacturing industries in close proximity to each other which minimized transportation costs. Concern over pollutants released by these firms was first publicized by fishermen, who demanded compensation for being unable to sell the strange-smelling fish they had caught in the area since 1958. By 1960 a number of victims of air pollution who were referred to as Yokkaichi asthma patients had been identified. It was already obvious that the widespread incidence of asthma was a result of the sulfurous fumes produced by industries in the *kombinat* zone.

In July 1963 the first citizens' assembly was held by the regional labour association in combination with leftist parties and others. This committee, which sought countermeasures to the pollution generated by Yokkaichi city, demanded that the city assembly take concrete measures to prevent air pollution and to force the polluting firms to install effective prevention equipment. A similar citizens' assembly was held in July 1964, in relation to the death of one victim. In 1965 and 1967 respectively, two victims who were no longer able to endure their agony committed suicide. On September 1st, 1967, nine of the hundreds of certified Yokkaichi victims finally filed suit against six of the *kombinat* enterprises. On July 24th, 1972, after almost five years in court, the plaintiffs won their case.

The major pollution lawsuits, including the 'Big Four' mentioned and the damages awarded are listed in Table 6–4. Table 6–5 gives details of designated pollution diseases and their effects on the victims (McKean, 1981, pp. 68–72).

Development of Citizens' Movements, and the Community in Transition

On the day the Yokkaichi district court verdict was delivered, residents bitterly noted that 'even though victims have been awarded their damages, we can never again restore cleanliness to the blue sky'. It must be remembered that the lawsuit though it is the main method, is not the only means employed by citizens' movements. Less effective and more typically passive anti-pollution movements also exist. Though people organize to rectify problems, a complete stabilization of the situation is difficult to obtain regardless of legal verdicts and compensation. It is both ironic and unfortunate that if the goal of the citizens' movement is the restoration of original environmental conditions, its achievements however great, can never attain that goal.

The citizens' movements of Mishima and Numazu cities and Shimizu town in Shizuoka prefecture in 1964, where residents prevented the introduction of a new petrochemical *kombinat*, may be regarded as the first truly successful anti-pollution movement.

The governor of Shizuoka prefecture, Toshio Saitō, proposed the amalgamation of Mishima, Numazu and Shimizu in May 1963. According to his initial prefectural plan, the post-amalgamation success of the new city would lead to further consolidation through the absorption of outlying towns and villages, and finally

Table 6–4 Damages awarded in pollution diseases litigation

Case	Number of plaintiffs	Total award (million yen)	Largest to a single plaintiff (million yen)	Date suit filed	Date of verdict
Cadmium poisoning Toyama DC	31	57	4	March 1968	June 1971
Mercury poisoning Niigata DC	77	270	10	June 1967	Sept. 1971
Air pollution Yokkaichi DC	12	88	15	Sept. 1967	July 1972
Cadmium poisoning Toyama HC	33	148.2	12	July 1971	August 1972
Mercury poisoning Kumamoto DC	138	930	18	June 1969	March 1973
PCB poisoning Fukuoka DC	46	683	25.7	Feb. 1969	Oct. 1977
SMON disease Tokyo DC–Wakai	35	870	47	May 1971	Oct. 1977
SMON disease Kanazawa DC	16	431*	38.4*	May 1973	March 1978
PCB poisoning Fukuoka DC	729	6,000	17	Nov. 1970	March 1978
SMON disease Tokyo DC	133	3,251	49.7	May 1971	August 1978
SMON disease Hiroshima DC	43	1,070	53.7	April 1973	Feb. 1979

Note: DC = District Court; HC = High Court; Wakai = Court-mediate settlement.
'Number of plaintiffs' refers only to the number of plaintiffs in the single civil suit in which the verdict was pronounced. These are additional PCB suits involving at least 331 plaintiffs, and in the case of SMON there are over 28 additional suits.
*Includes interest (250 and 28 million *yen*, respectively without interest).

135

Table 6–5 Pollution disease victims

Designated pollution diseases	Alive	Dead	Total	Application pending
Organic mercury poisoning				
Kumamoto and Kagoshima	1,478	287	1,765	5,982
Niigata	676	66	742	230
Cadmium poisoning				
Toyama (itai-itai disease)	230	120	350	
Tsushima	22		22	
Chronic arsenic-trioyide poisoning				
Miyazaki	99	10	109	
Shimane	17	3	20	
Air pollution disease				
41 designated zones (January 1979)	71,190	625	71,815	
Total victims shown above	73,712			
Other Environmentally related disease PCB (Kanemi cooking oil)*	1,578	51	1,629	
Morinaga arsenic powdered milk**	11,839	505	12,344	
Thalidomide***	253	?	?	
Hexavalent chromium****	191	41	232	
SMON*****	approximately 11,000			

* PCB or polychlorinated biphenyl, contaminated a large batch of rice bran cooking oil produced by the Kanemi Company in North Kyushu. The contaminated oil was sold throughout western Japan in 1968.
** The Morinaga Dairy Corporation accidentally allowed powdered arsenic to enter a large batch of powdered formula for babies in 1955, and babies all over Japan were affected.
*** The Japanese Thalidomide disaster was settled out of court in December 1974, with awards to individual survivors ranging from 3 million yen to 40 million yen.
**** Hexavalent chromium poisoning victims are confirmed only among those who have handled the toxin during the course of their work.
***** SMON or subacute-myelo-optico-neuropathy, is a disease resulting at least in part from the ingestion of large quantities of quinoform (or chinoform), a drug prescribed for stomach ailments. It produces a variety of chronic central nervous system disabilities up to and including paralysis and blindness.

result in an industrial city with a population of one million. When that goal was achieved, the comprehensive development plan called for the designation of an industrial zone onto which petro-chemical industries could be invited. This plan was announced in December 1963. However, in 1964 a movement began in both cities and in the town opposing the amalgamation and its associated proposal for attracting petro-chemical industries. Within the following year the movement succeeded in persuading the pro-development local officials to cancel their plan.

Miyamoto pointed out three important lessons which can be drawn from this movement (Miyamoto and Shōji, 1975, pp. 220–21). First, its success was due to the social power of the united residents. It was estimated that almost 80–90 per cent of the voting population supported the movement. The citizens' meeting in Numazu in September 1964, for example, mobilized 25,000 people, one-third of the city's voting population. In both cities and in the town, neighbourhood associations adopted anti-development resolutions, as did their municipal assemblies.

Secondly, the movement encouraged meetings of small groups to procure more exact information regarding pollution. High school teachers prepared slide and film presentations, nightly visiting various neighbourhood associations to explain the terrible consequences experienced in other industrial cities. Many groups also went to other industrial complexes such as Yokkaichi, to see first hand the effects of pollution, and to bring into stark reality the likely future of the industrial development proposed for Mishima-Numazu.

The third lesson concerns both the integration achieved with the movement and its diversity. Many associations were able to unite against development while still maintaining individual doctrines. Labour unions of national railroad workers, for example, school teachers, and local government workers, cooperative associations of farmers, fishermen, medical practitioners, and pharmacists, traditional regional associations of neighbours, housewives, young men and women, and various voluntary citizens' associations, all became involved. The success of the movement rested particularly on cooperation between the more radical activists from the younger voluntary associations and the older, more traditional leaders of neighbourhood associations.

In contrast to the Mishima-Numazu-Shimizu movement, the movement in Fuji city only began after industry had been attracted to the area and the amalgamation of cities was complete. However, it too can be regarded as having succeeded. Fuji city is highly industrialized; and its paper-pulp products account for 40 per cent of total national production. It is noted for its *hedoro* (waste from paper-pulp processing) problem, which has caused the decimation of the once beautiful Tagonoura Port on Suruga Bay. *Hedoro* (slime) is a mass of fine particles and other organic substances, including poisonous gases, that accumulate and solidify in shallow water.

Fishermen first began petitioning the local authorities for compensation in the late 1950s. At that time, however, no satisfactory results were obtained. In the meantime, Fuji City, Yoshiwara City and Takaoka town were amalgamated to form the new Fuji City in November 1966. The new mayor was the younger brother of the president of Daishowa Paper-Pulp Company, one of the major companies in the area. In March 1968, the Tokyo Electric Company announced plans to construct a thermal power plant on the Fuji River. At that time the existing anti-pollution movements aided in the organization of regional groups. These groups wanted the complete elimination of *hedoro* wastes and dredging of the bay. In April 1968, one month after announcement of the construction plans, a Citizens' Committee for Countermeasures to Pollution was formed by a combination of regional labour associations, leftist parties and existing anti-pollution activist groups.

Originally, the Tokyo Electric Company had planned to construct a thermal plant in Numazu city in 1964. The plan was cancelled because of opposition from the Numazu citizens' movement in 1964. This allowed the people of Fuji to learn from the Mishima-Numazu experiences, enhancing their ability to mobilize. The movements which demanded a cessation of the disposal of *hedoro* into the sea and to those who objected to the further construction of industries, combined and directed their efforts toward blocking the construction of the thermal power plant. Finally, in January 1970, the reformist candidate for mayor defeated the paper-pulp sponsored candidate, ensuring the success of the movement to block construction.

In November 1970 the movement filed a civil suit against the prefectural governor and the four major pulp companies. An out-of-court settlement in December 1976 awarded 1.1 billion *yen* to the Fishermen's Cooperative Association. And in September

1977, a Tokyo high court ruling declared that the dumping of *hedoro* was illegal, and ordered the pulp companies to find other waste disposal means and to reimburse the prefecture for the expense incurred in dredging Tagonoura Bay (McKean, 1981, p. 32).

The success of this movement, however, is rather exceptional. Citizens' movements since the mid–1970s have been faced with new difficulties. Firstly, the demand for simple withdrawal is no longer likely to be supported by residents from 'underdeveloped' areas. For example, the attitudes expressed by the residents of Tomakomai, in Hokkaido, on city development plans are summarized as shown in Table 6–6.

Tomakomai is one of five focal areas selected by the government according to its New Comprehensive National Development Plan in 1969. The basic strategy of the development plan was to establish gigantic industrial bases in remote areas. For example, according to the plan, the proposed gigantic Mutsu-Ogawara industrial base in Aomori prefecture was to refine two million barrels of crude oil per day. In the case of Tomakomai, one million barrels would be processed per day. No one knew what effect these huge petrochemical industries would have on the natural and social environment of the area. Central and local governments used every device available to them in persuading the local people of the advantages of an industrial-complex development.

As Table 6–6 indicates, however, most citizens of Tomakomai were conditional supporters of the development. Opposition was 16.7 per cent in 1973 and had declined to 6.3 per cent in 1978. After construction began in 1976, the column 'initially opposed' was added. From the questionnaire results, one may speculate that among those who once opposed the plan, conditional support had arisen. Although it is rather difficult to make a clearcut distinction between those who are anti-development and those who are conditional supporters of development from these statistics, the unconditional supporters of the plan comprised only a small portion of total population: 7.0 per cent in 1973 to 10.5 per cent in 1978.

In Tomakomai, the city authorities first attempted to promote the national development plan through the construction of an industrial harbour to the east of the city in 1968. When the master plan was announced by the national government in 1970,

Table 6-6 Results of development plan questionnaires

	Supporters		Opponents		D.K.		Total	
	Uncondi-tioned	Condi-tioned Initially opposed						
		(%)		(%)		(%)		(%)
Dec. 1973								
Municipal workers	10 5.0	136 67.3	50 24.8		6 3.0		202	
Employees of companies	22 6.8	233 72.4	46 14.3		21 6.5		322	
Entrepreneurs	14 10.3	101 74.3	14 10.3		7 5.1		136	
Others	10 7.1	89 63.6	24 17.1		17 12.1		140	
Total	56 7.0	559 69.9	134 16.7		51 6.4		800	
Dec. 1974								
Municipal workers	5 7.6	40 60.6	19 28.8		2 3.0		66	
Employees of companies	18 8.1	159 71.3	25 11.2		21 9.4		223	
Entrepreneurs	15 21.7	51 73.9	1 1.4		2 2.9		69	
Others	22 7.4	186 62.6	45 15.2		44 14.8		297	
Total	60 9.4	436 66.6	90 13.7		69 10.5		655	
Dec. 1975								
Municipal workers	2 2.8	47 66.2	14 19.7		8 11.3		71	
Employees of companies	24 9.9	195 80.6	10 4.1		13 5.4		242	
Entrepreneurs	15 16.0	71 75.5	5 5.3		3 3.2		94	
Others	18 7.0	186 72.4	22 8.6		31 12.1		257	
Total	59 8.9	499 75.1	51 7.7		55 8.3		664	

Dec. 1976											
Municipal workers	2	2.7	39	53.4	17	23.3	11	15.1	4	5.5	73
Employees of companies	25	9.7	164	63.8	50	19.5	10	3.9	8	3.1	257
Entrepreneurs	15	15.0	69	69.0	9	9.0	3	3.0	4	4.0	100
Others	17	6.8	153	60.9	50	19.9	14	5.6	17	6.8	251
Total	59	8.7	425	62.4	126	18.5	38	5.6	33	4.8	681
Dec. 1977											
Municipal workers	6	6.5	47	50.5	18	19.3	16	17.2	6	6.5	93
Employees of companies	46	14.0	174	52.9	46	14.0	26	7.9	37	11.2	329
Entrepreneurs	32	21.8	68	46.2	26	17.7	14	9.5	7	4.8	147
Others	41	9.8	178	42.5	73	17.4	44	10.5	83	19.8	419
Total	125	12.6	468	47.3	163	16.5	100	10.1	133	13.5	988
Nov. 1978											
Municipal workers	10	13.1	38	50.0	17	22.4	7	9.2	4	5.3	76
Employees of companies	49	14.0	170	48.7	71	20.3	21	6.0	38	10.9	349
Entrepreneurs	15	13.1	53	46.5	22	19.3	6	5.3	18	15.8	114
Others	28	6.5	197	45.4	102	23.5	27	6.2	80	18.4	434
Total	102	10.5	458	47.0	212	21.8	61	6.3	140	14.4	973

Motojima and Shōji, 1980, p. 21, initially from Tomakomai Minpōsha.

they were sorely embarrassed by its extraordinarily large scale, and suddenly reluctant to lend it support. Thus, in November 1973, the basic plan for the development of the eastern part of Tomakomai was announced as an independent action. Although referred to as 'the city plan', it essentially represented the 'first stage' of the national project. In 1973, an association to oppose the development was formed by labour unions and leftist parties. The strategy of the association was to demand the complete withdrawal of the plan. Reformists focused their campaign on the mayoral election of April 1975. However, the former mayor vowed in his election campaign that he would promote the development plan even at the risk of his political career, defeated the reformist candidate. At this point the movement, headed by the association of regional labour and by the socialist and communist parties, was left with no viable strategy to oppose the regional development. Although the movement had always stood ready to oppose the development, few efforts were made to identify the actual needs of local residents. Except for the few people who did not want further development of the city, most citizens fundamentally agreed with the locally proposed regional development plan if it could be implemented, even in the face of anxiety regarding developmental exploitation and subsequent pollution should the national government's plan go through.

The second difficulty facing citizens' movements concerns solidarity among residents. The issues with which citizens' movements are concerned usually split the residential sector sharply, due to differences in interests and values. For example, the attraction of new industries into a rural area may bring economic benefits to the local government, to shops which can expect new customers, to peasants who can sell their land to those who would welcome new job opportunities, and so forth. On the other hand, the attraction of new industries may economically disadvantage the local factories, be opposed by peasants who do not wish to sell their land, and by people who are simply fearful of the effects of pollution.

Another difficulty has to do with city-type pollutants where the relationship between the causes of pollution and its sufferers is often less simple than in the case of industrial pollution. Those living at busy road intersections, for example, may organize an anti-car-pollution movement, although at the same time they may also use cars. In this sense, the 'enemy' of the anti-pollution movement continually lives 'next door'; or put another way, each citizen is his own worst enemy. Thus anti-pollution movements have necessarily tended to develop into movements advocating residents' involvement in regional planning. Anti-pollution or anti-development movements need to be linked with community formation movements which promote consensus.

Community formation is one of the important goals of citizens' movements, in as much as they themselves are a part of, and require, the process of community formation. The community being based on democratic self-government. In this regard, Margaret A. McKean in her excellent study describes Japanese citizens' movements as follows:

> Their message is home-grown, not imported, indicating that Japanese political culture had an indigenous potential for democratic 'evolution'. To the Japanese who have become active in citizens' movements, the idea they have something called 'rights' which have been 'unjustly' trampled upon, that the system itself owes them some recourse, that democratic procedures are actually devices that exist precisely for the situation in which they find themselves, is attractive and satisfying. It helps them to interpret the situation and it gives them guidance in responding to it (McKean, 1981, p. 268).

She concludes by citing an elderly fisherman:

> In this kind of situation, we used to just put up with it and cry ourselves to sleep. But this time it affected our economic circumstances and our health. So we just had to rise up and protest against it. Why it went against the ideas of democratic politics! . . . The way things are now, the government tells the people what to do, but it's supposed to be the other way around, you know (McKean, 1981, p. 268).

Forty-five years ago in 1948, E. Herbert Norman was invited to address an anniversary celebration at Keio University in Tokyo. The title of his lecture, which was delivered in Japanese, was *Settoku Ka boryoku Ka – Gendai Shakai niokeru Jiyuna Genron no Mondai* (Persuasion or Force – The Problem of Free Speech in Modern Society). In it he explained that self-government 'means that people look upon government officials as their servants or as their deputies and not as their masters'. It is the very opposite of the old concept of *'kanson minpi'*. *Kanson minpi* means literally, 'official-revering, people-despising' or more properly, putting government above people, the overvaluing of government at the expense of people. Norman's argument is, I believe, still relevant to the present situation in Japan. He concluded his speech at Keio with these remarks:

> Once liberty is dead, people must lose their self-respect; despair, envy, deceit and malice will grow apace like weeds in a deserted garden . . . but no people who have lost their freedom can bequeath any lasting benefit to succeeding ages. They will leave behind no inspiration or generous work to which their descendants can look with pride and gratitude.
> . . . Persuasion is not only the way of reason and humanity, it is now the sole path of self-preservation. Thus we are, all of us, whatever our nation or status, faced with the stern alternative: PERSUADE OR PERISH (Norman, 1948, p. 146).

PART III

The chapters of Part III deal with the development of capitalism in relation to the religious cosmos of ordinary Japanese people. First an analysis is made of relationship between Japanese religion, the modern Japanese State, and the emperor system. In Chapters 7 and 8 the problems of Japanese capitalism and the emperor system are discussed. It has been assumed that the full development of capitalism would undermine the bases of pre-modern institutions such as the emperor the system. It has also been thought that Japan committed itself to wars of aggression because of a strong system of command in both military and civil organizations which was based on the emperor system. It has been said there would have been no wars of aggression had civilian control functioned in prewar Japan. But the development of capitalism itself is a cause of wars of aggression. Thus for example, there was civilian control in the United States at the time of the war against Vietnam.

Japanese capitalism is based not on individualism but on collectivism. In Japan the profit-making unit is the household or extended family. Rational pursuit of profit is not incompatible with groupism or familyism. Thus the market for a commodity may be remote from its place of production.

Households in Japan are perpetual groups within which people are born and die. Those who live together in the same household are to be buried in the same grave, as the family group extends beyond this world into the other world. Thus there are thought to be three kinds of people in the village: people presently living, dead ancestors, and people who will be born in this world. Similarly, the living inhabitants of a village may be divided into three categories: children who represent the future, adults who represent the present, and old persons who represent the past. The present is thought of not as a knife edge dividing past and future, but as including past and future.

As will be discussed in Chapter 9, the distinction between this world and the other world is one of the peculiar characteristics of the Japanese world view. 'I' is not an absolute individual in Japanese. Each 'I' represents one of the indispensable roles in the community. So there are many 'Is and accordingly many 'mes. 'We' (*ware ware*) in Japanese means 'I' (*ware*) and 'I' (*ware*). In Japanese 'you' is not the other person in front of 'I', with whom 'I' could not identify. Thus 'me' does not emerge from the perspectives of 'you' but that of 'I'.

7 The *Tennōsei* Ideology and Japan's Wars of Aggression

Japanese Views on War

Machiko Hasegawa recalled her younger days in her amusing vignette 'The Sazae-sans on tour', in the *Asahi* newspaper of 29 June 1987. Her mother used to cut her hair, believing that if Sazae-san went to a barber shop, she would become bald on account of the germs breeding on the scissors. Because of her mother's lack of skill, Sazae-san's hairstyle was appalling. She was mortified and cried. When her foreign friends came to say goodbye to her, she was not able to see them. Machiko herself said that she did not go to the barber until, in reaction against her mother's foolish fancies, she tried to have her hair permed.

This story symbolizes the traditional Japanese thought (common until quite recently) that while the inside is kept clean, the outside is soiled by bacteria. Emiko Ōnuki, an anthropologist at the University of Wisconsin, wrote in *Japanese Views on Disease* that it was very important for Japanese children, and was something in which they were strictly trained as a part of their socialization early in life, that when they returned home after playing outside, they must take off their shoes and wash their hands, and, if need be, gargle. They were so taught because it was thought that since there were many bacteria outdoors, one must remove one's shoes to avoid bringing them inside, and it followed that one should also wash the bacteria out of the mouth (Ōnuki, 1985, pp. 29–30).

This traditional Japanese idea that the source of pollution and the cause of disease is always external is reflected in views of relationships between the in-group and out-group, and is clearly discernible in Japanese views on war. While the inside is always thought to be at peace, harmonious and secure, the cause of trouble is always external. A moral and economic duality existing between the community and outsiders in pre-capitalist society was observed by many of the classical sociologists (for example

147

Karl Marx and Max Weber). Such a duality has been expressed in the views on war of some Japanese, even after the Meiji Restoration.

Recently a political scientist, Bakuji Ari, published a book in which he critically analyzed his own experiences in the battle of Luzon in the Philippines. It took him more than forty years to write analytically about his own war experiences. In the postscript to this book, he noted that the antagonistic relationship between the insiders (the Japanese military) and the outsiders (Philippinos) was paralleled by tensions between army units (Ari, 1987, p. 177). In the eyes of the members of one squad another unit was comprised of outsiders. A squad was a microcosm; if one stole from a fellow squad member, it was considered an unpardonable crime, but stealing from a member of another squad was condoned (Ari, 1987, p. 14).

Ari also points out that the cruelty of the Japanese army toward natives was closely related to that which it perpetrated on its own soldiers. As to military discipline, he was impressed by a commander's order forbidding the theft of native farmers' products. However, he soon realized the order was not obeyed by the Japanese soldiers, and pointed out that if the order had been adhered to, an aggressive war could not have happened (Ari, 1987, p. 52).

He explained his state of mind at the time he went to battle in the Philippines as follows:

> I hated the war. But apart from this fact, I accepted the tragic atmosphere of the surroundings, and thought: 'we must cut our way through the enemy now that Japan's position in the war is getting worse. This is the reason why we, the students, are drafted'. I went to the front neither for the sake of the emperor nor for the 'sacred war', but for the sake of my parents, brothers and sisters, and friends. If I were asked the reason why I was going to the war, I could only answer that all other students were going, so I was going (Ari, 1987, pp. 7–8).

What is deemed unique to the Japanese derives not from Japanese feudalism but from the Asiatic mode of production in Japan, whose common characteristic is the patriarchal hierarchy of extended families. Therefore, strictly speaking this foundation is not unique to the Japanese. Japan's uniqueness is attaining capitalism without individualism. In Japan, a highly developed capitalistic society co-exists with the *ie* (family) and *tennōsei* (emperor system) ideologies.

In modern Japan, naturalistic novelists such as Katai Tayama who in his youth read Emile Zola, were not essentially different from the ordinary people who respected the emperor and pledged loyalty to him.

The Tayamas were members of the clan of Akimoto near Tokyo. Tayama's father became a policeman in Tokyo after the Meiji Restoration of 1868. However, at the beginning of the Meiji government, there existed neither a modern military system nor a policing system. The civil war in 1877 was caused by discontented former *samurai* who engineered the greatest revolt in the early Meiji period. Even though he was officially a policeman, Katai's father fought in the war. He died in battle and was deified in Shōkonsha, literally the shrine to call and give rest to the spirits of the war dead (in 1879 it was renamed Yasukuni shrine). Although he was the second son, Katai was very conscious that he was a member of a war-bereaved family, a member of the Tayamas whose head had died for the sake of the state. In the book, he describes his own young feelings: 'Whenever I took a walk in the precinct of Shōkonsha, I always heard my own inner voice saying that I would be a great man soon; I could not but be a great man' (Tayama, 1917, p.69).

Professional soldiers and anyone who died in battle might be enshrined in Yasukuni. But the criteria determining who was to be enshrined were unclear. Generally speaking, only those who died a glorious death in battle for the sake of the emperor were enshrined. After World War II, the separation of religion (Shinto) and the state was instituted. Yasukuni shrines are now run by a private religious body. The emperor is no longer the highest priest of national Shinto. But freedom of religious belief, and the independence of the civil realm from the state, are not yet adequately realized in Japan. For example, since the war, whenever a prime minister plans to visit the Yasukuni shrine for a memorial service, his attendance becomes the focus of serious debate. Of course, if he attended a memorial service as a private citizen, not as the prime minister, there would be no problem. Thus, the late prime minister Ōhira once decided to visit the shrine as a private person. Ironically, he was a Christian who was not obliged to do so.

Since 1954, when Japan obtained 'defence forces', the soldiers who have died during military training have been semi-officially enshrined in the Gokoku shrine in their native prefecture. The Gokoku shrine is a prefectural Yasukuni shrine. On one occasion, however, the Christian wife of a dead soldier objected to her husband's enshrinement in the Gokoku shrine in Yamaguchi prefecture. She sued the defence agency and the association of veterans, both of which insisted that enshrining soldiers who died for the sake of the state was a matter of public concern, regardless of whether they and/or their wives were believers in the Shinto religion. Eventually the defence agency won the case. The Supreme Court dismissed the woman's suit for the expressed reason that enshrinement of her husband's soul in the Gokoku shrine was essentially the private business of the association of veterans, and was not incompatible with her religion. Enshrinement in a Gokoku shrine is a step towards enshrinement in a Yasukuni shrine.

After the war, the new Japanese constitution of 1946 renounced both war and the divinity of the emperor. However, it declared the emperor still to be the symbol of the state and of the unity of the people. According to the constitution the Japanese people could not exist without the emperor. Thus, the emperor, the war dead, and the Yasukuni shrine have remained closely related. Consequently, in Japan the nationalist stance is also accompanied by a religious and conservative stance. These elements are also associated with the military. When we consider the three pairs, nationalism vs. internationalism, religious orientation vs. secular orientation, and property rights vs. human rights, we find in Japan only two combinations of positions: nationalism, religious (Shinto) orientation and property rights, on the one hand, opposed to internationalism, secular orientation and human rights on the other. It should not be thought that these opposing stances align with the opposition between traditionalism and modernization. In Japan modernization from above coexists with nationalism, militarism and the *tennōsei* ideology. Furthermore, technological development occurred alongside the negation of freedom, equality and human rights. We should not naively assume that the modernization process is always accompanied by democracy and peace, rather than by militarism and nationalism.

In *Shosai no Mado* (April, 1987) Atsuko Takashima, a sociolinguist, wrote an essay on 'The role of English teaching'. She stated that when learning a foreign language it is very useful to know what things native speakers hold in high regard and value. She also pointed out how, in general, English speaking peoples' respect for independence and equal human relationships is reflected in their terms and customs, and how these contrast with Japanese terms and customs (Takashima, 1987, p. 46). According to Takashima, English speaking people value freedom, equality and individualism, whereas authoritarianism, discrimination, familyism and collective factionalism are esteemed in Japan. (Takashima, 1987, pp. 48–9).

Takashima also mentioned Yukichi Fukuzawa, one of Japan's most enlightened scholars, who more than a hundred years ago referred to the concepts of reciprocity and equality which, according to Takashima, did not exist in Japan. She promoted Fukuzawa's opinions, strongly urging that Japan should reform its tradition of overemphasizing the virtues of social relationships in order to become a truly civilized nation. Takashima believed that one of the great goals of teaching English is to change the values of the Japanese along the lines of the forgotten Fukuzawa (Takashima, 1987, p. 49). Masao Maruyama's book, *Reading Fukuzawa's An Outline of a Theory of Civilization* (1982), presents a similar, although more sophisticated, viewpoint.

The *Ie* Ideology and the *Tennōsei* Ideology

Some have argued that Japan's wars of aggression would not have happened had there been civilian control of the military and had civil society been matured by the development of modernization. However, if such arguments are correct, there could not have been a war of aggression waged against Vietnam by the United States, as the American people enjoy civil control over the military.

In Japan the major force which promoted war was monopoly capital, and the *tennōsei* ideology was used to mobilize the people for wars of aggression. Those who might have been reluctant to fight in foreign countries on behalf of a *zaibatsu*, went willingly to the front in the name of the emperor. It was the *zaibatsu* who were most enthusiastic in building up the myth of the emperor and using it for their own profit. For this reason, as Mark Gayn wrote in his *Japan Diary*, millions of *yen* were used to support the Shinto shrines, to underwrite propaganda and to promote movements which planned the great mission of Japan.

After the war, some big business people such as Aiichiro Fujiyama tried to represent themselves as part of the forces for peace, and to shift the responsibility for the war and war crimes on to the right-wingers, militarists and bureaucrats. In his *Autobiography* Fujiyama wrote:

> The majority of the business community is of the opinion that they did not cooperate voluntarily with the military authorities, but were forced to serve them. Indeed, most people of the business world opposed war with the United States from the very outset. No one supported the war with the U.S., such consciousness was revived after the war ended. Therefore, businessmen believed that when the American army occupied Japan, the militarists and the policemen would be blamed but not them. Even after the purge directive orders were issued, businessmen thought that they would be spared.
>
> Ryōzō Asano, a president of Asano Cement Corporation, who studied in an American university and had many American friends, never imagined that he would become a target of the purge and believed that he would be utilized by the American army of occupation. There were many others like him. When the war was over, businessmen in Karuizawa raised a champagne toast to the end of the war celebrating 'the coming of our businessman's age' (cited in Nakase, 1967, p. 10).

In the 1960s Japanese business confidence revived. It emphasized the unique features of Japanese management and business practice, whose spiritual ground is emperor-centric, advocating absolute obedience to the emperor enroute to the miracle of economic growth. Hajime Maeda, a managing director of Nikkeiren (the Japan Federation of Employers Associations) wrote in an article entitled 'To ensure the first year of stable economic development':

> Among the living, the living god, the emperor, is the object
> of reverence and obedience instead of gods in heaven. He
> is a descendant of the sun goddess, Amaterasu Ōmikami, and
> belongs to an unbroken line of emperors. The belief in
> absolute obedience to the emperor comes not only from the
> idea of heaven worship but also from the idea of the pure
> blood of the Japanese nation. The purity and homogeneity
> of the Japanese nation, which has never experienced
> mixed blood with alien nations, is the basis of emperor
> centerism.
>   Meiji Japan won the great victories of the Sino-Japanese
> and Russo-Japanese wars internationally, and achieved
> economic development and national prosperity domestically.
> Although the causes of the great victories owe much to both
> military and economic powers, the main drive to make
> manifest these powers is the thought of emperor-centerism,
> the thought of dying for the country and the spirits of fortitude
> and manliness.
>   After all, we are neither American nor European. We are
> Japanese forever. Even though they are small, the four
> islands are our own territory. Within this territory, the
> Japanese nation which is not mixed with alien nations places
> the emperor at its centre and makes this a foundation of
> national consciousness. This is a national trait which does
> not exist in other foreign countries. Under these
> circumstances, economic growth and the development of
> business enterprises are possible. If this fact could be
> admitted, then the Japanese way of management and the
> proper stance of the manager would be automatically
> understood by all (Maeda, 1964, pp. 16–17).

These remarks vividly illustrate the Japanese business community's nationalism. In coupling loyalty to the emperor with
loyalty to the enterprise, the idea of the family state emerges. It
is in this manner that Japanese capitalists have taken advantage
of the *tennōsei* ideology.

John Dower, an American scholar specializing in modern
Japanese history, wrote an article in a Sunday issue of the

Washington Post (5 October, 1986) reminding readers of the wartime slogan: 'One hundred million people should have one mind under the aegis of the emperor'. If all Japanese were the newborn infants (*sekishi*) of the emperor, their minds would be as the emperor's and hence as one.

The Japanese people believed in their own superiority which was owing to their supposed divine lineage. The concept of divinity was denied by the emperor himself, who pointed to the loss of the war. The renunciation of war in the new constitution is related closely to the emperor's renunciation of divinity. On 1 January 1946, immediately after the war, Emperor Hirohito made a declaration in which he acknowledged that he was human, not a god incarnate. The 1889 constitution of the Empire of Japan stated the emperor was sacred and inviolable. But in 1946 Emperor Hirohito repudiated 'the false conception that the emperor is divine and that the Japanese people are superior to other races and fated to rule the world'.

The concept of *kokutai* was used by the Meiji government to establish and affirm the centralized modern Japanese state while underscoring Japanese uniqueness. Hirofumi Itō, at a meeting of the Privy Council in 1888, explained the draft constitution of the Japanese Empire as follows:

> In Japan religion is too weak to be an axis of the state;
> Buddhism flourished once and was supported by the people
> but it is now declining; Shinto is not strong enough to win
> the hearts of the people as other religions, even though it
> emphasizes the importance of ancestor worship and celebrates
> forefathers. Thus, the only thing remaining to be the focus
> of the Japanese nation is the Imperial household. In the draft,
> therefore, I utilize the sovereignty of the emperor and try
> not to restrict it (cited in Hashikawa, 1962, p. 105).

When the *kokutai* of an unbroken line of sovereignty is emphasized, the Imperial household is deemed to have genealogical ties with each household of the nation. However, under the stem family system, each lineage group sees itself as unconnected with the Imperial household and its unbroken line. There is a similar dilemma presented in Chie Nakane's characterization of Japanese society as an hierarchical society which is also comprised of vertical relationships. According to Nakane, in Japanese society it is not horizontal relationships such as between managers and workers which are predominant, but vertical relationships such as those between company A and company B. Yet she fails to explain how these could constitute an integrated whole such as that in an hierarchical society.

Under the Asiatic mode of production, families are parts of the larger compound family whose property passes through the male line. Succession to the position of patriarch is by virtue of authentic genealogical descent from the divine founder of the line. However, this genealogical relationship can have fictitious components: the relationship between parent and child is often sociological. Originally, 'parent' in Japanese meant the leader of a cooperative work group (the extended family), and 'child' meant a follower. As the genealogical relation legitimates rule, that actual domination may be legitimated by appeal to the fictitious genealogical relationship.

In the Pacific war, the establishment of the Great East Asian Co-prosperity Sphere was regarded as bringing the whole world under one roof through lineage inclusion of the Japanese nation. Expansion by invasion was thought to be merely a spatial expansion of the lineage relationship. Thus, *kokutai* grows and becomes a whole cosmos or world. Consequently *kokutai* is synonymous with heaven and earth. In 1937, the Ministry of Education published *Kokutai no Hongi* (The National Entity of Japan), in which the concept is explained as follows:

> The unbroken line of emperors, receiving the Oracle of the Founder of the Nation, reigns eternally over the Japanese empire. This is our eternal and immutable *kokutai*. Thus, founded on this great principle, all the people united as one great family nation in heart, and obeying the Imperial will, enhance the beautiful view of loyalty and filial piety. This is the glory of our *kokutai*. This *kokutai* is the eternal and unchanging basis of our nation and shines resplendent throughout our history. Moreover its solidarity is proportionate to the growth of the nation and is, together with heaven and earth, without end. We must, to begin with, know with what active brilliance this fountainhead shines within the reality of the founding of our nation (Hall, 1949, p. 5).

Patriotism was identified by loyalty to the emperor: 'Our country originates with the emperor who is a descendant of Amaterasu . . . Obedience means casting ourselves aside and serving the emperor intently'. To take this path of loyalty is, for the subject, the sole way in which we legitimately live a life of our own, and the fountainhead of all energy. Hence, offering ourselves for the sake of the emperor does not mean self sacrifice, but the casting aside of our little selves to live under his august grace and the enhancing of the genuine life of the people of a state (Hall, 1949, p. 80).

The Ministry of Education book emphasized that our country is a land of divinities, governed by an emperor who is a deity incarnate; that the deities enshrined in Shinto shrines are the Imperial ancestors, ancestors of the clans descended from the heavenly deities or the Imperial family, and divine spirits who serve to guard and maintain the prosperity of the Imperial throne. These ideas led people to believe that 'all functions of the Shinto shrines are rendered by the emperor to the Imperial ancestors; and it is in this that we find the basis of our national reverence for the deities' (Hall, 1949, p. 141).

The authors of *Kokutai no Hongi* emphasized that to worship and deify ancestors intently is a form of service to the emperor. In *The Way of the Subject*, published by the Ministry of Education in July 1941, it was stressed that the worship of gods and ancestors manifests our submissiveness to the origin of our life, and is the basis of respect for the *ie* or family. We can be united in one – that is, in the emperor – through reverence for the gods. Just as the spirits of household ancestors are deified by their living relatives and guard their descendants, so the spirits of those sacrificed for the state are deified by the state and guard the nation. Ancestor worship in the household is related to emperor worship in the state, and the idea of the guardian gods of the state and its defence (*gokoku*) is connected with the protection of ancestor worship and the gods of the family.

The Yasukuni Shrine and the Traditional Service for the Repose of Souls

I would like to begin this section by citing the record of a round table conversation between mothers, all of whom were over sixty, who lost their sons in battle in northern China in 1937. In 1939, they went to Tokyo from Kanazawa where the 9th division was stationed, to attend a special festival at the Yasukuni shrine. The following conversation is recorded:

Saitō: My son eagerly wished that when he was called up for military service, he could willingly offer his life for the emperor. He wanted to lose no time in sacrificing himself for the sake of the state. He died a glorious death in battle in accordance with his wishes.

Morikawa: I am very thankful for seeing that the white sacred palanquin comes into the Yasukuni shrine. I am deeply indebted because the emperor makes good use of my son; otherwise he would be of no use.

Murai: We are indebted to the emperor. The emperor gives us more favour than we deserve.

Saitō: I heard that the emperor shares in our hardships and is eating boiled barley with rice because he loves us. I thought I must do something in return for his favour. When I look at the emperor I cannot help weeping with gratitude. I was able to visit the Yasukuni shrine and looked at the emperor. I have nothing to look back upon with regret. I would not regret even if I were to die now. I can die with a smile.

Nakamura: Today I am guided to the Imperial garden in Shinjuku. I am very grateful to the emperor who enshrined my son at Yasukuni and invited me to the garden.

Saitō: There are many flowers in the garden. It is very wide and beautiful like a paradise.

Takagi: My son would be pleased in the other world. He died a glorious death. I should not show weak eyes. If I cry for my son, I don't know what excuse to make to the emperor. I am cheerful every day thinking that my son died for the sake of the state.

Nakamura: That's true. I feel lonely when I think that my
son will never come back to life. But I am in high spirits when
I think that my son died for the sake of the emperor who in
turn complimented my son on his bravery (cited in
Hashikawa, 1974, pp. 195–7).

Referring to this document, Hashikawa said that he shuddered
to think of the mothers' pathetic bliss. They praise the emperor
for his benevolence and the Imperial garden for its beauty,
instead of complaining and grieving. He pointed out that 'prewar'
attitudes to the Yasukuni shrine are still alive, citing documents
written by war widows in the book *Ishizue* (A Foundation Stone),
edited by the association of the war bereaved. One widow wrote
that her teenage son was at the time at a difficult age. When
scolding him saying, 'Don't you think doing such things dis-
honours your father who died in battle?' he would always reply,
'What of death in battle?' He said that he felt humiliated whenever he was told he was a posthumous child. The mother
lamented the social atmosphere which made the meaning of her
husband's death in battle for the sake of the country so difficult
for children to understand.

In 1952 the war widows who visited the annual festival of the
Gokoku shrine in Matsue city, planned to visit the Yasukuni
shrine in Tokyo with their children. They believed that when
children came face to face with their fathers' souls, they would
understand the meaning of their fathers' death, and thereby be
inspired towards a better life. One mother wrote as follows about
her friend who visited the Yasukuni shrine with her eldest son:

She tells me with tearful eyes that the visit has been very
significant and she is thankful for it. She says that her son
became gentle and now joins his hands and prays at the family
Buddhist altar. Before his visit, he would become angry
when she mentioned his father's death in battle.

These war widows were not influenced by the ideas of militarism
or ultranationalism. Nor did they intend to glorify war. After the
war the Japanese tended to repudiate all kinds of war and felt
that the war dead had died in vain. Some Japanese base their
judgement of wartime attitudes and behaviour on the ease and

rapidity of Japan's defeat by the Allied Powers. However, it cannot be denied that those who died in battle did actually die for the sake of the nation. They all died for public reasons and a public cause, not for private ones. Given this fact, all Japanese still bear some responsibility for the war victims and must make sense of their death.

It should not be overlooked that in the fall of 1978, the Yasukuni shrine was secretly made sacred to the memory of fourteen A class war criminals including former prime minister Hideki Tōjō. The criteria for enshrinement were determined by the state in the prewar period, but at that time were set by the Yasukuni shrine's religious body. However, the state still decided who deserved to be enshrined and who did not, regardless of reputation. Thus, the state, for its own reasons, can enshrine those who, because of their behaviour before death, are not worthy of the gods.

According to Shigeyoshi Murakami, the author of *Kokka Shinto*, there was a tradition in pre-feudal Japan of holding a memorial service in honour of the war dead of both sides. People believed that the spirits of the war dead should be consoled and given repose. This tradition was abandoned after the Meiji Restoration, the state then not only distinguished between allies and opponents, but also between those who deserved to become sacred and those who did not. A new way of celebrating the memorial service for the war dead and for the repose of their souls needs to be found. We must find an alternative to the Yasukuni style of celebration.

In this regard we must stress our criticism of those who collaborated in the wars of aggression. In 1986 Yūko Suzuki in *Feminism and War: War Cooperation of the Leaders of Women's Liberation Movements*, criticized Fusae Ichikawa's support for the war: 'One cannot get out of it, once one has been drawn into the quagmire. Ichikawa who was drawn into the quagmire of the war was not able to escape from the war organization' (Suzuki, 1986 p. 135).

But it was not only Ichikawa who had been drawn into the quagmire of the war. Almost all Japanese, including the women, cooperated with the establishment to create the war organization. The Ichikawa's cooperation is an undeniable fact. As Suzuki pointed out, Ichikawa's *Readings of Wartime Women* (1943) included the following passage in its section 'Women and the

State':

> In the China war and the great East Asia war, the superiority
> of the Japanese nation has been recognized clearly and its
> position as the leader of the one billion Asian people has
> been established.
>
> To establish the great East Asia co-prosperity sphere and
> to test its sound development forever, it is important above
> all that the population of the Japanese nation further increases
> and its resources will be reinforced.
>
> The government published in 1941 *The Outline of
> Population Policies* as one of the most important national
> policies. According to it, the status of women, as the mothers
> of the Japanese nation, was recognized for the first time and
> the state asked women for their cooperation.
>
> To give birth and to raise children are now no longer the
> private task of the mother or her family but a public task
> for the country and the Japanese nation. As the gender who
> can give birth, we are pleased and proud of it.
>
> To answer the demands of the state, we women now are
> conscious of our role as mothers of the nation. . . . It is the
> service which only women can provide and is the most
> important contribution to Empire (cited in Suzuki, 1986,
> pp. 128–29).

This was by no means an extreme example of Ichikawa's many
wartime writings. But while supporting the war, Ichikawa acknowledged the irony that the war itself undermined the basis of
male supremacy. In 1943 she also criticized the prime minister's
statement that the 'drafting of women is not carried out because
it tends to undermine the Japanese family system. Women should
work voluntarily'. Ichikawa stated that if a female labour force
was necessary for the state to increase productivity, the state
should recruit it. She wondered how, if recruitment undermined
the family system, one could ensure that voluntary work would
not.

The war dead had thought and behaved no differently from
the ordinary Japanese. In the summer of 1985, the *Asahi* newspaper took a survey of members of the veterans' association in
Wakamatsu city in Fukushima, asking, 'Frankly speaking, how

did you feel when you went to battle?' Sixty per cent of 289 respondents felt they were obliged to do so. Twenty-nine per cent answered that they went willingly. Eight per cent gave other answers. It is noteworthy that only three per cent of the veterans answered that they had been very reluctant.

Sociology of War

Chōmin Nakae wrote *A Discourse on Government by Three Drunkards* in 1887. Three characters appeared in this book: the Gentleman of Western Learning, the Champion and Master Nankai.

At first the Gentleman said that:

if a small nation which is lagging behind the other civilizations were to stand up proudly on the edge of Asia, plunge into the realm of liberty and brotherhood, demolish fortresses, melt down cannons, convert warships into merchant ships, turn soldiers into civilians, devote itself to mastering moral principles, study industrial techniques, and become a true student of philosophy, wouldn't the European nations who take pride in their civilization feel ashamed? Suppose, however, those great nations are not only unashamed but also stubborn and villainous, and suppose they impudently invade our country, taking advantage of our disarmament. What could they do if we have not an inch of steel nor a single bullet about us, but instead greet them with civility? (Nakae, 1984, pp. 50–1)

Nakae wrote in the margin that national defence was the height of stupidity. Then upon hearing these words, the Champion said to the Gentleman, 'Have you lost your senses?' The Champion believed armaments were a measure of a nation's wealth and war was 'a measure of the strength of each nation's civilization': 'When two nations are about to engage in war, the one with superior learning and greater willpower surely shall win because it has superior weapons' (Nakae, 1984, p. 90).

The Champion stood for expansionism and recommended the

161

invasion of other Asian countries, especially China:

> My first proposal is to gather all able bodied men of the land
> and move into that big country. By seizing it, we would
> change our nation from small to large, from a weak to a
> strong one, and from a poor to a rich one. Then we'll pay
> a huge sum of money to buy the fruits of civilization, and
> with one bound will enter into competition with the
> European nations (Nakae, 1984, p. 115).

According to him, since a small nation cannot afford that purchase, it must seize a big country by force and thereby make
itself rich. Fortunately, by the grace of heaven, right before us
is a large country whose soil is fertile and whose soldiers are
weak – 'Could we possibly have better luck?' (Nakae, 1984,
p. 103).

Nakae contrasted the Gentleman's belief in democracy and
pacifism with the Champion's militarism and expansionism. The
Gentleman idealistically embraced modern thought, while the
Champion realistically insisted on expansion based on nationalism. From the Meiji restoration until 1945 Japanese leaders
always chose the use of aggression and repudiated democracy
and pacifism. However, after World War II a defeated Japan lost
all its colonies, its emperor renounced divinity and, in accordance
with the constitution, was disarmed and renounced war. But,
since the latter half of the 1950s, Japan has nonetheless experienced miraculous economic growth through 'study [of] industrial
techniques'. Thus, the Gentleman's view is to some extent vindi-
cated today.

Yukichi Fukuzawa's arguments in *Encouragement of Learning*
are also worth noting. He identified three courses of action open
to people under a tyrannical government: (1) obedience; (2)
armed resistance; and (3) martyrdom in the cause of justice. In
Fukuzawa's view martyrdom was the preferable course of action;
thus he admired those who had sacrificed their lives upholding
the principles of justice:

> There is a danger that resistance against the government by
> force of arms will destroy a hundred things in pursuit of one
> goal, but rational persuasion will sweep out those evils that
> should be eliminated.

He opposed the second course precisely because he believed violence achieved nothing. If a political faction tried to violently overthrow the government, it would need a greater armed force than the government. Thus, what becomes important is which side has the more power not which side is right. Even if such a political group were to succeed in overthrowing a tyrannical government, it would thereby merely substitute one form of violence for another. He insisted that persuasion should replace the use of violence. He was convinced that civil wars were not the purpose of civilization, because 'civilization means to advance the level of intelligence and virtue of the people, so that each and every person can be the master of his own affairs in his dealing with society' (Fukuzawa, 1968, p. 48).

This is even more true in our time, with a nuclear arms race between the superpowers. The large nuclear powers have engaged in an endless nuclear arms race on the assumption that if you don't want to be attacked with nuclear weapons, you should have more or better nuclear weapons than your opponents. There remains no other way but persuasion to abolish nuclear weapons.

In Hiroshima there is a monument with the words 'Please sleep peacefully; we shall never repeat this mistake'. In the Japanese language, the subject has been omitted, and there has been heated debate as to what the subject actually was. Because it does not make any sense to assume that it is either 'we Japanese' or 'we Americans', it has been said that it is 'we humans'. The victims of the atomic bomb, I believe, would opt for the latter interpretation. Thus, the message is directed not only to one's opponent but also to oneself.

It should be noted that the family-as-state ideology was established after the Russo-Japanese war. Before that, the doctrines of survival of the fittest and the right of the strongest were used to legitimize aggressive wars. For instance, Hiroyuki Katō delivered a lecture, 'Japanese and Russian fates from the vantage point of the theory of social evolution', in which he made a distinction between 'in group' and 'out group' in their struggle for survival, saying that 'the group which has strong solidarity and friendly relationships is stronger than the group which has less solidarity and contains more conflict relationships'. Japan is the fitter, he claimed, and Russia the unfitter. He contrasted the

163

virtues and strengths of Japan with the weaknesses of Russia as follows:

Japan	Russia
1 The people enthusiastically dedicate themselves to loyalty and patriotism.	1 Occasionally people try to revolt and destroy the state and overthrow the Imperial household.
2 Constitutional government is established and public opinion is respected.	2 Despotic government is established and public opinion is suppressed.
3 In regard to rights and duties, there is no distinction between the nobility and the people.	3 The powers of the nobility oppress the people.
4 Japan strives for peace, while trying to attain her own interests.	4 Russia destabilizes the world in pursuing her own interests.
5 Education and other civilized institutions are better.	5 Education and other civilized institutions are poorer.
6 Adheres to international laws in her military and diplomatic behaviour.	6 Does not mind violating international laws in military and diplomatic behaviour.
7 Attitudes towards the great powers are gentlemanly.	7 Attitudes toward the great powers are barbaric.
8 Japan's strengths enable her to survive and prosper in the coming years.	8 Russia's weakness will cause her to decline in the coming years (Katō, 1904, pp. 87–9).

Katō also held that there were no morals or laws between nations. Therefore, in the revolt of the 'outs' the final determinant is force. He also claimed that 'the fittest country is one that while keeping abreast of the world tries to pursue her own interests adroitly' (Katō, 1904, p. 56). (One should note that in this period he did not yet rely on the arguments that Japan was a divine land or that Japan was ruled by the emperor whose line is unbroken forever.) Nevertheless, he was also the first to distinguish between 'good' and 'bad' survival of the fittest, the latter being that which results in disadvantage for the hierarchical ordering of the family and society.

After the Russo-Japanese war, the *tennōsei* ideology became dominant among members of the Japanese Sociological Society. Tongo Tatebe, professor and chairman of the Department of Sociology at Tokyo Imperial University, tabled a 'research paper' at the annual meeting in 1914, in which he advocated a sociology for a strong nation as follows:

> Our national policy was determined by the oracle of the founder in heaven which was granted on the occasion of the descent to earth of the Imperial grandchild: 'The land of the plentiful reed plains, of the thousand-autumns and long five-hundred-autumn fresh rice-ears. This is the land over which our grandchildren are to reign. Go thou, Imperial grandchild, who shall reign over it. Go thou free of trouble. As endless as heaven and earth shall the Imperial Throne prosper'. The national polity of the Japanese Empire is well expressed by the phrase 'to guard and maintain the prosperity of the Imperial Throne which is coequal with heaven and earth'. For us as subjects, the only problem is how we can ensure this prosperity. . . . In the period of international competition, if we want to guard and maintain the prosperity of the Imperial Throne which is coequal with heaven and earth, we must make Japan a first-class power. To be a first-class power, Japan must have a population of at least one billion. Thus, our national policy demands the expansion of her territory (Tatebe, 1915, pp. 112–14).

As Shinobu Ōe has pointed out in his book *The Yasukuni Shrine*, the oracle is not mentioned in *Nihonshoki*; and in *Kojiki* it appears only as 'the land of the plentiful reed plains is the land you must rule. Descend to it according to my order', and 'the land of the fresh rice-ears has been entrusted to you as the land you are to rule. In accordance with the command, descend from the heavens!' (Ōno, 1968, pp. 137–8). There was no mention of 'the prosperity of the Imperial Throne which is coequal with heaven and earth'.

When the emperor-as-an-organ theory appeared in 1935, the

government made a statement clarifying the national polity in which *kokutai* was defined according to the oracle in which the expression 'to guard and maintain the prosperity of the Imperial Throne which is coequal with heaven and earth' occurred. The declaration maintained the sovereign power of the great Empire of Japan was held by the emperor, and that it would be contrary to the *kokutai*, which was unique to Japan, to state that the emperor was not sovereign but only an organ for the exercise of power.

In 1916 the Japanese Sociological Association established a research committee composed of seven members, including Tatebe. It published a basic plan for the education of the empire, in which the role of sociologists in a strong nation was also set out. In this program for the education of a strong nation, five principles were given:

1 One must respect and guard the Imperial household;
2 One must respect his household;
3 One must cultivate industry and the enterprising spirit;
4 One must acquire practical knowledge;
5 One must form and maintain warmhearted social bonds.

Under (2) it was said that 'the social unit of our nation is not the individual but the household (*ie*) . . . the individualistic society is one which tends to collapse'. This same argument appears in the *Kokutai no Hongi*:

> the basis of the nation's livelihood is, as in the Occident, neither the individual nor husband and wife. It is the household . . . The life of a family in our country is not confined to the present life of a household of parents and children, but begins with distant ancestors, perpetuated for ever by its descendants (Hall, 1949, pp. 87–8).

Further on it was added that Japan was a great family nation, and that the Imperial household was the head family of all Japanese subjects and the nucleus of national life. Thus, subjects revered the Imperial household with the tender esteem they had for their ancestors and, in turn, the emperor loved his subjects as his children (Hall, 1949, pp. 89–90).

In *The Way of Subjects*, it was emphasized that our nation was a family and that belief in *kokutai* was cultivated through the household, which was the embodiment of an eternal entity including ancestors and descendants. Thus, 'to be human is to be Japanese, and to be Japanese is to act according to the way of the subject and the way of the empire'. The way of the subject is that in which a hundred million people sacrifice themselves to the emperor, thus following the spirits of the gods who manifested themselves on the occasion of the first emperor's descent to earth.

Finally I would like to cite an example of the way in which the state-as-family ideology was presented in the field of sociology in academic disguise. Teizō Toda, a professor at Tokyo Imperial University, and family sociologist who had visited the U.S. in his youth to study empirical research methods, had made empirical studies of the modern Japanese nuclear family in the 1920s. But in the 1930s he began to change his stance. In 1942 he published *The Way of the Household*, in which he said that our task was not to earn money but to serve the country unselfishly. In ancient Japan, the clan was the work unit through which one devoted oneself to the emperor. This spirit of the clan had been replaced by the spirit of the household (Toda, 1942 p. 203). Thus, Toda insisted that the way of the household was to realize the spirit of the New Order of the Great East Asian Co-prosperity Spheres. The unification of all the souls of the world was to be based on the will of the emperor who wished to make the entire world household his domain. The expansion of the national household would realize world peace and give each nation a respectable status in the world. To achieve this, Japan had to eliminate the root of evil which England and America and their allies served under the guise of freedom (Toda, 1942, p. 48). In his youth Toda had opposed his teacher, Tatebe, with his nationalism and support for democracy and liberalism. But by the 1930s he had surrendered to the ideology of the state-as-family.

Toda's sociology became completely bankrupt when Japan was defeated by the Allied Powers. But after more than forty years, advocates of the old ultra-nationalism have again come to the fore. For example, a few years ago NHK broadcast a TV drama based on Toyoko Yamazaki's novel *Futatsu no Sokoku* (The Two Fatherlands). In this book the author justified Japanese ultra-nationalism by using as her hero a second-generation Japanese American. Even though the hero, Kenji Amou, was an officer of the occupation army, he was described as Japanese because

167

'Japanese blood flows' in his body. Thus, when he became a monitor for the International War Tribunal held in Tokyo from 1946 to 1947, the author made him write in a note that the 'atomic bomb and war criminals are made in the USA'. He also attacked the Japanese newspapers which regarded attorney Kiyose's opening statement as 'reactionary'. Amou thought Japanese newspapers unprincipled because while only recently they had made General Tōjō a hero, now that the Allied Powers occupied Japan, they cringed before GHQ and described Tōjō as a war criminal and promoted arguments for the elimination of Japanese imperialism. He criticized an editorial which said:

> On 24 February, 1947, Dr Kiyose held the views which were
> the basis of the defense for most of the accused. But it
> should be emphasized that these are only an ideal of old
> Japanese leaders and are not advocated by present
> Japanese . . . The terms 'all-the-world-one-family' and 'the
> Great East Asia Co-prosperity Spheres' and their associated
> justificatory rhetoric would lead us into this nightmare . . .
> Of course, today's Japanese cannot accept the argument that
> the Imperial way is nothing but democracy. If there had been
> true democracy, how could we explain the ascendancy of
> the military?

Yamazaki said through the vehicle of Amou that this was not a newspaper editorial but a case for the prosecution; one should not have forgotten that it was not only the accused but the whole Japanese nation (including the mass media) which was on trial. However, while no American could deny the newspaper's arguments, Kenji Amou rejected them because he had become aware of his 'Japanese blood'.

At the outbreak of the Pacific war, Amou had buried an old sword in the backyard of his home in Boyle Heights. During a break in the Tribunal proceedings, he returned to Boyle Heights to dig up the sword. At the time he had buried it, he had felt he had severed his bonds with Japan; upon recovering the sword Amou feels he has 'firmly reestablished his bonds with Japan' and simultaneously 'feels an upsurge of Japanese blood in him'. Thus, Yamazaki affirmed the mythical importance of Japanese blood.

The intention of the book's author was clear. Yamazaki

regarded the 'essential Japaneseness' as being the emperor system and the Imperial way. According to her, the people's sovereignty, human rights, international peace and the renunciation of war, were not part of the 'essential Japaneseness', and that the people who accepted such ideas were not real Japanese.

Arguments about Japanese culture are advanced in support of the 'good' Japanese tradition of patriarchal order. These arguments rest on the premise that Japanese loyalty toward the emperor is central, and that Japan's wars of aggression since the Meiji Restoration could be justified by the 'unique Japanese blood' and the emperor system. To counter these arguments we must develop alternatives and establish new arguments in favour of a Japanese culture based on the goals of peace and democracy.

8 Japanese Capitalism and the Extended Family System – Modernization and Tradition in a Local Community

Introduction

Social scientists in Japan tend to regard Japanese modernization as atypical or distorted compared with that of the West. It is true that the development of capitalism in Japan did not completely transcend traditional community structures such as the household and village. Furthermore, the Japanese have a communal religious ethos not found in the West. Therefore in Japan the development of capitalism did not encourage individualism and privatization but rather collectivism and socialization. Within the emperor system, which is the context of Japanese modernization, we can observe the simultaneous creation of tradition.

This chapter examines the relationship between the development of the Katakura Silk Company of the Suwa lake area and the Katakura extended family system. The example of the silk-reeling industry is discussed because an indigenous and spontaneous type of industrialization occurred in the Japanese silk industry.

No matter how modernization is defined it is clear that Japanese modernization occurred after Commodore Perry travelled to Uraga in 1853. Following the Treaty of Peace and Amity in 1854, the 1858 Treaty of Amity and Commerce between Japan and the U.S.A. was concluded. Subsequently, while Japan's cotton industry declined because of the importation of cheaper cotton thread, the silk industry thrived through foreign trade.

Modernization in the Suwa lake region began with the development of the silk industry. After the Meiji Restoration in 1868, the newly established government bought machines from technologically advanced countries and established government factories. It hired Western engineers and trained Japanese workers to develop an indigenous modern industrial system. The government bought spinning machinery, established a government silk factory in Tomioka in Gunma prefecture near Tokyo in 1872 and hired a French engineer at the same salary as the then Japanese prime minister. It would be naive to believe that once the machinery was introduced rational organization would develop automatically. Machines, raw materials, and workers are the means of production. When machinery was introduced from the West, it was imperative to establish a free labour force and to provide the raw material. But in Japan private capitalists in the silk industry tried to disassemble the machines and to build new ones that could be used in household businesses.

In England, where a massive free labour force was available and capitalists could organize rational labour groups, labourers worked in order to get money for their labour. In Japan there were neither capitalists nor labourers in the Western sense. Village and household communities still existed even after Meiji Restoration. The Japanese silk industry was at this time a domestic industry, there being no large modern industrial organization in Japan. Early capitalists in the silk industry first developed silk production as a domestic industry based on the family system. Initially the silk reeling industry was conducted by small nuclear families, but as the scale of business and management increased, production was carried out by the larger extended family.

For peasants living at the end of the feudal era, the silk industry was a secondary business. Before Japan opened to the West, silk and cotton were spun into yarn to form the raw material for woven textiles. However, the silk that was spun when trade with the West commenced was mostly exported. It had been assumed that when products multiplied and the production scale increased, wealthy farmers would hire labourers and introduce Western machinery, beginning capitalist enterprises. Traditional assumptions did not apply in the Japanese situation. When Japan borrowed Western technology it had also to develop the materials and labour that suited the technology. Machinery alone will not cause the development of a rational capitalist organization. The scholar must identify the indigenous factors which could cause this rationalization.

Robert Bellah sought these factors in the motivation for the development of Japanese capitalism. He concluded that Buddhism played a positive role in Japanese modernization, just as

Puritanism did in the West. But he later revised this view. In the 'Introduction to the Paperback Edition' of his *Tokugawa Religion*, he says:

> the book's weakness . . . came from my unwillingness to face
> the defects of the Japanese pattern or to count the costs that
> Japanese modernization would exact . . . However, the
> greatest weakness of the book has nothing to do with Japan
> but with a weakness in the modernization theory I was using:
> I failed to see that the endless accumulation of wealth and
> power does not lead to the good society but undermines the
> conditions necessary for any viable society at all (Bellah,
> 1985, p. xviii).

Bellah abandoned his early assumption that modernization in opposition to tradition was itself a desirable goal, and now believed that maintenance of tradition should be the goal, while modernization was merely a means to this end. Should modernization weaken tradition, he insisted, it must be checked.

Historical Background

Japanese Marxists tried to apply Marx's feudal land rent theories to Japanese rural villages. Marx identified three kinds of feudal rent, defined according to the method of payment: in labour, produce or money. The oldest form was labour rent where, for example, a serf in Europe had to work on his master's farm three days a week, and so could cultivate his own plot of land only on the remaining three days (excluding Sunday). However, whereas in Europe a serf typically had a small family, in Japan dependent peasants were included in their master's large extended family.

Kizaemon Aruga, a prominent Japanese rural sociologist much influenced by Kunio Yanagida, studied the Japanese landlord and household systems. In Japan small family farming only began in the seventeenth century. Before that time the farming unit had been a large extended household in which an *oya* was the leader and all other members of the extended family were the followers, *ko*. Aruga has argued that there had been no labour rent in the

Japanese land system, and that even after the Meiji Restoration, when landlords cultivated their land and enlarged their household labour force, each such estate still consisted of a large extended family. In a postscript to his *Japanese Household System and Tenant System* (1943), Aruga said that:

> As for the formation of Japanese capitalism, many Japanese scholars tend to think that only the developmental form of Western capitalism is universal. Even people who try to find phenomena unique to Japan tend to regard Japanese capitalism as a later development or atypical distorted form . . . We must look at capitalism taking into account two factors: one is its economic function and the other is the characteristic social relationships which exist under capitalism. Unless one can study the relationship between these two, one cannot understand Japanese capitalism . . . In the book the author studied the extended Japanese household system in rural areas, to prepare to solve this problem. Next, the big merchant families should be considered, because the development of Japan's capitalist economy was only possible through the development of the big merchant family into large company organizations (Aruga, 1943, postscript, p. 2).

One should note that Aruga focused on landlords and the privileged merchants and neglected entrepreneurs and wealthy farmers. It is unfortunate that he did not mention the development of the silk reeling industry in the Suwa lake area as a large extended family business. Aruga was born in that area in 1889 and entered Suwa High School in 1909. One of the main enterprises of the region was the silk reeling industry represented by Katakura and Company Limited, which was a family business (like other small companies in this area). It can hardly be assumed that Aruga did not know that the Katakura extended family ran Katakura and Company Limited. It is not clear why he failed to mention the Katakura family business.

The fact that he was born an heir of a large landlord family and of the role of the village head, might be related to his underestimation of the role of peasants in the achievement of modernization. This could also explain his disregard for modernization 'from below'. Aruga presented the same argument in his last article, 'Japanese Culture and Foreign Civilizations'.

> From 1876 to 1886, many government enterprises were established. The government employed foreign engineers to teach Japanese the manufacturing process. They were to teach managers how to run the factories and train workers. The Government later sold these factories at bargain prices to the big merchants. Thus the government allowed the powerful merchants to take over the businesses and manage them as a family business.
> As I mentioned before, James Abegglen wrote that in Japan the reason capitalist production developed is unknown. In the West there are theories that the cause of the development of capitalism was a rational world view, such as Puritan ethics. In Japan it seems that the cause of capitalist development was the governmental order to develop the factory as a family business. But one should not forget the fact that the government convinced the privileged merchants that this was the way to pledge their loyalty to the new Meiji state. It is important to see that the spirit of the Meiji Era emerged through contact with international circumstances (Aruga, 1980, pp.24- 25).

It is clear that Aruga made a serious mistake in concluding that the government could establish a rational profit making organization which would later be transferred to the hands of wealthy merchants. As we will later see, it was very difficult for the private modern Japanese factories to be profitable. This was why the government needed to establish factories. The situation did not improve even after the merchants had taken over.

According to Aruga, the extended family system was only required in the case of modernization 'from above'. He neglected to consider the fact that in Japan even farmers used the household and extended household systems as models for a new factory system. They could not create a new business form from nothing. This has coloured the development of Japanese capitalism and modernity.

Table 8–1 The silk industry in the Okaya area in 1875

Villages	No. of households	Population	No. of horses	Products cocoons	raw silk
Kawagishi	456	1,974	154	400*kan*	180*kan*
Nagachi	516	2,467	10	600	360
Hirano	987	4,501	45	1,200	1,440
Minato	341	1,572	5	–	10

Note: a *kan* = 8.267lbs.

Development of the Silk Reeling Industry in the Suwa Lake Area

The total production of cocoon and raw silk did not change rapidly, even after the Meiji Restoration. The amount of raw silk produced in 1875 by the four former villages of what is now Okaya city is shown on Table 8–1. Table 8–2 shows the amounts produced in the Suwa lake area from 1881 to 1912. Clearly, the rapid development of the silk industry in this area occurred at the start of the twentieth century. As shown in Chart 8–1, there were few silk producing factories in Okaya city in 1883, and most were in Hirano village. But ten years later, new factories were established in Kawagishi village on the large Tenryū river, and this village had the greatest concentration of factories from 1893 to 1918.

Prior to the 1890s, most factories were small, and a river as small as the Yokokawa was all that was needed to turn the water wheel powering a factory's machinery. The average number of basins for boiling cocoons in a factory was then between 10 and 20. From the 1890s the scale of factories increased, with the average number of basins rising to between 100 and 150. Since production of this scale required greater power, their water wheels were driven by the larger, Tenryū river.

In Japan the mechanization of the silk industry began in 1872, when the Meiji government established a factory in Tomioka, Gunma prefecture. This factory faced great difficulties. The people of Tomioka, seeing machines for the first time, thought they must be a product of Christian magic. Moreover, it was believed that those who worked under the control of foreign engineers had their blood drained for use in the red wine that the Westerners drank. Managers of this government business also had difficulty hiring trained labourers who could operate the

175

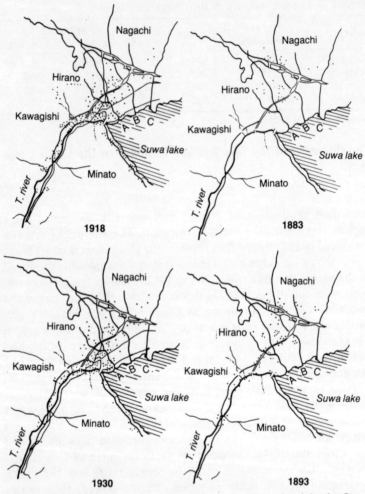

Chart 8–1 Distribution of factories (more than 10 workers) in the Suwa lake area

machinery. The Western engineers were unable to train the Japanese workers because they could not speak Japanese and were not accustomed to Japanese culture.

Red tape was also a problem. Kenso Hayami, who was the second director of the Tomioka factory, complained that officials were hampered by petty rules and thought only of protecting their own interests. It was impossible to make profits while the government imported expensive machines, paid foreign engineers

Table 8-2 Number of basins and silk produced by the workers in the Suwa areas

Year	Raw silk products	No. of basins	No. of workers	Year	Raw silk products	No. of basins	No. of workers
1881	6,661*kan*	1,369	1,602	1897	85,956*kan*	9,909	10,926
1882	6,670	1,290	1,510	1898	102,836	9,969	10,657
1883	7,274	1,301	1,522	1899	135,978	10,653	11,424
1884	11,107	1,524	1,900	1900	147,386	10,963	12,012
1885	17,966	2,242	2,622	1901	150,037	10,634	11,478
1886	24,779	2,752	3,009	1902	154,792	13,383	14,826
1887	29,427	3,159	3,696	1903	174,579	12,030	13,774
1888	41,634	4,234	4,953	1904	181,499	12,917	14,963
1889	53,252	5,352	6,262	1905	182,992	14,415	17,661
1890	70,087	7,337	8,584	1906	230,774	15,910	19,241
1891	79,392	7,452	10,445	1907	254,715	16,962	19,747
1892	102,646	8,420	10,890	1908	286,016	17,876	21,450
1893	110,133	10,883	12,881	1909	352,970	20,202	23,665
1894	144,131	13,426	14,995	1910	375,599	19,912	22,485
1895	153,657	13,499	15,110	1911	376,198	18,526	25,339
1896	126,335	12,212	12,415	1912	508,966	19,973	30,356

high salaries, hired unskilled workers and laid down troublesome bureaucratic rules.

In 1875, before becoming director, Hayami recommended to the Minister of Home Affairs, Hirofumi Itō, that the factory be transferred to private hands. Ito responded that losses were unavoidable. Hayami replied that it should not be a business hidden from the people, but rather could be a model factory which others would copy. His point was that if the government did not correct this loss, then regardless of the quality of its product, the industry would attract no interest.

The Tomioka silk factory did not make a profit, but the private sector did begin to introduce machines and establish similar factories. (The Tomioka factory had cost 198,572 *yen* to establish, and its French machines allowed for up to 300 attendant workers and handled the cocoons from the factory's 300 boiling basins.) However, while some merchants and landlords bought French and Italian machines and constructed large factories immediately after the establishment of the Tomioka factory, none of these factories continued in production. Instead, as in Okaya, new simplified machines (that were cheaply constructed with wood and tin, but based on the foreign models), were developed for use in small factories, which were linked together and powered by the factory's water mill. It was only in this last detail that mechanized spinning differed significantly from the traditional method using traditional spinning tools manipulated by seated workers.

The traditional cotton-spinning industry was seriously damaged by the importation of cheap cotton thread following the opening of Japan to trade. But later, although cotton thread was spun by machine, traditional cotton fabrics survived because Japanese favoured traditional clothes which felt good against the skin. The silk-spinning industry was developed because of rapid growth in demand from foreign countries. However, at that time silk was spun by peasant women on a wooden reeling instrument operated by one person. At the end of the Tokugawa period (in the 1850s) there were many rural silk merchants and wholesale dealers who provided peasant women with the silk cocoons and instruments for spinning thread. Additionally, some wealthy farmers hired women to work together in a cottage on their estates. Because each worker operated one spinning reel, this stage of production cannot be described as a manufacturing industry.

A Japanese history textbook pointed out that Japan's first cotton spinning mill was established by the government in 1878, and in 1886 was transferred to private ownership. In 1883 a large cotton mill using imported spinning machines and steam engines was privately established. Thereafter many merchants established large cotton mills and, by 1890, the product manufactured using domestic machines exceeded cotton imports.

While this much is accurate, the textbook later described the transfer of these government factories to the privileged merchants who organized the *zaibatsu* financial cliques. As shown in Table 8–3, Mitsui, Mitsubishi and Furukawa had mines and mills transferred to them by the government.

From this description readers might gain an impression that in the silk spinning industry, as in the other sectors, Mitsui succeeded in bringing about industrialization from above. People might also believe that the Katakura Silk Company followed a modernization process in which the initiative was taken by *zaibatsu* such as Mitsui and Mitsubishi. But in fact, the opposite was the case. The Tomioka silk spinning factory was transferred to Mitsui in 1893, but Mitsui sold it to a general partnership, Hara & Co. which in turn sold it to Katakura. In this respect, there was a great difference between the development of the silk industry and that of the cotton industry.

In the early Meiji period it was imperative for the government to introduce Western silk spinning machines, because the Western market demanded uniformly fine thread. Before the Tomioka silk factory was built, the Maebashi feudal clan established the Maebashi silk mill using an Italian designed machine in 1870, and later in the same year a private enterprise, Onogumi, established a factory in Tokyo with a similar machine that was capable of being operated simultaneously by sixty workers.

An inducement for the machine production of woven thread was the higher price it fetched, compared with the traditional tool-woven thread. The 1879 price of 100 *kin* (150 lbs) of machine woven thread was $710 while that of tool-woven thread was US$563. However the management of large factories using the Western machinery soon faced great difficulties. Mitsuru Takagi stated that the Italian silk spinning machine was first used in the Suwa lake area in 1872 by Onogumi, in its Miyamada factory (Takagi, 1975, p. 281). On this machine one hundred workers could spin thread simultaneously. But the Onogumi company went

179

Table 8-3 Main government enterprises transferred to merchants

	Enterprises	Year	Merchants	Price
Mines	Takashima Coal Mine	1874	Gotō later Mitsui	¥550,000
	Innai Silver Mine	1884	Furukawa	108,977
	Ani Copper Mine	1885	Furukawa	337,766
	Miike coal Mine	1888	Sasaki later Mitsui	4,590,439
	Sado Gold Mine	1896	Mitsubishi	} 1,730,000
	Ikuno Silver Mine	1896	Mitsubishi	
Ship-Building	Nagasaki Shipbuilding	1887	Mitsubishi	459,000
	Hyōgo Shipbuilding	1887	Mitsubishi	188,029
Cement	Fukagawa Cement Manufacture	1884	Asano	61,714
Textile	Shinmachi Cotton Mill	1887	Mitsui	150,000
	Tomioka Silk Mill	1893	Mitsui	121,460

bankrupt in 1874. In 1875 Nakayama Sha was established in Hirano village by nine persons in partnership. Its Western machines produced an output equivalent to that of 100 workers. This machine was a prototype in the Suwa style, which integrated elements of the French and Italian machines, and was modified to suit small Japanese household business. The total cost of construction for Nakayama Sha was 1,350 *yen* (an investment of 150 *yen* per partner) which may be contrasted with the 198,572 *yen* cost of the government-established Tomioka factory. The cost of construction per basin was 13.50 *yen* in Nakayama Sha, compared to 662 *yen* in Tomioka.

To understand the early conditions experienced by the silk industry in the Suwa lake area, Hirano village will be used as an example. As shown in Table 8–4, in the late nineteenth century the Hirano village had an overwhelmingly agricultural population. In 1872 the percentage of agricultural households was 82.2, but it fell to 48.1 in 1902, and 38.9 in 1912.

In Hirano village machine silk production exceeded the production of silk by traditional reeling tools in 1879. Table 8–5 shows the development of machine production in Hirano village. Although both production and the number of female workers increased in the 1890s, in general machine production did not rapidly develop.

As shown in Table 8–6 and Table 8–7, in 1879 most silk factories in the Suwa lake area were small. Factories with fewer than twenty basins comprised 80.6% of the total number, 83.3% had fewer than thirty employees and, as shown in Table 8–8, 74.1% produced less than fifty *kan* of raw silk. Therefore, we should not overestimate the amount of Western style machinery used in the Suwa lake area silk industry during the early Meiji period.

The introduction of machinery in the Suwa silk industry did not involve the development of large-scale mechanized factories, but increased in the number of small household factories. As we can see from Table 8–9 mechanized factories increased from 5 in number to 108 between 1873 and 1879. But most of these factories were small, with fewer than twenty basins and thirty employees, and produced less than fifty *kan* of silk.

Mechanization of the silk industry in the Suwa lake area was imperative not because of the need to reduce the cost of production but because of the need to make a uniform and fine thread. At that time it was impossible to profitably run a factory

Table 8–4 The change of population and occupation by household in Hirano village

Year	Population	Total	Agriculture	Household Industry	Commerce	Other
1872	4,412	972 (100)	802 (82.5)	46 (4.7)	65 (6.7)	59 (6.1)
1879	4,735	?	925	56	62	?
1892	114,069	?	1,035	?	326	?
1902	?	2,586 (100)	1,243 (48.1)	432 (16.7)	809 (31.3)	102 (3.9)
1912	37,461	3,088 (100)	1,202 (38.9)	572 (18.2)	748 (24.2)	566 (18.4)
1924	49,014	4,173 (100)	1,036 (24.8)	729 (17.5)	962 (23.1)	1,446 (34.6)
1930	53,878	6,453 (100)	722 (11.2)	2,318 (35.9)	1,568 (24.3)	1,845 (28.6)

Table 8–5 The mechanized silk factory in Hirano village

Year	Factories with 10 basins or more	No. of basins	Workers Total Number	Workers Cocoons as raw material	Silk production Amount (koku)	Silk production Money (kan)	Silk production Money (Y)
1875						1,125	Y25,000
1876						1,800	76,000
1877	30	455					
1878	57	940		455			
1879	28	655	102	940		1,638	
1880	60	941	194	655		1,882	176,000
1881	60	1,046	187	941		3,180	
1882	51	1,008	181	1,046		4,712	
1883	44	912		1,008		4,828	
1884	50	1,234		975		6,664	251,000
1885	53	1,399				8,544	299,000
1886	50	1,386					
1887	65	1,755					
1888	70	2,192					
1889	72	2,594			41,180	29,853	1,393,000
1890	84	3,362				38,223	1,401,000
1891	87	3,461				46,640	1,653,000
1892	89	3,977				57,591	2,741,000
1893	86	4,764			63,369	60,576	2,725,000
1894	106	6,176			96,238	89,038	3,828,000
1895	109	5,772			65,984	81,927	3,440,000
1896	89	5,332			73,809	70,613	3,177,000
1897	58	4,889	387	4,873		53,597	2,840,000

Note: a *koku* = 5.119 U.S. Bushels.

Table 8-6 Number of mechanized silk factories by number of basins in the Suwa lake area in 1879

No. of basins	Northern lake area villages						Plain area	Mountain area	Total
	Hirano	Kawagishi	Minato	Nagachi	Shimosuwa	Total			
10–15	7	4	3	8	4	27	16	6	49
16–20	15	1	1	4	3	23	11	4	38
21–25	1	1			1	3			3
26–30	1				1	2	2		4
31–35		2				2			2
36–40	2				3	5			5
41–45									
46–50	1					1		1	2
51–60					2	2	1		3
61–70									
71–80									
81–90									
91–100	1					1		1	1
	28	8	4	12	14	66	30	12	108

Table 8–7 Number of mechanized silk factories by number of employees in the Suwa lake area in 1879

No. of employees	Northern lake area	Plain area	Mountain area	Total
10–20	33	21	6	60
21–30	20	6	4	30
31–40	4	1		5
41–50	4	1		5
51–60	2			2
61–70		1	1	2
71–80	2			2
81–90				
91–100				
101–	1		1	2
Total	66	30	12	108

Table 8-8 Number of mechanized silk factories listed by the amount of production in 1879

Production	Northern lake area	Plain area	Mountain area	Total
5–10*kans*		1	2	3
11–20	1	8	3	12
21–30	17	6	1	24
31–40	16	6	2	24
41–50	13	4		17
51–60	4	1	1	6
61–70				
71–80	3	1	1	5
81–90	1	2	1	4
91–100	2			2
101–120	2			2
121–140	2			2
141–160	1			1
161–180	2			2
181–200				
201–250	2	1		3
251–			1	1
Total	66	30	12	108

Table 9–10 Number of mechanized silk factories by number of employees in
the Suwa lake area from 1873 to 1879

No. of employees	1873	1874	1876	1879
10–20	3	3	7	60
21–30				30
31–40				5
41–50			2	5
51–60	1	1	1	2
61–70				2
71–80				2
81–90	1	1	1	
91–100				
101–				2
Total	5	5	11	108

such as that at Tomioka. The Tomioka factory, which had iron machines with 300 basins and was designed to employ 300 female reel operators (210 were actually employed), could survive only because it was a government enterprise.

In the Suwa lake area, even a mechanized factory of one hundred reel operators was not viable. For example, Onogumi planned to employ one hundred female workers in its Miyamada factory, but could at most actually employ thirty-six and a minimum of seventeen. This was also the case for Nakayama Sha in Hirano village. The Suwa type of mechanized silk manufacture introduced by Nakayama Sha was not directly imported from the West and was very cheap compared with the cost of Western machines. Nevertheless, it still cost 13.50 *yen* per basin to set up and 300 *yen* per basin in operating costs. Thus, because of these costs it was common for 10–20 basin factories to be managed by farmers as family businesses.

Moreover, although considerable capital was needed to mechanize silk manufacture, there still remained technological limitations. Production of high quality goods was not possible because of the poor quality and variability of cocoons. A basic necessity of the silk industry was the supply of quality cheap cocoons. Therefore an improvement in cocoon breeding was a prerequisite for the development of mechanization in the silk industry.

The Katakura Silk Company and the Katakura Extended Family System

The Katakura Silk Company was organized in 1878 as a family business in Misawa hamlet of Kawagisi village in the Suwa Lake area, and reorganized in Tokyo in 1920 as a joint stock company, the Katakura Raw Silk and Spun Silk Manufacturing Company Limited. More than sixty per cent of the company stock was held by the Katakura families. Over this period the company had steadily expanded and become widely known as one of the largest and oldest raw silk spinners in the world.

The company's first president was Kanetarō I who was born in 1849. He had gone to Tokyo to study classical Chinese in 1868, but after few months returned to Misawa. In 1889 he became the first Kawagishi village head. In 1873 his father, Ichisuke, established a traditional silk mill in his yard. The management of this mill was soon handed to the second son, Mitsuharu. In 1874 Mitsuharu established a new family and moved the factory to his own household's yard.

In 1876 Kanetarō's cousin, Shuntarō, and three others established Ichinosawa Sha, a machine mill of 32 basins in Misawa hamlet. It was the first machine mill to be established in Kawagishi village. In 1878 Kanetarō and his brother, Mitsuharu, established Kaito Gumi, another machine mill of 32 basins. Both mills were dependent on a water wheel in the Tenyrū river for power. In 1879 Kanetarō I and twelve others established Kaimei Sha, a marketing cooperative which later became a silk company. In 1881 Ichinosawa Sha was amalgamated with Kaito Gumi, to later become a mill of 60 basins. Shuntarō became one of the chief joint managers of the Kaito Silk Company.

I would now like to draw the readers' attention to the Katakuras genealogical map in Chart 8–2. As we can see, Kaemon II had two sons, Ichisuke being the elder and Gonsuke the younger. While it may seem natural for the eldest son to inherit the household property, in this area inheritance by the youngest son had been common practice in the feudal era. In fact Gonsuke inherited Kaemon's household and Ichisuke established a branch family. The success of his son, Kanetarō I, in the silk business was sufficient reason to amend the genealogy with regard to which household was the main family.

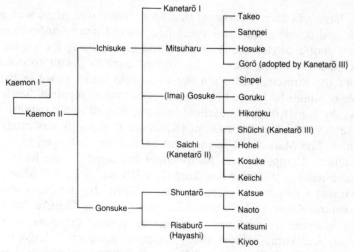

Chart 8–2 The genealogical map of the Katakuras

Ichisuke's third son Gosuke was born in 1859 and adopted by the Imai family as heir in 1876. But immediately after Gosuke married into the Imai family, his father-in-law had a son, causing Gōsuke a serious identity crisis. Gosuke attended a normal school and became a teacher in Matsumoto city near the Suwa lake area. In 1886, ten years after his marriage, Gosuke quit teaching and went to Tokyo, leaving his wife and children. Later that same year he went abroad to the U.S. and there engaged in agricultural labour for four years, learning the American way of life and acquiring a rational and pragmatic way of thought. He returned to Japan in 1890 and became the first president of the Katakura Company in Matsumoto, which had 48 basins. It is very important to understand that even though he learned to be pragmatic in the U.S., his identity was tied up in being a member of the Katakura family.

Ichisuke's fourth son, Saichi, was Kanetarō II. Since Kanetarō I had no child, Saichi was adopted as the heir of the Katakura family. He was born in 1862, when Kanetarō I was 14. In 1877, when he was fifteen, Saichi went to Tokyo to study at a private school. Within a few years he had to choose whether to stay in Tokyo to continue his studies or return to his home town and the family business. He decided to return to Suwa and the silk industry. In 1894 the Sanzen Sha began production in Misawa hamlet with 360 basins, Saichi became its first president. It was

189

the largest factory in Japan at that time. Saichi was gifted with a splendid physique and as a youth had worked much harder than most people at cultivating the land and grass cutting for fodder. As manager of the factory, he worked hard to obtain cocoons from the farmers, and when the water mill broke down in the cold of winter he jumped into the Tenryu river to repair it. Saichi was the leader of the household business as well as a capitalist.

In 1895 the Katakura Gumi (Katakura Company) was established. The Matsumoto factory and Sanzen Sha belonged to the Katakura Company, and Kaito Gumi belonged to the Kaimei Sha. Finally in 1920, the Katakura Raw Silk and Spun Silk Manufacturing Company Limited was established. Its president was Kanetarō Katakura II and its vice president was Gosuke Imai. Family members who were among the general directors were Takeo Katakura, Shinpei Imai, Kanetarō Katakura III, Naoto Katakura, Kiyoo Hayashi and Katsue Katakura.

In 1929 (just before the great depression) the Katakura Company, with its affiliated companies controlled more than 50 factories and 4 silkworm egg establishments, all located in different parts of Japan, Korea and China. At that time the company possessed approximately 22,000 reeling basins, and employed 31,000 women and 4,000 men. The company's annual output, including that of companies under Katakura's control, amounted to over 65,000 bales of raw silk, 1,000,000 pounds of spun silk yarn and 1,000,000 cards of silkworm eggs.

There were many family businesses in the silk industry in the Suwa lake area. But only the Katakura Silk Company was successful enough to become one of the biggest companies in Japan. It was successful because it could obtain quality cocoons and therefore produced a uniformly fine silk. It was for this reason that the Katakura Company, took the initiative of mass producing silkworm egg cards, and improving their quality through cross breeding. In order to reel clean and even silk, the cocoons needed to be carefully sorted according to quality and size, and imperfect cocoons eliminated. Rejected cocoons were sold for domestic consumption. Cocoon boiling was also essential, because it greatly affected the quality of the raw silk. Uniformity of size, evenness of thread and cleanness of silk were essential to maintain the company's reputation.

In 1913 the Katakura extended household framed a family constitution whose object, as stated in the first article of its first chapter, was to preserve the happiness of the household. Article two stated that even though the constitution included articles which were illegal under national law, family members should observe the constitution unless they would actually be punished for doing so. Article 4 defined the Katakura extended household as comprising eighteen families, of which the family of Kanetarō Katakura was the head family and the four families of Shuntarō Katakura, Mitsuharu Katakura, Gosuke Imai, Risaburō Hayashi were main (sub-head) families. Kanetarō I was the first son of Ichisuke and Kanetarō II was the fourth son and the adopted son of his eldest brother. Mitsuharu was the second son and Gosuke Imai was the third son. Shuntarō and Risaburō Hayashi were the sons of Gonsuke, the younger brother of Ichisuke.

Of the remaining thirteen branch families, only five were named in the constitution, these being those of Goroku Imai (the second son of Gosuke), Kōsuke and Keiichi (the third and the fourth sons of Saichi, Kanetarō II), and Hosuke and Gorō (the third and fourth sons of Mitsuharu). Of course these were not genuine genealogical families. Branch families not included among the specified eighteen were excluded from the Katakura extended household. The extended household system of the Katakura families was created to maintain the Katakura Company as a general partnership. After the constitution was framed, a covenant was made between Kanetarō, Shuntarō, Mitsuharu, Gosuke Imai and Risaburō Hayashi in 1923. According to this covenant, the headship of the household of Kanetarō Katakura was to succeed to Saichi and then to Shūichi.

The household of Shuntarō Katakura, one of the main families, was to succeed to Katsue, that of Mitsuharu to Takeo, that of Gosuke Imai to Mahira Imai and that of Risaburō Hayashi to Katsumi Hayashi. They were all eldest sons. Kanetarō had the right to establish four branch families. Three already existed: Hohei, Kosuke, Keiichi; the fourth was to be that of a male born into the Kanetarō family. Shuntarō had the right to establish three branch families. One was already established: Mahito; the other two were to be those of a male born into the Shuntarō family and a male born into the Naoto family.

Mitsuharu also had three branch families: Sanpei, Hosuke and Gorō. Gosuke Imai had two branch families: Goroku and Hiko-roku. Finally, Risaburō Hayashi had one branch family: Kiyoo

Hayashi. Thus at that time there already were ten branch families. Each share in the joint enterprise is shown in Table 8–10.

As exemplified by the Katakura Company, the prototype of the Japanese company was a household or a large extended household. The company does not consist of individual stock holders but precedes and transcends individuals.

In Japan, enterprise has not been based upon the rational organization of free and independent workers. Nor has it been a capitalistic profit-making organization. Rather, the enterprise is a unit of cooperative work, as is an individual household. In Japanese capitalism a leader is the *oya* and the workers are followers or *ko*. Workers work not to provide for their own living expenses, but for the sake of the enterprise, that is, the household with which they identify themselves. The enterprise as a household is not an ideological construct but a reality. In Japan even labour unions are specific to an enterprise and intended to create harmonious relationships within that enterprise. Thus, for example, a labour union in Ishikawajima Heavy Industries made the following appeal in 1930:

> We must put aside our stress on rights for a time and go back to *giri* (obligation) and *ninjō* (human feeling). Only an immoral fool would demand a pay raise or better treatment in such a depression as this. If the father is poor, so must the child be. We must accept lower pay, work as hard as we can, and with labour and capital united as one, overcome this adversity . . . Japanese workers must work for the sake of the nation and abandon the concept of labour and capital.
>
> Labour-capital fusion (*yūgō*) is not the same as labour-capital cooperation or harmony (*kyōchō*). *Kyōchō* assumes a prior conflict which may re-emerge at any time. *Yūgō* asserts a fundamental unity of one mind and spirit, fused in an inseparable solidarity. This gives birth to tremendous power. This alone can move Japanese industries forward (Gordon, 1985, p. 228).

This is an example of the ideological use of the household system of Japan. The relationship between capitalists and labourers has nothing to do with right-wing ultra-nationalism or fascism.

Finally I would like to refer to a document that accompanied a donation by the Katakura families to the Suwa shrine in 1931.

Table 8–10 The Katakura extended household and the share rate of common property of the members

	Head of Family	Share Rate of Common Property
Head Family		
Main Families	1 Kanetarō Katakura	10/72
	2 Katsue Katakura	8/72
	3 Takeo Katakura	6/72
	4 Shinpei Imai	5/72
	5 Katsumi Hayashi	4/72
Branch Families	6 Hohei Katakura	3/72
	7 Kōsuke Katakura	3/72
	8 Keiichi Katakura	3/72
	9 Son of Kanetarō	3/72
	10 Naoto Hayashi	3/72
	11 Son of Shuntarō	3/72
	12 Son of Naoto	3/72
	13 Sanpei Katakura	3/72
	14 Hosuke Katakura	3/72
	15 Gōrō Katakura	3/72
	16 Goroku Imai	3/72
	17 Hikoroku Imai	3/72
	18 Kiyoo Hayashi	3/72

Thirteen of the Katakuras were contributors: Kanetarō Katakura, Katsue Katakura, Takeo Katakura, Gosuke Imai, Katsumi Hayashi, Shūichi Katakura, Naoto Katakura, Sanpei Katakura, Shinpei Imai, Kiyoo Hayashi, Hohei Katakura, Goroku Imai and Kōsuke Katakura. The amount of the donation was 14,588 *yen* for the repair of the Spring shrine and 18,052 *yen* for the repair of the Autumn shrine. A note included with the donation said that Kanetarō Katakura II, who was a representative of the people under the protection of the community deity and a man of deep faith, consulted with the other Katakura families and had decided to donate money even though it was a time when people faced a serious depression. The document shows that the Katakura household had often donated money in the 1830s at the time of Kaemon II. The success of the Katakura household as world silk king made it possible for Kanetarō to be deemed a direct descendant of the deity of the Suwa shrine. Thus Kanetarō Katakura became a living Shinto god just like the emperor.

The Suwa shrine deity was Tateminakata who was the second son of Ōkuninushi. According to the myth Izanami and Izanagi made the world and other gods. Izanagi had three children after his wife's death: Amaterasu, Tsukuyomi and Susanō. Although they were siblings, Amaterasu and Susanō feuded, and Susanō was banished from the high plain of heaven to Izumo where he built a palace. Amaterasu, the female god, is the founder of the imperial household.

According to the myth, Susanō and Ōkuninushi were defeated by the deities in heaven, Amaterasu defeating Susanō and expelling him to Izumo. Ōkuninushi's first son, Yaekotoshironushi, agreed to yield the land to the heavenly deities. Ancestors of the emperor who were believed to come from heaven, seemed to conquer Izumo. Thus, knowing that Ōkuninushi's son was the progenitor of the Suwa shrine is important to understand the distinction between national Shinto and folk Shinto, and to understand why the Japanese modernization required the emperor system. The latter is not merely a remnant of the feudal system but is also a newly created tradition to promote modernization of the Japanese nation from above. In this process of modernization, the Katakura household needed to create a new tradition in which the Katakura families took powerful roles. Just as the *zaibatsu* utilized the national Shinto religion and the emperor myth, the Katakura family utilized the Suwa shrine and created

a new myth in which ancestors of Kanetarō Katakura played the
same role as emperors.

9   The Japanese Images of the World

Introduction

Charles Scott Brunger[1] listed the four defining characteristics of the Asiatic mode of production in his Ph.D. dissertation: (1) communal land ownership based originally on tribal relationships; (2) the communal control of labour eventually permits the appropriation of surplus labour by nonproducers; (3) division of labour is limited to the extended family or to the village; and (4) if exchange exists at all, it occurs at the boundaries of the community (Brunger, 1983, pp. 10–11).

He also pointed out that the tribal community based on blood ties maintained itself through land ownership and patriarchal social relations. He identified three variants of the Asiatic mode of production:

(a) In egalitarian kinship variants, family lineages recognized each other's rights to land. Family elders appropriated labour directly. They organized production and supervised the distribution of produce. When slavery occurred, captives would be incorporated into the family as junior members.

(b) In hierarchical kinship variants, the ruler placed the land at the disposal of lineages in return for symbolic payments to acknowledge sovereignty. Land ownership remained communal, though there was individual possession of the harvest. Control of the ruler by the lineages prevented exploitation through taxation. As a representative of the community, the ruler could preside

[1] This chapter is based upon the lectures at staff seminars of Maryville College. On those occasions, Charles Scott Brunger told me that everything I said about Japanese ideology had parallels in Africa. Brunger maintained that the unique contribution of Japan is to have capitalism without individualism. He also pointed out that the prototype of Japanese society was based on the Asiatic mode of production. Furthermore, when I later attended a Japanese Studies meeting of the Southern Atlantic States Association for Asian and African Studies in March 1987, an African specialist mentioned that the characteristics of Japanese society, which Japanologists claimed were unique to Japan, could also be found in African society.

196

over a number of villages and could carry out trade and military policy.

(c) In the despotic state, the ruler embodied the community, acting through an appointed officialdom rather than through council lineages. At the village level production was still organized by the real community. Within the higher community, the village was a territorial tax unit. The village headman's responsibilities for taxation reinforced his authority over villagers, while the surplus production was appropriated from the village by the state (Brunger, 1983, pp. 52–55).

However, what is peculiar to Japan is that during the long era of the Asiatic mode of production from the tribal period to the appearance of the bureaucratic state, the ruler was always the emperor. The fact that traditional Japanese society shares the characteristics of the Asian mode of production with African tribal societies, opens a new dimension for studies of Japanese society and culture. So far many Japan specialists have tried to understand the unique features of Japanese society and culture in terms of the remnants of feudalism in Japan. But the importance of the genealogical relationship, which is one of the most conspicuous characteristics of Japanese society, originated in the extended-family system of archaic Japanese societies. Feudal land relationships were established through the dissolution of the blood ties which functioned as the principle for the construction and organization of communities. What is unique to Japan is that such genealogical relationships are not only supplementary elements of feudal society but also of capitalist society.

Tradition and Modernization in Japan

Katai Tayama's 1917 autobiography *Thirty Years in Tokyo*, in the section 'On the death of the Meiji Emperor', includes the following reminiscence:

My father died in battle in the civil war of 1887, which broke out ten years after the Meiji Restoration began. In the Sino-Japanese War of 1894–95 and in the Russo-Japanese War of 1904–05, I went to the front as a member of a photographer's

team. In both wars, I witnessed the Emperor's armies
conquest of enemies everywhere, thus expanding the grace
of the Imperial Throne. When I saw a Japanese national flag
fluttering in the enemy's camp, I could not help jumping for
joy. At that time I became aware of my national identity and
was conscious that the hot red blood of the Japanese runs
in my veins. In thought I am a free thinker, but in spirit I
am an advocate of Japanism in the same way as any ordinary
Japanese. (Tayama, 1917, p. 288)

He wrote the phrase 'a free thinker' in English. As an intellectual
and a novelist of modern naturalism, he believed that he should
be a free citizen who had freedom of speech, assembly and
association. But according to Tayama, the ordinary Japanese folk
who were so-called 'Japanist' had only one thought – that it was
best to obey the emperor's order even at the expense of one's
own interests. As an intellectual, Tayama should not have been
like them; rather he should have been independent of the ideology of the 'emperor myth.' But he was not.

Of course this contradiction is not unique to Tayama. Since
the very beginning of the modern period in Japan, contradictory
relationships have existed between an individual's identity as a
member of a nation and their civil freedom. It is certainly true
that, in combination with the remnants of Tokugawa feudalism,
the emperor system established by the Meiji Restoration could
not accommodate civil freedom.

Katai's father, although officially a policeman, was mobilized
into the military in the civil war of 1877, and died in battle.
Although he was the second son, Katai was very conscious that
he was a member of a war-bereaved family whose head had died
for the sake of the state. As a matter of course, his father was
deified at the Yasukuni shrine. Yasukuni literally means 'to guard
the state': it was believed that the state was guarded by the dead
soldiers' spirits. At that time the shrine was called Shōkonsha,
literally 'the shrine to call and rest the spirits of the dead soldiers'.
In the book Katai recollects:

Whenever I took a walk in the precinct of Shōkonsha, I
always heard my own inner voice saying that I would be a
great man soon; I could not but be a great man. While I was
going up the stone stairs, I thought of heroes and great

characters. The soul of my father who died for the sake of
the state, seemed to be very near me whenever I went
through the precinct (Tayama, 1917, p. 69).

Thus whenever he passed the shrine, the young Katai swore in
his mind that he would succeed in the world and be a great man,
as a member of the honoured Tayamas. When his mother died,
his eldest brother decided on a Shinto funeral because her husband had been enshrined in Yasukuni. In Japan, the common
people have a Shinto marriage ceremony but a Buddhist funeral
ceremony. So it was significant that the Tayama brothers had a
Shinto funeral for their mother.

In his younger days Tayama was a close friend of Kunio Yanagida, who at that time was a student in the law school of Tokyo
Imperial University and wished to become a novelist. Later Yanagida became a founder of Japanese folklore studies and a great
scholar of indigenous disciplines. He was not a 'Japanist' as
Tayama called himself, but a moderate conservative. However,
when he wrote *The Age and Agriculture* in 1910, he argued that
the uniqueness of Japanese culture was rooted in the fact that
the Japanese people had served the emperor as an institution
for several thousand years. Were there no emperor system and
household system in Japan, people would not be able to understand how they could be truly Japanese.

Sohō Tokutomi, a leading journalist, also thought of the
Japanese as members of a family-nation whose foundation was
the unbroken line of the Imperial House. In this family-nation
the Imperial House was the parent of the people. He wrote in
the 1908 edition of *Yoshida Shōin*:

[At] the time of the foundation of the country, the Japanese
race grew out with the Imperial House at the centre . . .
[I]n which country in the world can one see a familial structure
like our imperial Japan? The imperial house is the main
trunk, and our Japanese state is the expansion of the family.
Our emperor is the sovereign of the Japanese race . . .
'Emperor, that is, the father' is but a common fact in Japan.
Emperor-centralism therefore, is not a fact deduced from
theory but a theory induced from the fact (Tokutomi, 1908,
pp. 124–125).

Summing up his view of the role of emperor-centralism through-out Japanese history, he said that the idea that the emperor was a divine being and that Japan was a divine country had grown up with the Japanese nation and with the Imperial House generation after generation. He pointed out that Japan had been reigned over by an unbroken line of emperors, whereas China had been subject to constant dynastic changes.

If 'Japanism' presupposed this hierarchical order with the emperor at its apex, essential Japaneseness would be incompatible with the ideas of freedom, equality, individuality and democracy which citizens of the West cherish so much. To examine this issue we must first analyse the Japanese conception of the world of myth.

The Prototype of the Japanese World View

At the end of the seventh century, the emperor Tenmu ordered that Japanese history be recorded. Two books were completed: one was the *Kojiki* (712) which was mostly written in classical Chinese and partly in Japanese with Chinese characters (because Japanese at that time did not have its own letters), and the other was the *Nihon Shoki* (720) which was written in classical Chinese. Here we will draw mainly upon the *Kojiki* to explain ancient Japanese thought and behaviour.

The *Kojiki* is divided into three sections. The first describes the creation of heaven and earth and the founding of Japan. The birth of the Japanese land is explained as the result of sexual intercourse of two sibling deities. A part of this story is as follows:

Izanagi-no-mikoto asked his spouse (younger sister) Izanami-no-mikoto saying: 'How is your body formed?' She replied, saying: 'My body, formed though it be formed, has one place which is formed insufficiently.'
     Then Izanagi-no-mikoto said: 'My body, formed though it be formed, has one place which is formed to excess.
Therefore, I would like to take that place in my body which is to excess and insert it into the place in your body which is formed insufficiently and [thus] give birth to the land. How

would this be?' Izanami-no-mikoto replied, saying: 'That will be good'. (Philippi, 1968: p.50).

Such creation stories are quite different from those of ancient Judaism. The Japanese believed that something cannot be created out of nothing. Sexual intercourse is the only conceivable cause of production. And the ancient Japanese language makes no distinction between sister and wife: the term *imo* means sister as well as wife. As we will explain later, this attempt to produce the land was unsuccessful because the female deity had spoken first. This represented the decline of the matriarch and the rise of the patriarch.

The *Kojiki* began with the story of the origin of the cosmos. Originally there was no clear distinction between heaven and earth. Both heaven and earth were created from chaos, and in the high plain of heaven (Takamagahara) seven deities came into existence but their forms were not visible. They had no spouses and no corporeal bodies. They were then followed by ten divinities, five of whom were male and five female. We may suppose them to have been five couples among whom Izanagi and Izanami held a privileged position as patriarch and patriarch's wife. Thus only the children of Izanagi and Izanami had a legitimate right to succeed to the position of patriarch.

According to the *Kojiki*, Izanagi and Izanami were bidden by the heavenly deities to solidify the drifting land and were given a heavenly jewelled spear. Standing upon the floating bridge of heaven, they plunged the spear into the brine below them and stirred it. As they lifted it out, the drops falling from it formed the island. Descending to the island, they erected a pillar and a palace. Then, as mentioned earlier, they had sexual intercourse in order to produce the land. But because the woman spoke to the man first the result was a *hiruko*, a deformed leech child, which they discarded by sending it off in a boat of reeds.

Then they returned to heaven where it was announced that because the woman had spoken first, the child was not good. The heavenly deities said, 'Descend once more and say it again.' This time they produced a number of islands and other deities. Finally, in giving birth to the fire deity, Izanami was badly burned and died. Izanagi buried her but, desiring to see her again he went to find her in Yomi, the land of the dead. He reproached her for not helping him complete their work in creating land

and implored her, unsuccessfully, to return with him. When he returned, Izanagi purified his body in a river. He washed out his left eye and Amaterasu, the sun goddess, was born (she was the progenitor of the imperial line). From his right eye came the moon deity, Tsukuyomi, and from his nose emerged the deity of the oceans, Susanō.

Izanagi regarded these three last-born deities as noble children. Giving Amaterasu his necklace, he bestowed on her the mission of ruling the high plane of heaven. Susanō was to rule the oceans but did not obey his father's exhortations. Although they were siblings, Amaterasu and Susanō feuded. On one occasion Amaterasu became angry at her brother's mischief and retired to the heavenly rock cave, and in the high plain of heaven all became dark. Before long she left the cave and light was again restored. The gods decided to expel Susanō from the high plain of heaven. Banished, he descended to Izumo where he built a palace. His descendant was Ōkuninushi.

Amaterasu ordered her heir Oshihomimi to descend and rule the central land of the reed plains which was under Ōkuninushi's control. But from the floating bridge of heaven the land seemed to be in uproar. Soon, another deity was dispatched to prevail upon Ōkuninushi but instead flattered Ōkuninushi and did not return for three years. After that time elapsed another deity was sent, but he plotted to obtain land for himself and did not return for eight years. Next, two deities were dispatched to inquire what Ōkuninushi intended to do with the land. After various incidents, his son, Yaekotoshironushi, agreed to yield the land to the child of the heavenly deities.

Amaterasu gave birth to a male child, Ninigi, whom she bade to descend to the land and rule. When Ninigi was about to begin his descent to the peak of Mt. Takachiho, Amaterasu bequeathed to him the three regalia which he in turn passed on to his descendants, the emperors of Japan. Ninigi had three children, and the third son, Hoori, was the grandfather of the legendary first emperor, Jinmu.

In 1872, four years after the Meiji Restoration, the government officially inaugurated the use of the imperial era estimated as commencing in 585 B.C., the year in which the legendary first emperor, Jinmu was said to have ascended the throne. The date of Jinmu's accession was calculated as the first day of the first (lunar) month – January 29 of the Gregorian calendar – and

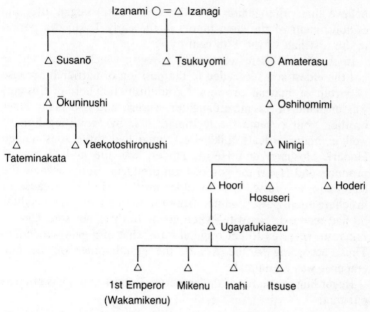

Chart 9–1 Genealogy of the Emperor's household

declared a national holiday. In 1873 it was officially named Kigen-setsu (founding of the nation day) and recalculated as the 11th of February. After the Second World War this holiday was abolished, but was restored in 1966.

This myth was used to legitimate the hierarchical order of society with the emperor at its zenith. Despite the fact that a goddess founded of the imperial household, the establishment of patriarchy well demonstrated in the beginning of the *Kojiki*. Izanagi could be considered the patriarch of an extended family, clan or tribe. In Japan the 'family' referred to the extended family until the 16th or 17th century. In this type of family, all male members remained in their native family.

When the family became too large it would be divided into two parts, each of which would also be an extended family. In this instance, the distinction between lineal descendants and collateral descendants had some importance, and the former held the dominant position. However, the patriarch within the extended family is not necessarily succeeded by his eldest son, and might be succeeded by his brother or a younger son. In either case the heir was one of his collateral descendants. We believe that primogeniture (in the strict sense) began after the establishment of the stem family in the early Tokugawa period in the first half of the 17th century.

In the *Kojiki* there were many cases in which a man who is not the eldest son succeeded to the position of patriarch because of virtue or martial prowess. Ōkuninushi (an heir of Susanō) was husband of Susanō's daughter, Suseri, and had many elder brothers, but became the legitimate heir by acquitting himself well in many ordeals. Likewise, Ninigi had three sons named Hoderi, Hosuseri and Hoori; Hoderi was the god of marine products and Hoori the god of farm products. Hoori became the legitimate heir instead of his older brother Hoderi, because of his charismatic power, gained from the sea-deity whose daughter he had married. His wife, when giving birth to her son, Ugaya-fukiaezu, reverted to her original form, that of a giant crocodile. Thus, according to the *Kojiki*, the grandmother of the first emperor was an animal.

Regarding the status of the emperor, Robert Smith has pointed out that:

> Given the nature of the claim to the throne, usurpation is simply not possible, for it is occupied not by divine right of the Mandate of Heaven, but by virtue of authentic genealogical descent from the divine founder of the line. Indeed, the Japanese imperial house advances the rather unusual and possibly unique claim of being able to trace its ancestry back in cosmic time before the establishment of the state over which it was to exercise sovereignty (Smith, 1983, pp. 12–13).

Smith was correct in his the statement about usurpation. We cannot say that usurpation would be impossible, for on the contrary, there were many consanguine usurpers within the imperial household. Of course, Smith was quite right when he pointed out that none of the breaks in succession of the imperial house was ever claimed to be a dynastic change. Usurpation is closely connected with the position of leadership within the large extended family; genealogical position has nothing to do with the charisma required of a patriarch.

Gods, the Emperor and the Household

The reason why the founder of the imperial household is the mother not the father, can be explained by the importance of shamanism in ancient Japan. Amaterasu had the dual character of being both a deity and a shaman. As a shaman, a virgin consecrated to a deity, she was a wife of the sun god, and so was considered the sun goddess. Her feud with her brother Susanō had nothing to do with the legitimate order of the patriarch, or the paternal clan-tribe system. In the *Kojiki*, Susanō and Ōkuninushi were described as gods and rulers of Izumo province. Both were defeated by the deities in the high plain of heaven. Amaterasu defeated Susanō and expelled him to Izumo, and Ōkuninushi's son agreed to yield the land to the child of the heavenly deities before the descent of Ninigi. Ancestors of the emperor who were considered to have come from heaven, first conquered Kyūshū province and then Izumo province before their expedition to Yamato.

The assumption that Amaterasu was a virgin consecrated to a deity, the highest priestess, and that her status as queen was not incompatible with patriarchy, is well supported by the historical documents concerning a queen Himiko in Yamatai. She was described by Chen Shau in the section 'Wei Chih' (History of Wei) of his book *Sankuo Chin* (History of the Three Kingdoms). There he wrote about the Japanese Wa people. According to Chen Shau, the Wa were once ruled by a king. At some time during the 170s and 180s there had been a civil war which ended with the Himiko's ascension. She devoted herself completely to religious affairs and was able to 'delude the crowd'. She had no husband but was assisted by her younger brother, who exercised power on her behalf. She lived in a towered palace behind forbidding walls and was constantly guarded; few ever saw her. She died sometime in the late 240s. A huge burial mound was raised for her, and over 100 servants were killed and interred with her. She was at first succeeded by a king, but the country would not accept him and a civil war erupted. Ultimately a 13 year girl, Iyo, was made queen, whereupon the strife ceased.

Himiko and Iyo were shamans, and their power did not threaten the political system of the clan-tribe ruled by patriarchy. According to Chen Shau there were over thirty tribal countries, and Himiko was both queen of Yamatai and at the same time queen of the federation. Likewise, in the case of Amaterasu, the rule of a queen did not mean there was any legacy of matriarchy.

The Japanese term for family originally meant house and lot, and then meant people living together in that place. Members of the family were not necessarily related to each other by blood ties; one could easily enter the family as a servant. The family was regarded as a group that has eternal continuity, succession passing down through male descendants of the group. Given such a patrilineal household system, a patrilineal clan system was possible.

Needless to say, a husband and wife belong to different clans, because members of the same clan cannot marry each other. Therefore females who are born into an extended family must marry out and become members of another family. Thus, clans whose unit is the patrilineal extended family are semi-consanguineous (from the male viewpoint),and semi-local (from the female viewpoint).

But the concept of blood relationship through the male line was not restricted to biological relationships. The lineage group may include members with fictitious blood relationships. The relationship between *oyakata* and *kokata* may be of this sort, as in the case of adoption. Significance lay in the mutual recognition of the *oya* and *ko* (leader and follower) relationship. The relationship between the main or head family and branch family was also based on mutual recognition of lineage among the families' members.

Not surprisingly there have been many disputes within clans as to which was the main family. A self-styled main family might even forge genealogical documents. When the head of one family asks for another family's protection, his family becomes a branch family. And when one clan or tribe is conquered by another and becomes dependent, it becomes *oyakata* in relation to the conquering clan. Thus, lineage may include fictitious or pseudo-lineage relations, while in turn the relationship of domination and subordination is coloured by lineage.

The concept of the eternal continuity of the family and the rule of the patriarch can easily be related to that of the Japanese nation and the rule of the emperor. The idea that the Japanese nation preserves, unaltered, its ancient social structure based on genealogical relationships, gained much popularity in the 1930s, when the fascist movement became active. For example, the right-wing activist Kōzō Tsuda, in an article called 'The Present Conditions of Japanese Fascism' wrote of a distinctive characteristic of Japanese nationalism at that time:

> In the family-system the keynote of society is not the demand for individual rights, as in the modern countries of the West, but service to the family as a whole. Socially each family is an independent animate body, a complete cell in itself. The individual is no more than a part or an element of this complete cell. Our nationalism should be the extension and enlargement of this family-system principle. This is perhaps because our nationalism is nothing but the union of these families at the national level. The emperor is the sovereign, family head, centre, and general representative of the state as a unified body (cited in Maruyama, 1963, pp. 37).

Of course such arguments did not flourish only in the 1930s and in wartime. For example, when Yatsuka Hozumi, professor of the law school of Tokyo Imperial University, criticized the original draft of the civil code, which was based on the French model, in an article with the inflammatory title, 'If the Civil Code Comes in, Loyalty and Filial Piety Will be Destroyed.' He wrote:

> The Japanese had a long history of ancestor worship. Japan is a country based on the household system and the law and power originate in the household. They do not originate from the war of every independent and free individual in the primitive field or forest. The clan, the tribe and the state can be considered as an extension of the household. Their head is a representative of the ancestor's souls in this world. The patriarch is to be sacred and inviolable in the same way as the souls of ancestors are to be sacred and inviolable. The Western family after the introduction of Christianity is the place of communal living of man and woman based on romantic love. Our draft of the civil code is based on such a principle of family life. But it is quite different from our indigenous household system. In Europe, because of Christianity in which the Omnipotent in heaven monopolizes the whole love and respect of mankind, descendants never worship ancestors, hence there is no filial piety. In Europe,

where the principles of egalitarianism and philanthropy are prevailing, people think little of their kin and folks, hence the household system has died. In Europe they build and maintain egalitarian and individualistic society in which the legal system also is based on individualism (Hozumi, 1891, pp. 223–5).

Hozumi believed that indigenous Japanese values were incompatible with the values that facilitate the emergence of modern democratic society.

Nationalism and 'Japanese' Culture

Ōgai Mori, one of the most famous men of letters in modern Japan, wrote a short story entitled 'Kano yōni' (As if it were) in 1912, immediately after the high treason incident of 1910. At that time the government arrested and prosecuted anarchists and socialists for plotting to assassinate the emperor. Among the 26 prosecuted, Shūsui Kōtoku and eleven others were executed as alleged conspirators in 1911. Intellectuals were concerned that government suppression of socialist and communist thought might spread to other areas of thought. But they took no strong stand or direct action against the government. Instead of advocating freedom of speech, Mori recommended that one act 'as if it [some divinity] were' there.

The story concerned a young scholar of Japanese history who had studied abroad in Germany (like the author) and who was the heir of a noble family whose former head had rendered distinguished services to the early Meiji state. As an historian Mori made a clear distinction between myth and history, and rejected the belief that ancestors became deities and proper objects of worship upon death. But doubting the existence of the sacred spirits of ancestors was the same as doubting the divinity of the emperor. This was a dangerous thought. Thus the hero tried to compromise with tradition, elaborating the philosophy of acting as if it were true:

I can believe in the bright future of the evolution of mankind.

In the same way I can look backward as if the ancestors' spirits were there. Thus I can indulge myself in such an idea as ancestor worship. I am a man just as is an unsophisticated and unenlightened peasant who lives in the countryside and believes his ancestors' souls return to their descendants' household every summer. How I differ from him is in having a clearer head. Don't you think that there could be no more undangerous or safer thought than this?

Another novelist, Kafū Nagai, was more sincere than Mori when, in his 1921 essay 'Hanabi' (Fireworks), he expressed his feeling of helplessness in regard to the high treason incident:

Among many incidents which I have experienced, this is the most awful one. I could not well explain my hateful feeling. As a man of letters I should have spoken freely about this issue and stood against the government for this oppressive incident, as the French novelist of naturalism, Emile Zola, fought in the cause of justice in the Dreyfus incident. I should keep in mind that for this reason Zola had to flee from his own country. But I did nothing, like many other men of letters. I was tormented by a guilty conscience, and as a man of letters I was ashamed of myself. Since then I thought I had better degrade the dignity of my art to the level of the artists in the end of the Edo feudal period . . . I tried to respect, rather than be disgusted by, the novelists and painters of that time who worked on pornography with composure thinking that it was not their business as little men that the black warships came to Uraga port, or that the chief minister of the shogun was assassinated at the Sakurada gate, because these were matters commoners should not be concerned about.

Recently Andrew Gordon introduced the subject of labour relations in Japanese heavy industry in the 1930s to Western readers. His research included the case of Ishikawajima Harima Heavy Industries Company and the Jikyōkai labour union. A Nogi Society had been established within this company (General Nogi was a hero of the Russo-Japanese War who followed a feudal custom by committing suicide when the Meiji emperor died) and the Jikyōkai labour union. In 1930, when Japanese felt their nation to be isolated and under pressure from other imperial powers, the following appeal was made in the name of the union by the founder of the Nogi Society:

> Only an immoral fool would demand a pay rise or better treatment in such a depression as this. If the father is poor, so must be the child. We must accept lower pay, work as hard as we can . . .

Thus it is that at present, no less than in wartime, that Japanese capitalists and managers can freely exploit the ideology of 'Japanism'. Even now, those who stress the importance of individuals' rights are regarded as un-Japanese, disturbers of the unity of the whole. The truly 'Japanese' should sacrifice themselves for the sake of the nation and the company.

Bibliography

Abegglen, James 1958, *The Japanese Factory: Aspects of Its Social Organization*, The Free Press, Glencoe.

Akimoto, Ritsuro 1971, *Gendai Toshi no Kenryoku Kōzō* (Political Power Structure of the Modern City), Aoki Shoten, Tokyo.

Anesaki, Masaharu 1963, *History of Japanese Religion*, Charles Tuttle Company, Tokyo.

Ari, Bakuji 1987, *Rusonsen* (The Battle of Luzon), Iwanami Shoten, Tokyo.

Arichi, Tōru 1977, *Kindai Nihon Kazokukan* (Views of the Family in Modern Japan), Kōbundō, Tokyo.

Ariga, Nagao 1883, *Shakai Shinkaron* (Theories on Social Evolution), Vol. 1 of *Shakaigaku* (Sociology), 3 vols, Toyokan, Tokyo.

— — 1884, *Zokusei Shinkaron* (Theories on Evolution of the Patriarchal System), Vol. 3 of *Shakaigaku* (Sociology) Toyokan, Tokyo.

Aruga Kizaemon 1933, 'Nago no fueki' (A Corvée of the Nago), *Shakai Keizaishi*, Vol. 3, No. 7, pp. 25–69, No. 10, pp. 1–44.

— — 1943, *Nihon Kazokuseido to Kosakuseido* (The Japanese Family System and Tenant System), Kawade Shobō, Tokyo.

— — 1980, *Bunmei Bunka Bungaku* (Civilization, Culture and Literature), (Takashi Nakano ed.) Ochanomizu Shobō, Tokyo.

Befu, Harumi 1971, *Japan: An Anthropological Introduction*, Chandler, San Francisco.

Bell, Daniel 1974, *The Coming of Post Industrial Society*, Heineman, London.

— — 1976, *The Cultural Contradictions of Capitalism*, Basic Books, New York.

Bellah, Robert N. 1957, Paperback edition 1985, *Tokugawa Religion: The Cultural Roots of Modern Japan*, The Free Press, New York.

— — 1983, 'Cultural Identity and Asian Modernization', in *Cultural Identity and Modernization in Asian Countries*, Kokugakuin University, Tokyo, pp. 16–27.

Benedict, Ruth 1946, *The Chrysanthemum and the Sword*, Houghton Mifflin, Boston.

Bestor, Theodore C. 1985a, 'Tradition and Japanese Social Organization', *Ethnology*, Vol. 24, pp. 121–135.

—— 1985b, 'Suburbanization in Tokyo, 1920–1940', Paper presented to the annual meeting of the American Anthropological Association.

—— 1989, *Neighborhood Tokyo*, Stanford University Press, Stanford.

Brunger, Charles Scott 1983, *The Development of the Internal Market in Algeria, Nigeria, and the Ivory Coast*, University Microfilm International, Ann Arbor, Michigan.

Bunka no Jidai Kenkyū Gurūpu 1980, *Bunka no Jidai* (The Age of Culture), Ōkurashō, Tokyo.

Commission of Inquiry into the Basic Problems of Agriculture, Forestry and Fisheries (ed.) 1961, *Nōgyō no Kihonmondai to Kihontaisaku* (Basic Problems and Basic Policies of Agriculture), Nōrintōkei Kyōkai, Tokyo.

Dahl, Robert A. 1961, *Who Governs?* Yale University Press, New Haven.

Domhoff, William G. 1967, *Who Rules America?* Prentice Hall, New Jersey.

Domhoff, William G. and Hoyt B. Ballard (eds) 1968, *C. Wright Mills and the Power Elite*, Beacon Press, Boston.

Dore, Ronald P. 1958, *City Life in Japan*, Routledge & Kegan Paul, London.

—— 1973, *British Factory – Japanese Factory*, University of California Press, Berkeley.

Dower, John (ed.) 1975, *Origin of the Modern Japanese State: Selected Writings of E.H. Norman*, Pantheon Books, New York.

—— 1986, *War Without Mercy: Race and Power in the Pacific War*, Pantheon Books, New York.

Embree, John F. 1964, *Suye Mura: A Japanese Village*, University of Chicago Press, Chicago.

Fukutake, Tadashi 1946, *Chūgoku Nōsonshakai no Kōzō* (The Social Structure of a Chinese Village Community), in *Fukutake Tadashi Chosakushū* (The Writings of Tadashi Fukutake), Vol. 9, Tokyo Daigaku Shuppankai, Tokyo, 1975.

—— 1949, *Nihon Nōson no Shakaiteki Seikaku* (The Social

Characteristics of Rural Japan), Tokyo Daigaku Shuppankai, Tokyo.

— — 1962, *Man and Society in Japan*, University of Tokyo Press, Tokyo.

— — 1967, *Japanese Rural Society*, translated by R.P. Dore, Oxford University Press, London.

— — 1974, *Japanese Society Today*, University of Tokyo Press, Tokyo.

Fukuzawa, Yukichi, 1968, *An Encouragement of Learning*, translated by David A. Dilworth, and Umeyo Hirano, Sophia University, Tokyo.

Gayn, Mark 1948, *Japan Diary*, William Sloane, New York.

Gluck, Carol 1985, *Japan's Modern Myth*, Princeton University Press, Princeton.

Gordon, Andrew 1985, *The Evolution of Labor Relations in Japan Heavy Industry, 1835–1955*, Harvard University Press, Cambridge, Mass.

Hall, Robert King (ed.) 1949, *Kokutai no Hongi: Cardinal Principles of the National Entity of Japan*, Harvard University Press, Cambridge, Mass.

Halliday, Jon 1975, *A Political History of Japanese Capitalism*, Pantheon Books, New York.

Hashikawa, Bunzō 1962, 'Kokutai Ron' (National Polity of Japan), in *Hashikawa Bunzō Chosakushū*, Vol. 2, Chikuma Shobō, Tokyo, 1985, pp. 98–119.

— — 1974, 'Yasukuni Shisō no Seiritu to Henyō' (Establishment and Changes of *Yasuku ni* Belief), *Chosakushu*, Vol. 2, pp. 194- 225.

Hata, Hiromi 1976, 'The Development of the Residents' Movements in Japan in the 1970s'. A paper presented at the first Conference of the Asian Studies of Australia.

Hofstadter, Richard 1955, *Social Darwinism in American Thought* (Revised edition), Beacon Press, Boston.

Hosumi, Yatsuka 1891, 'Minpō idete Chūkō horobu' (If the Civil Code Comes In, Loyalty and Filial Piety Will Be Destroyed), *Hōgaku Shinpō*, No. 5, in *Hozumi Yatsuka Hakase Robunshū* (The Collected Papers of Dr Yatsuka Hozumi), revised and enlarged edition, Yuhikaku, Tokyo, 1943, pp. 223-7.

Hunter, Floyd 1953, *Community Power Structure*, University of North Carolina Press, Chapel Hill.

Ichioka, Yūji 1984, 'A Nisei Critique of Futatu no Sokoku', Typescript, unpublished.

Iijima, Nobuko (ed.) 1979, *Pollution in Japan: Historical Chronology*, Asahi Evening News, Tokyo.

Inoue, Mitsusada, Kazuo Kasahara and Kōta Kodama 1979, *Shōsetsu Nihonshi* (A Textbook of Japanese History), Yamakawa Shuppan, Tokyo.

Isoda, Susumu (ed.) 1955, *Sonrakukōzō no Kenkyū* (A Study of Village Structure), Tokyo Daigaku Shuppankai, Tokyo.

Jansen, M.B. 1962, 'On studying the modernization of Japan', *Asian Cultural Studies* No. 3, International Christian University, Tokyo, pp. 1–11.

Katakura Company 1929, *The Katakura Company Limited*, The Katakura Co. Ltd., Tokyo.

Katayama, Sen 1918, *The Labor Movement in Japan*, Charles H. Kerr and Company, Chicago.

Katō, Hiroyuki 1900, 'Aikoshugi to Chūkun Aikoku no kankei' (On the Relationship Between Self-Love and Patriotism), in *Katō Hiroyuki Kōen Zenshū* (The Complete Collection of Lectures delivered by Hiroyuki Katō), Vol. 3, Maruzen, Tokyo.

—— 1904, *Shinkagaku yori Kansatsushitaru Nichiro no Unmei* (Japanese and Russian Fates from the Vantage Point of the Theory of Social Evolution), Hakubunkan, Tokyo.

Kawamura, Nozomu and Hasumi, Otohiko 1958, 'Kindai Nihon niokeru Sonraku Kozo no Tenkai Katei' (The Developmental Process of Village Structure in Modern Japan), *Shisō*, May-June, 1958, pp. 55–71, 87–103.

Kawamura, Nozomu 1973–75, *Nihon Shakaigakushi Kenkyū* (Studies on the History of Japanese Sociology), 2 vols, Ningen on Kagakusha, Tokyo.

—— 1976, 'Nihon Shihonshugi to Kankyō Hakai' (Japanese Modern Capitalism and Environmental Distraction), *Shakaigaku Hyōron* (Japanese Sociological Review), Vol. 27, No. 2, pp. 2–20.

—— 1980a, *Sociology and Society in Early Modern Japan*, La Trobe University, Melbourne.

—— 1980b, 'The Historical Background of Arguments Emphasizing the Uniqueness of Japanese Society', *Social Analysis*, Vol. 1, No. 5–6, pp. 45–56.

—— 1982, *Nihon Bunkaron no Shūhen* (Some Arguments on Japanese Culture), Ningen no Kagakusha, Tokyo.

214

Kawashima, Takeyoshi 1950, *Nihon Shakai no Kazokuteki Kōsei* (The Familial Structure of Japanese Society), Nihon Hyōronsha, Tokyo.

Kolko, Gabriel 1963, *The Triumph of Conservatism*, Macmillan, New York.

Kotoku, Shūsui 1910, *Shakaishugi Shinzui* (The Quintessence of Socialism), Iwanami Shoten, Tokyo.

Locke, John 1975 edn, *Two Treatises on Government*, Dent, London.

Lummis, C. Douglas 1982, *A New Look at the Chrysanthemum and the Sword*, Shohakusha, Tokyo.

McKean, Margaret A. 1981, *Environmental Protest and Citizen Politics in Japan*, University of California Press, Berkeley.

Maeda, Hajime 1964, 'Antei Seichō eno Daiichnendo taru Ninshiki o' (To Ensure the First Year of Stable Economic Development) *Keieisha*, February, 1964, pp. 14–19.

Maruyama, Masao 1963, *Thought and Behaviour in Modern Japanese Politics*, edited by I. Morris, Oxford University Press, London.

— — 1982, *Bunmeiron no Gairyaku o Yomu* (Reading Fukuzawa's 'An Outline of a Theory of Civilization'), 3 vols., Iwanami Shoten, Tokyo.

Mill, John Stuart 1912, *On Liberty*, in *Three Essays by J.S. Mill*, Oxford University Press, Oxford.

— — 1871, *Jiyū no Ri* (On Liberty), translated into Japanese by Keiu Nakamura, in *Meiji Bunka Zenshū* (Collection of Works on Meiji Culture), Vol. 5, Kaizōsha, Tokyo, 1927.

Mills, C. Wright 1956, *The Power Elite*, Oxford University Press, Oxford.

Miyamoto, Ken'ichi (ed.) 1970, *Kōgai to Jūmin Undō* (Pollution and the Residents' Movement), Jichi Kenkyūsha, Tokyo.

Miyamoto, Ken'ichi and Hikaru Shōji (eds) 1975, *Nihon no Kogai* (Pollution in Japan), Iwanami Shoten, Tokyo.

Mori, Ōgai 1912, 'Kano yōni' (As if it Were), in *Mori Ōgai Zenshū* (Complete Works of Ōgai Mori), Vol. 10, Iwanami Shoten, Tokyo, 1963, pp. 45–78.

Motojima, Kunio and Kokichi Shōji (eds) 1980, *Chiiki Kaihatsu to Shakaikōzō* (Regional Development and Social Structure), Tokyo Daigaku Shuppankai, Tokyo.

Murakami, Shigeyoshi 1970, *Kokka Shintō* (The State Shinto), Iwanami Shoten, Tokyo.

—— 1974, *Irei to Shōkon* (Dead Man's Soul and Its Invitation) Iwanami Shoten, Tokyo.

—— 1977, *Tennō no Saishi* (Emperor as Priest), Iwanami Shoten, Tokyo.

Nagai, Kafū 1921, 'Hanabi' (Fireworks), in *Kafū Zenshū* (Complete Works of Kafū Nagai), vol. 15, Iwanami Shoten, Tokyo, 1963, pp. 7–17.

Nakae, Chōmin 1984, *A Discourse on Government by Three Drunkards*, translated by Nobuko Tsukui, Weatherhill, New York.

Nakase, Juichi 1967, *Sengo Nihon no Keiei Rinenshi* (Post-war History of Ideas of Management) Hōritsu Bunkasha, Kyoto.

Nakamura, Hachirō 1980, 'The Concept of Community Transplanted in Japan', in Shōgo Koyano et al. (eds), *Asian Perspectives on Social Development*, University of Tokyo Press, Tokyo.

Nakane, Chie 1968, *Tateshakai no Ningen Kankei* (Human Relations in Vertically Structured Society), Kōdansha, Tokyo.

—— 1970, *Japanese Society*, Weidenfeld and Nicolson, London.

Nihon Shakai Gakuin Chōsabu 1916, 'Teikoku Kyōiku no Konpon Hōsin' (The Basic Principles of National Education), *Nihon Shakai Gakuin Nenpō*, Vol. 4, Nos. 1–2, pp. 4–29.

Nishi, Amane 1870–71, 'Hyakugaku Renkan' (An Encyclopedia), in *Nishi Amane Zenshū* (The Complete Writings of Amane Nishi), Vol. 1, Nihon Hyōronsha, Tokyo, 1954, pp. 11–37.

—— 1873, 'Seisei Hatsuro' (Creation of Human Life), *in Nishi Amane Shū* (Selected Writings of Amane Nishi), Vol. 1, Munataka Shobō, Tokyo, 1960, pp. 29–127.

Norman, E. Herbert 1940, 'Japan's Emergence as a Modern State', in *Selected Writings of E.H. Norman*, edited by John W. Dower, Pantheon Books, New York.

—— 1948, 'Settoku Ka Bōryoku Ka' (Persuasion or Force), in *E.H. Norman Zenshū* (The Complete Writings of E. Herbert Norman), Vol. 4, 1978, Iwanami Shoten, Tokyo, pp. 139–60.

Ōe, Shinobu 1984, *Yasukuni Jinja* (The *Yasukuni* Shrine), Iwanami Shoten, Tokyo.

Ōno, Yasumaro, 1968, *Kojiki*, translated by Donald Philippi, University of Tokyo Press, Tokyo.

Ōnuki, Emiko 1985, *Nihonjin no Byōkikan* (Japanese Views on Disease), Iwanami Shoten, Tokyo.

Ōsugi, Sakae 1914, 'Sei no Sōzō' (Creation of Living), *Ōsukgi*

Sakae Zenshū (The Complete Writings of Sakae Ōsugi), Vol. 2, Sekai Bunka, Tokyo, 1964, pp. 53–62.

Ōta, Masao (ed.) 1971, *Shiryō Taishō Demokurashii Ronsōshi* (The Debates on Taishō Democracy), (2 vols.), Shinsensha, Tokyo.

Ōtsuka, Hisao 1946, 'Kindaiteki Ningen Ruikei no Soshutsu' (The Necessity of Creating the Modern Civic Type of Person), reprinted in Ōtsuka, 1968, *Kindaika no Ningenteki Kiso* (A Personal Bases for Modernization), Chikuma Shobō, Tokyo, pp. 11–19.

—— 1963, 'Gendai Nihonshakai ni okeru Ningenteki Jōkyō' (Social Conditions of People in Present Day Japanese Society), *Sekai*, August, 1963, pp. 73–80.

Parsons, Talcott 1968, 'The Distribution of Power in America' in G.W. Domhoff et al. (eds), *C. Wright Mills and the Power Elite*, pp. 60–88.

Reick, Charles A. 1970, *The Greening of America*, Random House, New York.

—— 1976, *The Sorcerer of Bolinas Reef*, Random House, New York.

Saitō, Shigeo 1974, *Daikigyō to Rōdōsha* (Big Business and Workers), Gendaishi Shuppansha, Tokyo.

Small, Albion W. and Vincent, George E., 1894, *An Introduction to the Study of Sociology*, American Book Company, Chicago.

Smith, Robert J. and Wiswell, Ella Lury, 1982, *The Women of Suye Mura*, University of Chicago Press, Chicago.

Smith, Robert J. 1978, *Kurusu: The Price of Progress in a Japanese Village 1951–1975*, Stanford University Press, Stanford.

—— 1983, *Japanese Society: Tradition, Self and the Social Order*, Cambridge University Press, Cambridge.

Smith, Thomas C. 1959, *Agrarian Origin of Modern Japan*, Stanford University Press, Stanford.

Suttle, Gerald D. 1972, *The Social Construction of Communities*, University of Chicago Press, Chicago.

Suzuki, Yūko 1986, *Feminizumu to Sensō* (Feminism and War), Marujusha, Tokyo.

Takabatake, Michitoshi 1986, *Chihō no Ōkoku* (Kingdoms of the Provinces), Ushio Shuppan, Tokyo.

Takada, Yasuma 1911, 'Shakaiteki Hosoku ni tuite' (On the Social Laws), *Geibun*, Vol. 2, No. 1, pp. 86–102.

Sociology and Society of Japan

—— 1912, 'Shakai Shinkaron no Seishitu' (Nature of Theories on Social Evolution), *Tetsugaku Zasshi*, No. 307, pp. 55–71.

—— 1913, 'Shakai Hōsokuron' (Theories of Social Laws), *Tetsugaku Zasshi*, No. 319, pp. 55–69, No. 320, pp. 41–68.

—— 1914, 'Shakai Hōsoku no Seishitu' (Nature of Social Laws), *Kyoto Hōgakkaishi*, Vol. 9, No. 7, pp. 159–82.

—— 1919, *Shakaigaku Genron* (The Principles of Sociology), Iwanami Shoten, Tokyo.

—— 1922, *Shakaigaku Gairon* (Theories of Sociology), Iwanami Shoten, Tokyo.

—— 1925 *Kaikyū oyobi Daisan Shikan* (Social Class and the Third View of History), Nihon Hyōronsha, Tokyo.

—— 1934, 'Shisō Ruten no Ki' (Notes on Changing Thoughts), in *Hinja Hisshō* (Certain Victory of the Poor), Chikura Shobō, Tokyo.

—— 1938, 'Nihon no Tsuyomi' (The Strength of Japan), in *Kaisōki* (Reminiscences), Kaizōsha, Tokyo.

—— 1940, *Hinja Hisshō, Kaiteiban* (Certain Victory of the Poor: Revised Edition), Chikura Shobō, Tokyo.

Takagi, Mitsuru 1975, *Suwa Keizai Hattatsushi* (The Economic Development of the Suwa Area), Kasahara Shoten, Tokyo.

Takashima, Atsuko 1987, 'Eigo Kyōiku no Yakuwari' (The Role of English Education), *Shosai no Mado*, April 1987, Yūhikaku, Tokyo.

Tatebe, Tongo 1906, *Sensōron* (The Arguments on the War), Kinkodō, Tokyo.

—— 1915, 'Teikoku no Kokuze to Sekaino Senran' (National Policy of the Empire and Disturbances of the World), in *Nihon Shakaigakuin Nenpō*, Vol. 2, Nos. 3 and 4, pp. 507–18.

—— 1916, 'Teikoku Kyōiku no Konponhōshin ni tuite' (Comments on the Fundamental Policy of Education in the Empire), in *Nihon Shakaigakuin Nenpō*, Vol. 4, Nos. 1 and 2, pp. 31–53.

Tayama, Katai 1917, *Tokyo no Sanjŭnen* (Thirty Years in Tokyo), Iwanami Shoten, Tokyo, 1981.

Toda, Teizō 1926, *Kazoku no Kenkyū* (The Study of Family), Kōbundo, Tokyo.

—— 1942, *Ie no Michi* (The Way of the Household), Chūbunkan, Tokyo.

Toffler, Alvin 1980, *The Third Wave*, Morrow, New York.

Tokutomi, Sohō 1908, *Yoshida Shoin*, in *Tokutomi Sohō Shū*, Kaizōsha, Tokyo, 1930.

Tominaga, Ken'ichi 1964, *Shakai Hendō no Riron* (Theories of Social Change), Iwanami Shoten, Tokyo.

Ui, Jun 1974, *Kōgai to Jūmin Undō* (Pollution and the Residents' Movement), Aki Shobō, Tokyo.

Vinh, Sinh 1986, *Tokutomi Sohō (1863–1957): The Later Career*, University of Toronto-York University Joint Centre on Modern East Asia, Toronto.

Vogel, Ezra F. 1979, *Japan as Number One*, Harvard University Press, Cambridge, Mass.

Weber, Max 1968, *The Protestant Ethic and the Spirit of Capitalism*, translated by Talcott Parsons, Allen and Unwin, London.

Yamakawa, Hitoshi 1917, 'Minshushugi no Nōritsu Zōshin ka Shakaishugi no Nōritsu Zōshin ka' (Increase of Efficiency of Democracy or Capitalism), in Masao Ōta (ed.), *Shiryō Taishō Demokurashii Ronsoshi* (The Debates on Taisho Democracy), Vol. 2, Shinsensha, Tokyo, 1971, pp. 64–9.

— — 1918, 'Sojō no Demokurashii' (Democracy on Trial), Masao Ōta (ed.), *Shiryō Taishō Demokurashii Ronsōshi* (The Debates on Taisho Democracy), Vol. 2, pp. 197–210.

— — 1920, 'Nihon no Rōdō Undō to Handōshisō' (Reactionary Ideologies and the Labour Movements in Japan), in *Yamakawa Hitoshi Zenshū* (The Complete Writings of Hitoshi Yamakawa), Vol. 2, Keisō Shobō, Tokyo, 1966, pp. 348–59.

— — 1922, 'Futsū Senkyo to Musan Kaikyū no Senjutsu' (Universal Suffrage and the Tactics of Proleteriat), in *Zenshū*, Vol. 4, 1967, pp. 211–18.

Yamazaki, Toyoko 1983, *Futatsu no Sokoku* (Two Fatherlands), 3 vols, Shinchōsha, Tokyo.

Yanagida, Kunio 1902–05, *Nōseigaku* (Agronomy), *Yanagida Kunio Shū* (The Selected Writings of Kunio Yanagida), Vol. 28, Chikuma Shobō, Tokyo, 1964.

— — 1910, *Jiai to Nōseiu* (The Age and Agriculture), *Yanagida Kunio Shū*, Vol. 16, 1962.

— — 1919, *Toshi to Nōson* (Urban and Rural Societies), *Yanagida Kunio Shū*, Vol. 16, 1962.

— — 1925, 'Seinen to Gakumon' (The Youth and Scholarship) in *Seinen to Gakumon*, Iwanami Shoten, Tokyo, 1976, pp. 13–42.

— — 1927, 'Nōson Kazokuseido to Kanshū' (The Rural Household System and Customs), *Yanagida Kunio Shū*, Vol. 15, 1963, pp. 343–69.

— — 1934, 'Josei Shigaku' (The History of Japanese Women), in

Momen Izen no Koto (Before Import of Cotton), Iwanami Shoten, Tokyo, 1979, pp. 250–96.

—— 1940, 'Daikazoku to Shōkazoku' (A Large Family and A Small Family), in *Ie Kandan* (A Free Talk on Households), Kamakura Shobō, Kamakura, 1946, pp. 113–45.

—— 1949, 'Tamashii no Yukue' (The Abode of the Departed Souls), *Yanagida Kunio Shū*, Vol. 15, 1963, pp. 553–61.

—— 1954, 'Ie no Kannen' (The Concept of the Household), in K. Yanagida (ed.) *Nihonjin* (The Japanese), Heibonsha, Tokyo, pp. 33–57.

Yoneda, Shōtarō 1919a, *Gendai Chishiki Kaikyū to Narikin to Demokurashii* (The Modern Intellectual Class Movement, the Upstart Millionaire and Democracy), Kōbundō, Tokyo.

—— 1919b, 'Demokurashii to Wagakuni' (Democracy and Japan), in M. Ōta ed., *Shiryō Taishō Demokurashii Ronsōshi* (The Debates on Taisho Democracy), Vol. 1, pp. 125–42.

Yoshimi, Yoshiaki 1987, *Kusanone no Fasizumu* (Grassroots Fascism), Tokyo Daigaku Shuppankai, Tokyo.

Yoshino, Sakuzō 1914, 'Minshuteki Shiiundō Ronsō' (Arguments on Mass Demonstration), in M. Ōta ed. *Shiryō Taisho Demokurashii Ronsōshi* (The Debates on Taisho Democracy), Vol. 1, pp. 208–27.

—— 1916, 'Kensei no Hongi' (The True Meaning of Constitutionalism), in M. Ōta ed., *Shiryō Taishō Demokurashii Ronsōshi* (The Debates on Taisho Democracy), Vol. 1, pp. 244–312.

—— 1919, 'Minponshugi Shakaishugi Kagekishugi' (Democracy, Socialism and Radicalism), in M. Ōta ed. *Shiryō Taishō Demokurashii Ronsōshi* (The Debates on Taisho Democracy), Vol. 2, pp. 448–55.

Index

Abe, Isoo 35, 45, 47
Abegglen, James 77, 174
agriculture 87–92, 172–3; farmers'
  unions 66, 98; *see also* land
  tenure
air pollution 133–4, 135–6
airports 117–18
Akahata 38
Allied Occupation 99
Amakasu, Masahiro 34
Amaterasu 156, 194, 202, 205–6
American Federation of Labour
  59
AMPO demonstrations 94
anarchism, 59, 60
ancestor worship 67, 71, 154, 156,
  208–9
Anezaki, Shōji 30
anthropology 10
Arahata, Kanson 59
Ari, Bakuji 148
Arichi, Tōru 73
Ariga, Nagao 41
Arishima, Takeo 34, 48
Aruga, Kizaemon 69, 70–2, 75,
  84–5, 172–4
Asahi Shinbun 29
Asano, Ryōzō 152
Ashio Copper Mine 32
Association of Japanese Sociology
  (Nihon Shakai Gakuin) 8, 52,
  166
Association of Socialist Studies
  (Shakaishugi Kenkyūkai) 45
Association of Socialists
  (Shakaishugi Kyōkai) 47, 50
Association of Sociological
  Studies (Shakaigaku
  Kenkyūkai) 46–7

Basic Agriculture Law (1961) 88

Bell, Daniel 100
Bellah, Robert 15, 16–17, 171–2
Benedict, Ruth 2, 12–13
Bentham, Jeremy 5
Bestor, Theodore C. 99
Bolshevism 2, 60
Bougle, C. 58n
Brunger, Charles Scott 196–7
Buddhism 154, 199
*Bulletin of the Institution of
  Sociological Studies* 51

cadmium poisoning 132–3, 135–6
capitalism: development 6, 19–20,
  145, 149, 170–3; Japanese 80
Chen Shau 205
Chisso Corporation 131–2
Christianity 7–8, 41, 45, 150, 207
Citizens' Association, Shimoda
  113–14
Citizens' Committee for
  Countermeasures to Pollution,
  Fuji 138
citizens' movements 122–3, 134–44
class: middle 54, 64, 92; structure
  92–3
communal relationships 13
communism 1–2, 24, 48, 60–1
Communist Party *see* Japanese
  Communist Party
community: case studies 105–19;
  historical background 97–9;
  power structures 76, 102–5;
  social reconstruction 99–102;
  term 97
Comprehensive National
  Development Plan 125
Comte, Auguste 5, 49
conservatism, political 101–2
Constitution, Japanese (1889) 18,
  24, 53, 154

221

Index

Cooley, C.H. 58n
Co-prosperity Sphere, 29, 155, 167, 168
cotton-spinning industry 178–9
Council of Japan Labour Unions (Nihon Rōdōkumiai Hyogikai) 36
creation stories 200–1

Dahl, Robert 103
Dainihon Joshi Seinendan *see* Japan Female Youth Association
Dainihon Rengō Seinendan 35
Dainihon Rōdō Sōdōmei Yūaikai *see* Japan Federation of Labour
Daishowa Paper-Pulp Company 138
Darwinism, social 5, 46, 48, 101–2
Democracy 30
Democratic Socialist Party (DSP) 109, 116, 120
democratization, postwar 10–11, 82–3, 87–95, 98, *see also* election system
Dewey, John 3
Diet 104, 111, 115, 120
Domhoff, G. William 103
Dore, R.P. 12–13, 15
Dower, John 153
Durkheim, Emile 12, 14, 58n

Edo period 106, 209
education system 2, 10, 60, 69
election system: bribery 118–19; rights 24, 61–2, 103–4; universal suffrage 7, 24, 27, 60–2
elites 102–3
emperor system: after WWII 2, 153; conservative policies 101; Constitution 18, 24, 150; divinity 81, 153–4, 156, 162, 200; effects of capitalism 6, 145; family system 9, 20–2, 154; kinship relations 6, 58, 72, 85, 155; myth 81, 149, 152, 194, 197–8, 202–4; patriarchal order 166–7, 169; principle of

Japanese culture 28–9; state-as-family 166–9; study of sociology 42, 49, 52; WWII 28
Endō, Ryūkichi 29, 33
Engels, Friedrich 38
enterprise as household 20
environmental concerns 76–7, 122–4; citizens' movements 122–3, 134–44; emergence of protest 128–34; ideology and growth 124–8

factories 19–20, 79, 174–87
family system: after WWII 10, 98–100; ancestor worship 67, 71, 157, 208–9; effects of capitalism 6; emperor system 9, 20–2, 154–5, 167; extended 203–4; hierarchy 72–3, 85–6; history 206–8; household 18–19, 41–2, 52, 58, 65–8, 145; Katakura extended household system 173–4, 188–95; land ownership 23, 86–7, 196–7; legal rights 10; nation as lineage group 6, 164–9; patriarch 203–4, 206; principle of Japanese culture 28–9; sociological study 12, 52, 57–8; women's role 68–9, *see also* women; WWII 28; state 164–9; *see also* paternalism, patriarchal system
farmers *see* agriculture
fascism 9, 28
Feminism League 31
feudalism 4, 14, 18, 69–70, 79, 197, 198
Fishermen's Cooperative Association, Fuji 138
fishing communities 117, 126, 133, 138
Five Year Plan for Economic Independence 124–5
folklore 66, 67–8
Folklore Society 39
forests 117, 126
Friedrichs, Robert Winslow 11
Fuji citizens' movement 137–9
Fujiyama, Aiichirō 152

222

Fukuda, Tokuzō 30, 33
Fukumoto, Kazuo 36, 37
Fukutake, Tadashi 75, 78–96
Fukuzawa, Yukichi 46, 151, 162
Furukawa 179

Gayn, Mark 152
Gemeinschaft 5, 14, 55–7, 75–6,
   97, 120
German: socialism 8; sociology 10,
   42
Gesellschaft 5, 14, 55, 75, 97
GHQ (General Headquarters) 10
Giddings, F.H. 46, 53, 58n
Gōndō, Seikyō 37
Gouldner, Alvin Ward 11

Hagino, Noboru 132–3
Hall, Robert King 155–6, 166
Halliday, Jon 80
Hamaguchi, Osachi 39
Hani, Gorō 38
Hara, Kei 24, 30, 32, 59
Hara & Co 179
Hasegawa, Machiko 147
Hasegawa, Nyozekan 30, 32, 33
Hashikawa, Bunzō 154, 158
Hata, Hiromi 125–6
Hattori, Shirō 38
Hayami, Kenso 176–8
Hegelian thought 42
Heimin Shinbun 50
Hideyoshi 70
Himiko, Queen 205–6
Hirabayashi, Hatsunosuke 34
Hirai, Keiichi 34
Hirano, Yoshitarō 39
Hirano village 181
Hiratsuka, Raichō 31
Hirohito, Emperor 154
Hiroshima 163
Hoderi 204
Honjō, Eijirō 34
Hoori 202, 204
Hosokawa, Hajime 131
Hosuseri 204
households *see* family system
Hozumi, Yatsuka 207–8
Hunter, Floyd 102, 104

Ichikawa, Fusae 31, 160
Ichinosawa Sha 188
Ihara Institute of Studies on Social
   Problems 30
Ikeda, Hayato 125
Imori, Rikuhei 38
Imperial: Family 6; House
   199–200; Household 66, 166–7;
   Throne 8, 52, 166
individualism 8, 28, 41, 77, 100,
   145
industrial development 77, 79–80
Inomata, Natsuo 36, 38
Inomata, Tsunao 35
Iron Workers' Union 42
Ishikawa, Sanshirō 35
Ishikawajima Heavy Industries
   192, 209
Isoda, Susumu 86
itai-itai disease 132–3
Itō, Hirofumi 154, 178
Ito, Noe 34
Iwanami Shoten 29, 32
Iyo, Queen 205
Izanagi 194, 200–2, 203
Izanami 194, 200–1

Jansen, Marius 11
Japan Communist Party (JCP) 24,
   33, 38, 39, 61, 109
Japan Fabian Society 35
Japan Farmers' Association
   (Nihon Nōmin Kumiai) 33, 63
Japan Federation of Employers
   Associations 152
Japan Federation of Labour
   (Yūaikai, *later* Dainihon Rōdō
   Sōdōmei Yūaikai, *then* Nihon
   Rōdō Sōdōmei) 31, 33, 34, 59,
   60
Japan Federation of Youth
   Associations (Dainihon Rengō
   Seinendan) 35
Japan Female Youth Association
   (Dainihon Joshi Seinendan) 37
Japan Psychological Society
   (Nihon Shinri Gakkai) 36
Japan Socialist League (Nihon
   Shakaishugi Dōmei) 32, 60

Index

Japan Socialist Party (JSP) 50, 60, 91, 109
Japan Sociological Society 9, 31, 165
Japanese Society Today 91, 94
Japanism *see* nationalism
Jikyōkai labour union 209
Jinmu, Emperor 202
Josei Dōmei 31

Kada, Tetsuji 37
Kaihō 31
Kaimei Sha 188, 190
Kaito Gumi 188, 190
Kakushin Club 34
Kameido incident (1923) 34
Kaneko, Yōbun 32
Katakura family 188–95
Katakura Silk Company 170, 173, 179, 188–95
Katayama, Sen 7–8, 42, 44–5, 47, 51
Katō, Hiroyuki 5–6, 46, 48–9, 164–5
Katō, Kōmei 29
Kawada, Tsugurō 30, 35
Kawai, Gitora 34
Kawakami, Hajime 29, 30, 32, 33, 37, 38
Kawamura, Nozomu 48, 51
Kawashima, Takeyoshi 83
Kenseikai 29, 34, 37
Kindai Shisō 59
Kinoshita, Naoe 45, 47
Kita, Ikki 33
Kiyoura Cabinet 34
Kobe-Kawasaki Shipbuilding Co 31, 32
Kōchikai 35
Kōchisha 35
Koike, Shirō 39
Koizumi, Shinzō 31, 33
Kojiki 200–4, 205
Kokka Shakaishugi 31
Kokushō, Iwao 37
kokutai 154–6, 165–7
Komaki, Ōmi 32
Kōmei Party (KP) 109, 116, 120

Kōtoku, Shūsui 45, 47, 51, 55, 60, 208
Kuki, Shūzō 39
Kumamoto University 131
Kunikida, Doppo 65
Kurashiki city 126
Kurata, Hyakuzo 32
Kyōchōkai 38
Kyōdō Printing Co 36
Kyoto Imperial University 38, 53, 54
Kyushū Imperial University 38

Labour-Farmer Party (Rōdō Nōmin Tō) 36, 39
labour movement 7, 59–61
labour unions *see* unions
land tenure: effects of capitalism 7; farmers' unions 66, 98; feudal 18, 69–72, 78, 86; landlord system 22–3, 86–7, 172–3; Marxist theories 172; Meiji reforms 17–19, 98, 117; modern 87; modernization 78; ownership 18–19, 66–7, 80, 86–7, 98, 196–7; Public Peace Law (1900) 47; reforms after WWII 10; Taisho period 80–1; tenant movement 24, 26–7, 43, 47, 62–4, 80; traditional paternalistic 6–7, 22–3
Law for the Maintenance of Public Peace (1925) 24, 62
Lenin, V.I. 1
Lewis, Arthur 8
Liberal Democratic Party (LDP) 92, 109–10, 115–16, 118, 120
Liberal Party (*Jiyūto*) 18
liberalism 5, 9

McDougall, W. 58n
MacIver, R.M. 58n
McKean, Margaret A. 139, 143
Maebashi silk mill 179
Maeda, Hajime 153–4
Maine, Henry James Sumner 12, 14
Manchurian Incident (1931) 28
Maruyama, Masao 9, 151, 207

Marx, Karl 1, 10, 12, 38, 70, 102, 148, 172
Marxism 1, 10, 12, 65, 69, 70, 94
Mead, George Herbert 3, 12
Meiji period: calendar 202; civil war (1877) 149; civil war (1887) 197; Constitution 18, 24, 53, 154; expansionism 161–2; factory system 79, 170, 174, 179; Katō's career 46; *kokutai* 154; land reforms 17–19, 98, 117; land tenure 71–2; new order 17–18; railways 106; rights movement 7, 18; wars 149, 153, 169, 197–8
Meiji Restoration: community structures 76, 171; continuity of household 66; development of capitalism 79; emperor's charter oath 2; modernization 17; ruling bloc 81; silk production 171, 175; traditional elements 12; Western influences 4
Meirokusha 46
mercury poisoning 131–2, 135–6
methodology, research 10, 11
Miki, Kiyoshi 37, 38, 39
Mill, John Stuart 4, 5
Mills, Charles Wright 11, 102–3
Minamata disease 131–2
Minamata Disease Counter Measures Council of Democratic Groups 132
Ministry of Education 155–6
Ministry of Health and Welfare 132, 133
Minobe, Tatsukichi 33
minponshugi 53–4
Minzoku 36
Mishima citizens' movement 134, 137
Mitsubishi 10, 32, 179
Mitsui 10, 179
Mitsui Mining and Smelting 132–3
Miyamoto, Ken'ichi 128–9, 137
Mizushima district 127–8
modernization: characteristics in Japan 17–19, 170–2; from

above/below 75, 174; policies 11, 15–17; postwar 93–4
Moore, Barrington Jr 11
Mori, Ōgai 208–9
Morgan, L.H. 58n
Mori, Yoshitarō 38
Morito, Tatsuo 31
Motoyoshi, Yūjirō 46–9
Murai, Tomoshi 45
Murakami, Shigeyoshi 159
Mushakōji, Saneatsu 30, 58

Nagai, Kafū 209
Naitō, Konan 34
Nakae, Chōmin 161–3
Nakamura, Keiu 4
Nakane, Chie 79, 85–6, 154
Nakayama Sha 181, 186
Nasu, Kō 34, 35
National Levelling League 33
National Plan for the General Development of Land Act 124
nationalism: beliefs 101–2, 207, 208–9; business community 153; Japanism 15, 27–9, 56, 58, 81, 198, 199–200, 210; kinship relations 6; modernization 150; right-wing 15; sociology 8, 9, 10
New Comprehensive National Development Plan (1969) 139
New Industrial City designation 126–7
New Women's Association 31
NHK (Nihon Hōsō Kyōkai) 37, 167
Nihon Gakki 36
Nihon Nōmin Kumiai *see* Japan Farmers' Association
Nihon Rōdō Sōdōmei *see* Japan Federation of Labour
Nihon Rōdōkumiai Hyogikai *see* Council of Japan Labour Unions
Nihon Shakai Gakuin *see* Association of Japanese Sociology
Nihon Shakaigaku Nenpō 52
Nihon Shakaigakuin Chōsabu 31

Index

Nihon Shakaishugi Dōmei *see*
  Japan Socialist League
*Nihon Shihonshugi Hattatsushi
  Kōza* 69
Nihon Shinri Gakkai *see* Japan
  Psychological Society
Nihon Shoki 200
Niigata Minamata disease 131–2
Niigata University 132
Nikkeiren 152
Ninigi 202, 204, 205
Nishi, Amane 4–5, 40–1
Nishida, Kitarō 29
Nogi Society 209–10
Norman, E. Herbert 14–15, 143–4
Noro, Eitarō 39
nuclear weapons 163–4
Numazu citizens' movement 134,
  137, 138

Ōe, Shinobu 165
Ōhira, Masayoshi 101, 145
Ōno, Yasumaro 165
oil shocks 108
Ōishi, Heitarō 39
Ōkawa, Shūmei 34
Ōkuninushi 194, 202, 204, 205
Ōno, Takeo 36
Onogumi company 179, 181, 186
Ōnuki, Emiko 147
organicism *see* social organicism
Origuchi, Shinobu 38, 39
Osatake, Mō 35
Oshihomimi 202
Ōsugi, Sakae 29, 34, 59–60
Ōtsuka, Hisao 83
Ōya, Sōichi 36
Ōyama, Ikuo 33, 35, 39

Parsons, Talcott 11, 12, 14, 94,
  102–3
paternalism 6–7, 20, 23, 72, 120
patriarchal system 14, 166–7, 169,
  201, 203–4, 206
Perry, Matthew Galbraith 170
Plan for the Pacific Belt
  Industrialization 125
pluralism 103
pollution 76–7, 122–4

power structures 76, 102–5
Public Peace Law (1900) 47, 60

railways 106, 107–8
Reimeikai 30, 31
Reischauer, Edwin 94
religion 8, 41, 145, 150–1, 154–7,
  170, *see also* ancestor worship,
  Buddhism, Christianity, Shinto,
  Suwa shrine, Yasukuni shrine
Rice Riot (1918) 24, 59, 62
Rikkenminseitō 37
Rōdō Kumiai Dōmeikai 31
Rōdō Kumiai Kiseikai 42
Rōdō Nōmin Tō *see* Labour-
  Farmer Party
Rōdō Shinbun 59
Rōnō 37, 60, 61, 70
rural community 12, 17–18
Russia: comparison with Japan
  164–5; socialism 1–2, 8;
  Revolutions (1917) 59
Russo-Japanese war (1904–5) 7,
  48, 49–50, 51, 165, 197, 209

Saitō, Toshio 134
Sakai, Toshihiko 29, 31, 35
Sakisaka, Itsurō 38
Sakurai, Jikei 34
samurai 17–18, 19
Sano, Manabu 32, 33
Sanzen Sha 189–90
SCAP (Supreme Commander for
  the Allied Powers) 10, 98
Seiyūhontō 37
Seiyūkai Party 24, 30, 34, 59
Seki, Eikichi 33
Shakai 46–7
Shakai Gakkai *see* Sociological
  Society
Shakai Mondai Kenkyū 30
Shakai Zasshi 43, 44, 45
Shakaigaku Kenkyūkai *see*
  Association of Sociological
  Studies
Shakaigaku Zasshi 46
Shakaishugi Kenkyū 35
Shakaishugi Kenkyūkai *see*
  Association of Socialist Studies

226

Shakaishugi Kyōkai *see*
   Association of Socialists
shamanism 205
Shibaura Manufacturing Co 36
Shichi 29
Shiga, Naoya, 58
Shimazaki, Tōson 65
Shimizu citizens' movement 134,
   137
Shimoda city, case study 105–14
Shin Sakai 60
Shinfujin Kyōkai 31
Shinjinkai 30
*Shinkō Kagaku no Hata no
   motomi* 38
Shinmei, Masamichi 34, 37, 38
Shinrigaku Kenkyū 36
Shinshakai 29
Shinto 155, 156, 194, 199
Shinyūkai 31
Shirakaba 58–9
Shisō 29, 32
Shōkonsha 149–50, 198
Showa Denkō 131, 132
Showa Depression 28
Showa era 80
silk industry 170–1, 175–87
Simmel, Georg 53, 58n
Sin Shakai 31
Sino-Japanese war (1895) 7, 197
Small, A.W. 8, 44–5, 53
Smith, Robert 123–4, 204
Social Democratic Party 47–8, 50
social organicism 6, 48–9
socialism 7–8, 42, 73; early 20th
   century 43–51, 54–5; labour
   and peasant movements 58–64
Socialist Manifesto (1901) 47–8
Socialist Party *see* Japan Socialist
   Party (JSP)
society (term) 40–1
Socio-economic Basic Plan 129
Sociological Society (Shakai
   Gakkai) 43, 45
sociology: early 20th century
   43–51; European-derived
   liberal 51–8; importation of
   Western 4–6, 40–2; influence of
   American 10–12; psychological

46; relationship with socialism
   6–9, 42–3; tasks indigenous to
   Japanese 12–13
Souda, Kiichirō 29
Spencer, Herbert 5, 14
Stalin, Joseph 12
Strategic Point Development
   method 125
Structural Improvement Program
   88
Students' Federation 35
Suehiro, Gantarō 36
Suekawa, Ganjirō 34
Sugimori, Kōjirō 37
Sugiyama, Eitarō 39
Sugiyama, Sakae 35, 37
Suihei 33
Sumitomo 10
Sumiya, Etsuji 36
Sumner, William Graham 5
Susanō 194, 202, 204, 205
Suseri 204
Suwa lake area 170, 173, 175–86,
   188
Suwa shrine 192, 194–5
Suzuki, Bunji 59
Suzuki, Eitarō 75
Suzuki, Yūko 159–60

Tagonoura Port 138–9
Taisho Democracy Movement 24,
   80
Taisho era 9, 80–1
Takabatake, Motoyuki 29, 31
Takada, Yasuma 30, 33, 35, 36,
   54–7
Takagi, Masayoshi 46, 49
Takagi, Mitsuru 179
Takashima, Atsuko 150–1
Takayama, Iwao 39
Takigawa, Seijirō 38
Tanaka, Odo 30
Tanaka Cabinet 39
Tanemaku Hito 32
Tarde, J.G. 58n
Tatebe, Tongo 49–51; Association
   of Japanese Sociology 8, 52;
   organic theory 49, 53;
   publications 29, 30, 31, 37, 49;

Index

Russo-Japanese war 48, 49–50;
tennōsei ideology 165–6, 167
Tateminakata 194
taxation 18–19, 98, 126, 197
Tayama, Katai 65, 149–50, 197–9
Tazoe, Tetsuji 51
tenant movement *see* land tenure
Tenmu, Emperor 200
tennōsei ideology 151–154, 165
Terauchi Cabinet 59
Toda, Teizō 9, 36, 57–8, 167
Toffler, Alvin 100
Tōjō, Hideki 159, 168
Tokugawa period 1, 4, 17, 20, 40,
70–2, 106, 198
Tokutomi, Sohō 199
Tokyo Electric Company 138
Tokyo Imperial University:
Department of Sociology 9, 42,
49, 57, 165; law school 65, 199,
207; political activity 31, 39, 46;
Shinjinkai organization 30
Tokyo urban community 99
Tomakomai citizens' movement
139–42
Tominaga, Ken'ichi 94
Tomioka factory 175–86
Tönnies, Ferdinand 12, 14
Tosaka, Jun 38
Toyama, Shōichi 46
Treaty of Amity and Commerce
(1858) 170
Treaty of Peace and Amity (1854)
170
Tsu, Junichirō 37
Tsuchiya, Kyoson 33, 35
Tsuchiya, Takao 37
Tsuda, Kōzō 9, 207
Tsuda, Soukichi 29
Tsukuyomi 194, 202

Ugayafukiaezu 204
Ui, Jun 123
unions: farmers' 66, 98; labour 8,
10, 24–5, 42–3, 47, 60, 129–31;
tenant 24, 27, 63, 66, *see also*
land tenure
Universal Suffrage Law (1925) 24,
61–2

Unno, Kōtoku 39
US-Japan Security Treaty 94n

village: mountain communities
117; society 18–19, 82–4; status
98
Vincent, G.E. 8, 44–5
Violence Control Law (1926) 24,
62
Vogel, Ezra F. 16
voting *see* election system

wakon-yōsai 16
war: ideological positions 151–6;
Japanese views 147–52; widows
157–9; sociology 161–9
Ward, L.F. 53
Warera 30
Weber, Max 10, 12, 14, 58n, 148
women: education 69; liberation
68, 73; New Women's
Association 31; status 7, 68–9,
159–60, 201, 205–6; Taisho
Democracy Movement 80; war
widows 157–9
Women's Suffrage League 34
World War I 24, 43
World War II 2, 10, 98–9, 152–3,
168–9

Yaekotoshironushi 194, 202
Yama, Ikuo 30, 37
Yamada, Mōritarō 39
Yamakawa, Hitoshi 31, 34, 35, 37,
59–61
Yamakawa, Kikue 35
Yamamoto, Senji 34, 38
Yamazaki, Kesaya 35
Yamazaki, Toyoko 168–9
Yanagida, Kunio 65–9;
ethnographic approach 75;
folklore studies 2, 66, 67–9, 98,
199; influence 172; publications
35, 36, 37, 99–100; support for
unions 98
Yasukuni shrine 149–51, 156–61,
198–9
Yasuoka, Seitoku 34
Yawata Iron Manufacture 31

Yobimatsu Harbour 127
Yokkaichi asthma 133–4, 137
Yokoshiba-town, case study 115–19
Yoneda, Shōtarō 30, 31, 32, 33, 52–4, 55
Yoshino, Sakuzō 29, 30, 37, 53–4, 61
Yūaikai *see* Japan Federation of Labour

zaibatsu: after WWII 10, 82; emperor myth 152, 194; factory system 79–80, 179; formation 20; Japanism 27–8; modernization 24, 28; status 81
Zenkoku Suiheisha 33
Zola, Emile 149, 209